CYBERLINES
LANGUAGES AND CULTURES OF THE INTERNET

JAMES NICHOLAS
Publishers

Cyberlines

Languages and Cultures of the Internet

edited by
Donna Gibbs and Kerri-Lee Krause

JAMES NICHOLAS PUBLISHERS

P.O. Box 244, Albert Park Australia 3206

Design: Text Machine
Production: High Press Academic

National Library of Australia
Cataloguing-in-Publication (CIP) Data

Cyberlines : Languages and cultures of the Internet.

Bibliography.
Includes index.
ISBN 1 875408 26 6.

1. Internet users. 2. Communication and culture. 3. English language - Terms and phrases. 4. Internet (Computer network) - Terminology. 5. Online chat groups - Terminology. 6. Internet Relay Chat - Terminology.
I. Gibbs. Donna. II. Krause. Kerri-Lee Dawn.

004.678014

JAMES NICHOLAS
Publishers

JAMES NICHOLAS PUBLISHERS

For
James, Oliver and the future
D.G.

For
Rhoda, Milton and the past
K.K.

Acknowledgements

To all those who shared their knowledge and ideas with us during the course of *The Cyber Project*; to our contributors who have worked with good humour and patience; to our colleagues both near and far, who have given their advice and wisdom so generously, particularly the staff of the School of Education at Macquarie University, and Dr David Butt and Sue Butler; to our families and friends who have sustained us through the difficult times; to Julie-Ann Tapper who came to our rescue in preparing the manuscript at the last minute; to Rea Zajda of James Nicholas Publishers for her enthusiasm, encouragement and responsiveness: to these people we offer our warmest thanks. We are in your debt. Our greatest debt of gratitude, however, is to Professor Tony Gibbs whose imaginative suggestions, skilful advice, and love of fine scholarship have been an inspiration to us both.

Donna Gibbs and Kerri-Lee Krause
Macquarie University
2000

Table of Contents

Part 3: Cultures and Communities in Cyberspace

Notes on Contributors

Ray Archee is a Lecturer at the University of Western Sydney, Nepean. He has published widely in the area of computer mediated communication. His research interests include Internet communities, electronic decision making, and computer-based writing. In his spare time Ray works as a computer journalist and Internet consultant.

Dr Anne Cranny-Francis is Associate Professor in English and Cultural Studies at Macquarie University. Her research interests include critical and cultural theory, feminist cultural production, popular fiction (science fiction, fantasy, detective fiction), film, television, popular music, nineteenth-century fiction, and English as a discipline. She publishes in the areas of feminist fiction, engendered fiction and popular culture. Her most recent work includes articles on Star Trek novels, the erotics of the cyborg, Charlotte Perkins Gilman, and the pedagogy of English.

Scott Fitzgerald has been an editor at the Macquarie Dictionary Research Centre where he worked on various versions of the *Macquarie Dictionary*, the *Macquarie Encyclopedia of Australian Events*, and the *Australian Infopedia CD-ROM*. His research interests include stylistics, the application of systemic functional grammar to language and other semiotic systems and lexicography, including the ramifications of new technology upon dictionaries. He is currently developing a thesaurus of terminology related to the language of the Internet and expanding his collection of neologisms.

Dr Donna Gibbs is a Senior Lecturer in Postgraduate Studies in the School of Education at Macquarie University. She has taught in primary, secondary and tertiary systems and was an Inspector for the NSW Board of Studies from 1990-1995. Her publications are in the fields of Renaissance studies, Curriculum Studies, language and literature. She has recently received funding to work with the School of Education to put their postgraduate units online. Her current research interests include English curriculum in national and international contexts, boys' underachievement in English, and the impact of technology on curriculum, particularly in schools and at tertiary level.

Dr Kerri-Lee Krause lectures in the areas of educational psychology, sociology and language development in the School of Education, Macquarie University. She has taught in secondary and tertiary contexts and is particularly interested in the needs of first year tertiary students in relation to their use of technology to access information. Her research interests include adolescent literacy, writing anxiety and cognitive processes, and the metalinguistic features of second language writing in English.

Juliet Mar was awarded the University medal (UNSW) for her BA (Hons) thesis entitled *Interpersonal Meaning in Personal Letters* in 1996. She has taught undergraduate linguistics since 1996 at both the University of NSW and Macquarie University. She was a co-author and researcher for the *Grammar in School Textbooks* research project (1996) with Associate Professor Peter Collins and Carmella Hollo. Currently, she is investigating the unique language of prayer for her doctoral thesis.

Juliet McLean has held co-ordinating and advisory posts in School Library Services in the UK and Australia. Her research interest in aspects of language development led her to complete an MA in Language and Literature in Education at the University of London in 1985. As County Youth Librarian in Bedfordshire she had extensive involvement with the development of information technology in school libraries and the professional development of teachers and librarians in online information searching. She now holds the post of Head Librarian at Abbotsleigh in New South Wales and is engaged in doctoral research involving a study of students' use of language in the information searching context.

Jennifer Thurstun has extensive teaching and writing experience in both Spain and Australia. Since 1991 she has lectured in English for Academic Purposes and worked in related research at Macquarie University and the National Centre for English Language Teaching and Research. She has published books and articles on academic English including in 1997, with Professor Chris Candlin, *Exploring Academic English*. Her research interests include bilingualism, language maintenance, academic writing, the practical application of concordancing and the language of computer mediated communication.

Dr Ross Todd is Head of the Department of Information Studies at University of Technology, Sydney in the Faculty of Humanities and Social Sciences. He has had experience in secondary teaching and teacher librarianship. Dr Todd has published widely in the area of the integration of information literacy into learning. More recently his focus has been the development of information and critical literacies relating to the World Wide Web and student learning.

Annette Wong has worked as a commercial artist and graphic designer. She is currently engaged in researching the topic of the visual representation of self and the ways in which identity is expressed in relation to the Internet for her doctoral thesis. Other research interests revolve around cross-cultural studies and the formation of cultural identity. She is particularly interested in the concept of hybridity and its role in cultural change and adaptation. Her work as a research assistant has involved her in projects related to George Bernard Shaw and Irish cultural identity.

Introduction

The idea for this book had its origins in a modest project inspired by the editors' curiosity about the fascinating linguistic phenomena and practices generated by the Internet[1]. In order to further explore and share information about this subject we launched *The Cyber Project* in 1997 and invited responses from anyone, anywhere in the world, to requests for information presented on our webpage. Respondents were invited to comment on a range of language matters, including the origin and meaning of the term *cyberspace* and whether they considered that the jargon of the Internet acted as a barrier to their use of the technology. They were also invited to give examples of the words and expressions they used to talk about the Net and the values and attitudes these suggested to them.

The results were informative and useful, and at the same time we discovered a community of scholars, some of whom were almost on our doorstep, who shared our fascination for this new language. As the project developed it began to assume multidisciplinary dimensions and we realised that a larger scale study of the language of the Net from a range of cultural and intellectual perspectives was needed. The technology which brought us together with others who had an interest in the field then became an expeditious means for locating, collecting and shaping the ideas which are the basis of the present book.

Both the linguistic and visual dimensions of human communication, as well as ideas of what constitutes human identity itself, are being transformed by the information technology revolutions of recent times. The Internet has generated a multitude of new discursive practices: the aim of this book is to explore the discourses of the Net from a range of conceptual approaches, and the viewpoints of various disciplines.

As systems of communication create new practices and new forms of interaction between language users, so the reflective society needs to examine the implications of this transformation. Language is at the heart of every aspect of the processes involved. Yet, as Neil Postman (1993) accurately points out in *Technopoly* 'most of us, most of the time, are unaware of how language does its work. We live deep within the boundaries of our linguistic assumptions and have little sense of how the world looks to those who speak a vastly different tongue' (pp. 123-124). The present study strives to bring into the open a greater awareness of the significant social, cultural, political and educational ramifications of the linguistic choices we make in a new and powerful technological world.

In the past few decades various terms such as *technobabble*, *compuspeak*, *techspeak*, *techno-talk*, *computer jargon*, *Net talk*, *Netspeak*, *Silicon Valleyese* have fallen in and out of favour to describe the language of the Net. We have chosen a new term, *cyberlanguage*, to describe this language, though no doubt alternative terms will be coined, and in time this usage superseded. In the context of this book, however, cyberlanguage refers to the language used to communicate on and about the Internet. An understanding of how this language works can offer insight into the societies and cultures from which it has sprung.

In conceptualising notions about cyberlanguage and how it functions we have been influenced by the idea of communication systems and pathways which are employed in the culture of indigenous Australians, and which Bruce Chatwin (1987) has described in his work, *The Songlines.* As Chatwin describes this system, Aboriginal ancestors or 'Ancients' sing their way all over the world wrapping it in a 'web of song' (p.73). The pathways which are forged simultaneously reinforce the identity of individual communities and make links between them. Such a metaphor, with its emphasis on the importance and value of connections, has particular meaning for those investigating a cyber medium which is highly prized for its web-like linkages and its creation of new communities. The cyberlines of communication in the technological world have the potential to serve similar functions, though as is argued below in chapter 11, its language at present appears to function as both connecting pathway and dividing line. In adapting this notion for use in this book we are sharply aware of the limitations of the analogy. The predominantly Western version of communication used on the Net does not commonly reflect the deeply spiritual underpinning of indigenous cultures or the respect for difference which the indigenous term conveys. Hence our title, *Cyberlines: Languages and Cultures of the Internet*, is both a celebration of an idea provided by the example of indigenous cultures but also in a sense an apology to a culture which conceptualises the nature of communication between peoples and cultures in such a sophisticated way.

Like Julius Caesar's ancient Gaul, this book is divided into three parts. Part One deals with the language of cyberspace. In the introductory chapter to this section, 'Cyberlanguage: What it is and what it does', Donna Gibbs explores the phenomenon of cyberlanguage with an emphasis on its social and educational implications. An analysis of the origin and formation of terms used to talk about all things connected with communicating in cyberspace, and a consideration of the influences which have shaped content and style on the Net is presented. It is argued that new forms of thinking, perceiving and recording are being constructed at some speed with far reaching effects on our evolving formations of cultures and subcultures.

In 'Metaphor and meaning: Values in a virtual world' Donna Gibbs and Kerri-Lee Krause extend this focus on language by examining the range of metaphors in use and the often surprising sources from which they are drawn. The familiar superhighway metaphor is analysed in terms of the values it carries, the spawning of related images and its links with other metaphor clusters in order to demonstrate common patterns of metaphoric coinage in the cyberworld. A discussion of the ways in which metaphors function—to familiarise the unfamiliar, to create a sense of reality in a virtual world, to express emotion in an impersonal medium, to attract attention—leads into an analysis of the values associated with metaphorical terms used in relation to the Internet and their cultural and educational implications.

This section concludes with Scott Fitzgerald's 'Re(de)fining dictionaries: From paper to pixel', an analysis of the ways in which technology has dramatically changed how we store, present and digest information. His focus is on the 'warehouse' of language, the dictionary. He argues that the ability to publish dictionaries in electronic formats eliminates some of the restrictions associated with the book format such as size, space, the compression of information contained, and the amount of time between editions, making it difficult for a dictionary to be a contemporary record of the language. He shows how in addition to eliminating restrictions there is an opportunity to make the dictionary a better publication, not simply a bigger one. Publishers can provide links between different dictionaries, and links to external sites, include a more liberal use of graphics, and introduce the use of sound—practices which have the potential to benefit the well-established tradition of lexicography.

Part Two offers a closer look at the range of new literacies required to navigate and understand the Internet and the information it contains. Jennifer Thurstun's 'Screen reading: Challenges of the new literacy' traces the ways in which the development of the computer, the World Wide Web and the Internet is changing our conception of literacy and challenging the reader in many powerful ways. She takes up the issue of the perceptual difficulties posed by the new technology and the need for the reader to develop entirely new skills and habits of thought. The chapter explores the challenges associated with the reading of electronic texts and in particular draws attention to the need for critical thought about the current conventions for web design and the electronic presentation of information.

In 'Cyberseeking: Language and the quest for information' Juliet McLean examines the related issue of electronic information searching and its literacy demands. She notes the dramatic shift in the vocabulary of information access in the digital age compared with pre-electronic times which reflects changes in and extension of access to a new population of information users. She outlines the major literacy challenges for educators which result from the ways in which learners are inducted into the knowledge pathways offered by electronic information searching, especially on the Internet. The literacies she discusses include coming to terms with the nature of automatic keyword indexing and the retrieval mechanisms of search engines. She argues that the teaching of information skills strategies, particularly at the stage of preparing students for searching, by asking questions which help to clarify purpose and meaning, is of crucial importance in the cyber age.

Ross Todd's 'Negotiating the Web: Language, critical literacies and learning' complements McLean's chapter by providing a discussion of the information and critical literacies underpinning effective connecting to, interacting with, and utilisation of World Wide Web information. He argues that the development of information and critical literacies is fundamental to assisting learners in making decisions about what information to believe, what to doubt, what to pay attention to, what to be concerned with and what to reject. His chapter draws on current research in the fields of cognitive information processing, information seeking behaviour, information access and retrieval, and information utilisation to explore a series of real-life classroom scenarios highlighting the challenges of locating and using information on the Web.

Part Two concludes with Anne Cranny-Francis' chapter, 'Connexions'. An exploration of the literacies demanded of users of cyberspace texts allows her to theorise the role of the user in the electronic context. By analysing a contemporary institutional website, she is able to identify many of the literacy demands imposed upon Internet users which she sees as being highly conventionalised and rule-governed. She argues that some are generated out of familiar literacies (verbal, visual, aural) and based in our readings of books, magazines, film and television, whilst others arise specifically from the nature of this new medium—its focus on design, its use of default settings and its use of hypertext links. Using the image of the rhizome to depict the user's journey through cyberspatial texts, she argues that a complex of literacies is needed to enable the user to negotiate a site critically, and to generate, creatively, a response to the site.

Part Three is concerned with the cultures and communities of cyberspace. Juliet Mar's chapter 'Online on time: The language of Internet Relay Chat' explores the nature of language characterising the interactions of synchronous computer-mediated communication (CMC). Using an actual transcript downloaded from the Internet, she employs the theoretical framework of register theory to analyse its linguistic patterns in terms of field, tenor and mode and identifies a range of linguistic differences between the synchronous interactions of Internet Relay Chat rooms and other forms of communication. She shows that this new and increasingly popular form of interaction is very different not only from CMC such as email, but also from other real time speech activities such as face-to-face casual conversation.

In 'Cyberself: Identity, language and stylisation on the Internet', Annette Wong examines the processes of cultural identity formation and experimentation in the context of the Internet. She analyses the role of language and stylisation in such processes, and the cultural changes that are occurring through the influences of Internet technology and the immense cyberspace image production that weaves in and around the Internet. Her discussion focusses on 'bodilessness', default identities and assumptions of identity; the relationship between style and utility; the influence of cartoon cultures and 'adolescent identity' on the style of cyberspace; and the global rhetoric surrounding the Internet and its communities.

Ray Archee's chapter 'Critiquing <the> Internet 2000: Knowledge, language and freedom' raises questions about the problems that have accompanied our rush for Internet presence. In particular, ~~he argues~~ that information has in fact become devalued as issues of reliability are considered. After examining the relationships between language, democracy and community, the author cautions readers to consider carefully and critically why we use the Web, urging us to ask: what are its benefits and what are its costs?

In 'Cyberlines', the last chapter in this section, Kerri-Lee Krause presents an examination of the nature and roles of the language that links the worlds of the virtual and the real. Drawing inspiration from the Aboriginal belief in mythic Songlines which connect tribes across vast expanses of terrain— both physical and spiritual —she discusses ways in which this analogy can be applied to the cyberlines of communication on and about the Internet. Using an analysis of cyberpunk communities and hacker subcultures on which to base her argument, she claims that while the Internet by definition facilitates interaction and connections across previously immutable barriers of time, space, language and ethnicity, these pathways are not as smooth and unimpeded as they may seem. This final chapter explicates the book's title in greater detail and draws together a range of themes explored throughout the book.

Endnotes

1. Whilst the Internet and the Web are often used synonymously, it is important to distinguish between them. The Internet is a network of networks that connects computers around the world into a giant communication system. It includes various computer-mediated technologies such as email, newsgroups, Bulletin Board systems (BBSs), Internet Relay Chatlines (IRCs), and MUDs (Multi-User Dungeons/Domains/Dimensions). These are all different from the World Wide Web, although they are sometimes linked to websites. The World Wide Web is only one kind of cyberspace technology. It is accessed through browser software which uses hypertext to link information together.

References

Chatwin, B. (1987). *The songlines*. London: Jonathan Cape.

Postman, N. (1993). *Technopoly: The surrender of culture to technology*. New York: Vintage Books.

Part 1

The Language of Cyberspace

Chapter 1

CYBERLANGUAGE: What it is and what it does

Donna Gibbs

Both the linguistic and visual dimensions of human communication, as well as ideas of what constitutes human identity itself, are being transformed by the information technology revolutions of the late twentieth century. In the new world of information technology, traditional forms of written and spoken communication are combining with images, pictures, linguistic shortenings of all kinds, repackaging of bits and pieces of related words, typographical signs and other inventive usages to form a new language and new literacies. The aim of this chapter is to explore the phenomenon of cyberlanguage with a particular emphasis on its social and educational implications.

Dr Johnson, eighteenth century essayist, poet and famous lexicographer, declared in an essay in *The Rambler* (1752, No. 208, as cited in Bronson, 1966) that in his writings he 'laboured to refine our language to grammatical purity, and to clear it from colloquial barbarisms, licentious idioms, and irregular combinations'. If he were living today Dr Johnson would find this goal even more difficult to achieve than in the eighteenth century. The rapid accretion to the language of terms spawned by information technology in recent decades, often instantly seen as indispensable, has brought with it an extraordinary acceleration of related linguistic change, and a cascade of new, and frequently 'irregular', usages.

The living, changing nature of our language is nowhere more apparent than in the language we use for talking about all things connected with communicating in cyberspace. The language of the Net, or *cyberlanguage*[1], as we have chosen in this book to call the words, expressions and linguistic phenomena associated with information technology, provides an instant mini research laboratory where the processes which create language can be put under the microscope. New terms and expressions, or words borrowed from other contexts, enter this language with unprecedented speed—some to flare into life before fading from sight, others to become more permanent signs in the language landscape.

As communicators in cyberspace multiply, cyberlanguage is no longer the sole province of technocrats or people variously referred to as computer *nerds*, *geeks*, and *hackers*. Cyberlanguage, a term not yet recorded in traditional dictionaries, is encountered by a majority of people daily in the media, and regularly in the workplace, as well as in a multiplicity of other outlets.

Cyberplay: Variations on a prefix

The impact of information technology on language, and its power to generate a rapid spread of new usages, is well illustrated by the permutations of meaning and application of the term *cyber*. It is first recorded in English as part of the word *cybernetics,* a term derived from the Greek word *kubernetes*—oarsman, steersman (c.f. Latin, *gubernator*—steersman or governor). Norbert Weiner introduced this term to describe the science of communications and automatic control systems in both machines and living things in his book: *Cybernetics, or control and communication in the animal and the machine* (1948). The primary sense of *cyber* might be expressed as 'governor, or controlling agent or agency' when that agency is the result of information being looped back to the machine without necessitating human intervention. But in its semantic development the term has come to take on various senses as a kind of multi-purpose linguistic tool for a variety of phenomena relating to the machinery, cultural products and concepts in the field of information technology.

In the late 1940s and early 1950s, Isaac Asimov, biochemist and author, was publishing science fiction in which the term *cybernetics* was used to describe the workings of the brains of his fictional robots—a possible source for the cybermen of *Doctor Who* (late 1960s). These *cyborgs* (cybernetic organisms; persons whose physical abilities are extended beyond normal human limitations by machine technology[2]) populated sixties and seventies imaginations, and appeared in various forms in science fiction series such as *Doctor Who* and *Star Trek* or fantasy films such as *Blade Runner*, *Cyborg* and the TV show *The Bionic Woman.*

William Gibson is commonly credited with coining the term *cyberspace* in his science fiction (cyberpunk) tale, *Neuromancer* (1984), though in fact he had also used the word to label a simulator machine—the Cyberspace Seven—in his earlier short story 'Burning Chrome' (1982)[3]. The language of cyberspace in the late 1980s and early 1990s still had very strong scientific and/or science fiction connections. But the original semantic inflexion of 'control' in words which employ *cyber,* and which derive originally from *cybernetics,* began to disappear. In *Neuromancer* Gibson often draws on concepts of light and space to establish the other worldly, hallucinatory nature of the experience of entering the cyberworld: 'Lines of light ranged in the non-space of the mind, clusters and constellations of data. Like city lights receding . . .' (Gibson, 1984, p. 51). When Dan Josefsson interviewed Gibson on a TV news program in Stockholm, Sweden in 1994, Gibson defined *cyberspace* as a 'metaphor that allows us to grasp this place where since about the time of the second world war we've increasingly done so many of the things we think of as civilisation. It's where we do our banking . . .' (Interview by Dan Josefsson, November 23, 1994). In these later 'definitions' the initial sense of *cyber* implying control has been replaced by senses relating to territory, phenomena and events which are largely 'out there' and possibly out of control, in a new conceptual dimension created by technology[4].

The shift in meaning observed here is evident in the mid-90s when popular newspapers around the world began to include cyberwords in the headlines of articles:

- Flying Bimbo Leads Blitz on Cyberporn (*Independent on Sunday*, USA, December 3, 1995);
- Stop the Cyberworld, I Want To Get Off (*The Times*, UK, December 9, 1995);
- Cybernauts Survive in a World About To Make Santa a Navigational Hazard (*South China Morning Post,* December 26, 1995);
- Singapore's First Cyberpub Will Open This Month (*Straits Times*, January 1, 1996);
- Cyberbusking Becomes a Net Reality (*Sydney Morning Herald,* July 30, 1996); and
- Cyber Babe (*Daily Telegraph,* Sydney, April 26, 1997).

A sudden proliferation of these coinages (e.g., *cyberbabble, cyber-*

swill, cybercafe, cybervacation, cyberworshippers, and *cyberbusking*) saturated the media and filtered more and more frequently into everyday conversations. The faint sense of exhilaration which sometimes accompanies the coinage and usage of these new terms may derive from a feeling that the user is somehow venturing into, or challenging, the unknown. In spite of the shift in meaning to almost the reverse of its original sense, the question as to who is in control, or who is controlling what, often hangs in the air in discourse associated with technology.

A search of *Sydney Morning Herald* databases between 1992 and 1997 confirms an increase in the middle of that decade in the appearance of the term *cyberspace,* as well as the use of words containing *cyber** (e.g., cyber as adjective, prefix or in hyphenated form) in a variety of formations. The increase steadies towards the end of the period under review as demonstrated in Table 1 below.

Table 1.1 Number of occurrences of the term *cyber*

Year	Word	Number
1992	cyberspace	8
	cyber*	22
1993	cyberspace	5
	cyber*	23
1994	cyberspace	59
	cyber*	100
1995	cyberspace	136
	cyber*	333
1996	cyberspace	173
	cyber*	435
1997	cyberspace	179
	cyber*	488

Coinages, including the term *cyber,* are now quite commonplace. Some examples have been dignified by being included in formal reports and taken quite seriously. The Commonwealth Inquiry into Teaching (Senate Employment, Education and Training References Committee, 1998, p. 149), for example, includes reference to a submission which names *'cyber-violence'* and *'cyber-sexual harassment'* as causes of difficulties for women who want to become computer literate.

Creating cyberlanguage

Words and expressions employed to refer to the new electronic world under construction, and to all its associated parts, have to be borrowed or invented. The society of Net users has found ways to do this by drawing on all the devices commonly used for describing new concepts. One of the most common of these involves the process of borrowing words from other more familiar contexts to describe new phenomena, or similar phenomena in a new context. Words such as *bookmark, address, mouse, crash, homepage* and *icon* are the result of this process, and would be familiar to most computer users, or even non-users.

Consideration of the variety of ways in which these words are adapted from ordinary language reveals that there is nothing predictable about how the process will operate. In some instances terms are borrowed because there is a similarity of purpose in the actions being described (e.g., *bookmarking*); in others there is a similarity of physical appearance (e.g., a computer *mouse* has a shape and 'tail' like a 'real' mouse); others draw on the emotional associations a word usually carries (e.g., *home, homepage* evoke the familiar, the comfortable, a secure and central base); whilst other words have their usual associations discarded and a selected aspect focused upon (e.g., *icon* is often associated with the sacred or devotional, though in computer language the visual sign or graphic representation element tends to overshadow this connotation).

Other ways in which words are added to the store include:

- creating metaphors (*Net, Web*);
- anthropomorphising the computer and its workings (*memory, parent, handshake*);
- creating acronyms (*MUDs*—Multiple User Dungeon/dimension/ domains, *html*—hypertext markup language, *MOOF*—Modem Offline. This latter term has itself given rise to further related terms, another familiar process of word creation in the cyberworld (e.g., *MOOF Monsters* and *MOOF Meat*, terms to describe those responsible for causing a sudden disconnection from the Net, and those who have been disconnected);
- coining new words (e.g., *cruft, foo*[5]);
- repackaging bits and pieces of related words (e.g., *download, bloatware, cybrarian, yahooligan, internaut, pixel*); and

- creating playful blends and inventions (e.g., *digerati/digiterati* — the literati of the digital age[6], *linkola*—link/payola—a bribe paid to gain computer links to the briber's website, *cyberwannabees*—young, usually male teenagers, who have access to a bulletin board where they use grandiose pseudonyms and boast of their achievements).

The creativity and inventiveness of the coinages are evidence of an extraordinary energy and vitality released by this new environment and source of linguistic change.

That cyberlanguage has now become firmly established in language communities can be observed in the practice of turning common, everyday expressions into technical metaphor: *not enough time* is to be *short of bandwidth*, *talking personally* is *to use facemail*, and *having a short concentration span* is *to think in sound bytes*[7]. Other evidence of widening familiarity with cyber expressions is reflected in the way that advertisers of products unrelated to information technologies have begun to assume an audience who knows its technical jargon. This is strikingly represented in the advertisement, reproduced in miniature opposite, for a luxury island holiday.

A single computer key with *esc* at its centre, is surrounded by a hot pink background, with some discreet wording and a web address in the bottom right hand corner. The advertisement depends for its success on a number of assumptions—that to escape to this island hideaway is as easy as pressing the escape key on a computer; that it is the computer literati who can afford luxury holidays; and that the person who responds to this advertisement has good taste and is part of the cognoscenti (i.e., is in the 'know' about computers etc.). Light-hearted, witty headlines such as that used in 'Stay in Touch' in the *Sydney Morning Herald* (November 11, 1998, p. 24), *wow.charleshitscyberspace.pom*, (referring to Prince Charles of the United Kingdom's new website), which assume a certain familiarity with the Internet from a general audience, are also becoming increasingly common.

American influence

America has loomed large in the generation and control of information technology and consequently has had an enormous influence on the uses to which it is put and the style, spelling and content of its messages. Freedom of speech and choice, and the fundamental

Figure 1.1 Advertisement from *Gourmet Traveller*, August, 1998. (Produced by Kelly Gee Advertising, Brisbane for P&O Australian Resorts 1998.)

equality of individuals, the stated ideals of American society, are consistently represented in a language which favours the use of first names, surrounds information in a plethora of friendly colloquialisms (e.g., *'Let's take a peek at this site'; 'Talk to us'*), and frequently includes language which is larger-than-life, and promises the world, not in some utopian future, but instantly (e.g., *Find it here!*; *Real-Time News*; *Catch it all at IW Live*; *Buddylist instant messaging*).

The influence, so prominent in American public and social life, of 'sales talk', is strongly present in the cyberworld. Web pages, for example, frequently carry actual advertisements (e.g., *Powered by Bottom Dollar*), where words and images pulsate, or move across the screen, as in lit-up cityscapes where billboards or neon lights promote commercial wares. The language and layout used for sales pitches, navigational instructions, links to other sites, requests to the viewer to use services, win 'cookies' and so on, often imitate the visual and verbal language of the marketplace: there is little distinction between publishing and advertising on the Web. Competition is inbuilt in this medium because there is seemingly infinite choice for the viewer and it takes only the touch of a key or button to move on to new places or spaces. The image projected by the Net is of a society dominated by what Thomas Carlyle, the nineteenth century English essayist and social thinker called the 'cash nexus' society with the profit motive as the prime bonding agent of human society.

Cyberlanguage contains a high proportion of brand and trade names for software, search engines and the like. Brand names often hold out promise of transformation, success and/or perfection (e.g., *WordPerfect, Successmaker*, *Visionquest*). Some product names imply this transformation can be achieved from babyhood. The CD-ROM package, *Jumpstart Baby*, for example, picks up on the notion of the computer as a machine-like extension of the human body. The name plays on the assumption that the link between human and machine can be animated by further machinery, jump leads, capable of jolting the embryonic adult to instant superiority and success: Mary Shelley's Gothic horror tale, *Frankenstein*, comes to mind. These brand names, which are omnipresent in cybercultures, carry assumptions about what is valuable and necessary for success in society with the implication that you will be left out, or left behind, if you do not use them. Bernard Shaw's satirical invention, in *The*

Apple Cart (1929), of a company called Breakages Ltd which creates products designed to be obsolescent in a short period of time, is recalled with a vengeance. The implication in the cyberworld is that the computer user, as well as the software, will be obsolete if s/he does not buy the latest product.

The 'maleness' of cyberlanguage

A particular concern with the evolution of cyberlanguage is that much of it has been coined by scientifically oriented males (e.g., A'herran, 1996; Cole, Conlon, Jackson, & Welch, 1994; Spender, 1995). Dale Spender argues that if the language used to refer to the Net did not rely on 'revhead' images of superhighways, and instead used metaphors of the village community, women would feel and be less excluded. Her book *Nattering on the Net: Women, power and cyberculture* deliberately marries a stereotypical notion of women communicating (nattering) with a technological image (the Net) in order to provocatively challenge and counter prevailing notions of the Net as male territory (Spender, 1995, p. 166).

Paul Nicholson raises doubts about some of Spender's views in his recording of the activities of a small group of teenaged, female computer-users who label themselves *Web 'masters'* and *cyber virgins*: they 'frequently tested their skills against males—usually teachers or technical staff—and usually won' and they 'absolutely rejected stereotypes of themselves— including feminist stereotypes' arguing that 'Spender had got it all wrong' (Nicholson, 1995, p. 223). As Nicholson acknowledges, his female computer users may have been atypical, but even so his observations raise gender issues which need further exploration.

That the language of computing provides an imagery of sex and violence which is contrary to girls' conditioning is put forward by Cole et al., (1994) who cite Spavold's research (1990) to support this claim. Words such as *abort*, *chaining*, *thrashing*, *execute*, *head crash* and *kill* are quoted as examples of terms which produce an 'undercurrent of violence' (Cole et al., 1994, p. 81). Anne A'Herran's (1996) study of language in the electronic environment also suggests that the language of the new technology, 'invented by technical males for technical males', in the past at least, has created an unfriendly, alienating environment. Her examples of 'male' language include words like *bits*, *mips*, *Tbase* (which she labels 'wheelbrace and spanner words'), brand names such as *MicroTech,* and *CompuServe,* software names such as *Stuffit, Unstuffit,* or *HotMetal* and words from working environments with powerfully male connotations such as *toasting CDs, frying boards, building firewalls* and *zapping the parameter RAM.*

Whilst there is a degree of truth in these assertions about the alienating effect of much of this language, the arguments are not quite as straightforward as they may seem. Some of the words cited as having strong male connotations, for example, can equally be associated with traditionally female activities (e.g., *toasting* and *frying*). It may be that the language of the Net carries a range of ambiguous metaphorical meanings which are interpreted in myriad ways in this new environment.

A survey in 1998 of 89 preservice teachers from the Teacher Education Program at Macquarie University, 94% of whom were female, lends further support to this view (see p. 25). A majority of these preservice teachers did not perceive the technical language associated with computers to be alienating. This may be attributed to a lack of awareness about language and its implications, but on the other hand, it may be that, over time, the male 'hold' over the invention of computer language has weakened. It seems that the issue of the 'maleness' of cyberlanguage is more complex than has been recognised to date and that further research in the area is warranted.

Cyberlanguage and meaning

The Cyber Project, set up in 1997, was designed to collect examples of language used to refer to, and talk about, the Net, and to explore and analyse the ways in which this language influences attitudes and behaviour[8]. The website used to collect the information was available to the general public but three particular groups of respondents were invited to contribute via requests in journals with a focus on language and education: *Australian Style*, *Australian Language Matters* and *English Today* (an international journal). Analysis of sections of the data collected sheds light on perceptions about how individuals perceive the status and meaning of cyberlanguage terms.

A question which required respondents to give their definition of the term *cyberspace* (a sample of responses is provided in Table 1.2) revealed a degree of commonality of meaning, though idiosyncratic or outrider elements occurred in about 10% of definitions (see definitions 4 and 6) posted to the website. The variation in personal understanding of the terms may partly be explained by the speed with which these new terms come into the language, and the different levels of technical understanding held by users of the terms.

Table 1.2 Definitions of cyberspace

The word *cyberspace* means:

1. the environment of the Net. "Space'" as in outer, inner, cyber – that pertaining to computers and the assortment of computers connected together to form the Net.
2. a kind of imaginary space where machines "talk" to each other so people can communicate with someone, somewhere, using their own machine.
3. a place containing artificial intelligences.
4. the endless source of information that I have access to through my computer.
5. a non-physical realm of electronic existence that can be occupied only by the reality that we superimpose on to it by means of our messages and interactions.
6. anything concerned with the Net when used by people who don't have a clear idea of what it all means.

More general comments offered by respondents included a perception that there was a certain 'fuzziness' of meaning to the new terms: 'it is the very fuzziness of the language that makes it so useful'. Others commented that users with different backgrounds were likely to have different understandings but that this was liberating rather than restrictive. There was also a recognition that the creation of terminology can come from anyone, anywhere on the Net: no-one has the right to be more authoritative than anyone else in the 'democratic'[9] world of cyberspace.

Linguistic conventions

The Net provides a more informal and less exacting forum than many others where language is available to public scrutiny, though the electronic world (like letters to the Editors pages in newspapers) also has its language cops, police-like persons who take responsibility for linguistic crimes committed in cyberspace. As Reva Basch reports (*Sydney Morning Herald,* August 27, 1996) the conventions that govern Net language continue to change:

> It is like riding a unicycle on a highwire juggling five flaming torches, as I lurch desperately trying to keep my balance and trying to reinterpret which way I fell last time. Is it *Gopher* or *gopher*, *FTP* or *ftp*, *online* or *on-line*, *e-mail* or *email*?

The tendency of modern societies to favour speed and convenience over Johnsonian niceness and correctness in language use is reflected in the reliance on abbreviation and shortcuts taken with linguistic conventions in the information technology environment. There is a degree of experimentation, flexibility and tolerance in allowing varying ways to spell and represent ideas in writing which is reminiscent of Elizabethan times when different spellings of the same word and even of one's own name were quite acceptable[10].

The conventions used in email, chat rooms and the like, evolve fairly rapidly. This is partly caused by growing levels of familiarity and confidence which is quickly developed by the users of these mediums and partly by the speedy changes in the technology itself which create the potential for new forms of communication. Email communications, for example, generally reveal a very relaxed approach to grammatical and graphological conventions—as though convenience and speed of delivery, and the fact that the communication apparently disappears into the ether, makes it unnecessary to check for typographical or other errors. Chat room users, too, have developed ways to turn the written medium in which they communicate into something as close to conversation as possible. The personally developed vernaculars of the different chat rooms usually include a high proportion of abbreviated forms including:

- invented acronyms (e.g., *BRB*—Be right back, *IMHO* In my humble opinion);
- invented abbreviations (e.g., where *r u* from?, will u b there by 6?);
- *emoticons*, or icons to indicate emotions (e.g., a sad person is represented by :(or ☹, and a happy person by :) or ☺. The examples provided here are of the simplest kind but it should be noted that over time emoticons have become increasingly detailed, elaborate and playful. The effect, of course, is to both include and exclude according to 'local' knowledge[11]; and
- deliberately informal spellings and absence of punctuation (e.g., *coulda*, *dunno*).

The written record of chat rooms is similar to, though not the same as, a play script—'characters' are named, dialogue is recorded mainly as direct speech, and actions are indicated separately[12].

New literacies

Literacies which have been adequate in the past for the construction and interpretation of traditional forms of text are no longer fully adequate for texts presented through the Internet or on the Web, and they will become less so in the future as the medium continues to evolve and as new forms of texts emerge. Email and chat rooms, for example, provide possibilities for communicating which have much in common with previous modes of communication, but which also include new and different combinations of elements. 'Talk' between people on the Net is typed in so that it can be interpreted through a pixellated interface as conversation, and it can take place in real or delayed time. Web-based texts, usually nonlinear in structure with hyperlinks to other texts/graphics/sounds have their own set of conventions which vary from those which govern traditional text structures[13]. Multiple pathways within and beyond a document create open-ended, continuous forms of text which can be structured by the user as well as the author and which require new kinds of navigation. This also involves different ways of conceptualising notions of the author and the reader/user, and different strategies for positioning the reader in relation to the material being presented. Both Internet and web-based texts combine verbal, visual and aural elements with a facility, availability, and opportunity for modification not previously possible. Developing the ability to create and to 'read'[14] these new texts, to understand how they are constructed and how they operate, involves both old and new literacies.

Classroom practices

Developments in technologies create possibilities of new contexts for language use and for new literacy conventions, and it is these which must be incorporated into literacy pedagogies. A disadvantage of cyberlanguage is that it may be perceived to offer a running and superficially attractive undermining of educational attempts to foster generally accepted decorums of linguistic convention. Yet technology also has the potential to bring subjects to life with an immediacy which has not been previously available and can provide an exciting arena in which pedagogical aims can be effectively advanced. Consider, for example, how teaching concepts about meaning, or the way language changes, could be enhanced by access to electronic versions of dictionaries, including online dictionaries compiled by students themselves[15].

Research into whether lack of familiarity with the language of the Net actually inhibits computer use, or prevents teachers, for example, from making use of computers in the classroom has not yet produced any definitive answers. It is a question often left out of surveys which ask about the barriers which prevent Net use. On the other hand, a submission to the *Commonwealth Inquiry into Teaching* recorded from the School of Education at James Cook University points out that some Australian students have taught themselves:

> abstract and complicated computer programming language, which they then use to complete a number of Net related tasks from constructing a web site to establishing webzones. Interestingly, however, many of these students have been streamed by their state high schools into low level mathematics and English classes (Commonwealth of Australia, 1998, p. 149).

Recent research (1998) carried out by the editors with 89 Macquarie preservice teachers, indicates that these students have a reasonably high level of confidence about being able to deal with the language of technology in the classroom. The group surveyed was made up of 6% male students (all under 30 years of age) and 94% female (13% over 30 years of age).

When asked to rank, from the most problematic (1) to the least problematic (8), factors which might prevent their using technology in classrooms, 'unfamiliarity with computer language' was placed sixth out of eight possibilities. It scored an average of 5.5. Table 1.3 illustrates the average ranking accorded to each factor by the students.

Table 1.3 Survey of preservice teachers

Factors inhibiting technology use	Average rank order Most problematic (1); Least (8)
Lack of access to equipment	2.6
Timetabling difficulties	3.3
Lack of available time	3.8
Lack of technical support	4.2
Unfamiliar with computer usage	5.3
Unfamiliar with computer language	5.5
Lack of confidence in front of class	6.3
Distrust of usefulness	6.5

Only 14.6% of the student group reported that this unfamiliarity would prevent them from using computers in classrooms, while 85.4% claimed it would not affect them. This was mirrored in a fairly high level of confidence in using technical language to guide children to use technology being reported: *Very confident* (24.7%); *Somewhat confident* (63%); *Not at all confident* (12.3%). The reasons given for not being deterred, even when familiarity with technical language was lacking, included that:

- they could read up and learn what they needed to know;
- they could get help from in-service;
- they would learn along with the children; and
- they would not need much technical language and would either use everyday language or experiment.

Only 2% of the university students surveyed indicated any awareness that the rapid rise in the use of technology had made an impact on their language use, and none of the responses showed any recognition that language choices carry values and associations. It is difficult to know how to interpret these findings—but lack of language awareness, and possibly lack of experience in the field, may well be contributing factors.

Conclusion

What cyberlanguage *is* can partly be explained in terms of existing understandings and principles of language use, though it does present a complex challenge to conventional notions. Cyberlanguage is a new language, with its own brand of quirky logic, which evolves with unprecedented speed and variety and is heavily dependent on ingenuity and humour. The pace at which changes occur is indicative of a society on the move, with little time for reflection. The language choices which are made, and which survive, albeit temporarily, in a Net environment, and the shifts in grammatical and syntactical practice which occur, reveal a great deal about how a society perceives itself and the attitudes, values and associations on which people draw to construct their virtual worlds.

Fashions, trends, media usage and technological developments affect the meanings of cyberlanguage very quickly, probably at a much faster rate than is the case with other groups of words, and presumably because of the speed with which new processes are developing. Many people use terms related to the Net quite confidently but when pressed are not necessarily able to define what they mean. This may be true of all language use, but the fuzzy edges around the meanings of many of the new terms seem to be particularly pronounced and even welcomed. Some terms may change in meaning but continue to be used, whilst others gain a use-by date very early in their history and then drop out of sight. The conventions which surround their usage often differ from those involved in traditional writing and speaking practices.

What cyberlanguage *does* is an even more complex issue as it affects so many aspects of human experience in its social, political, economic and cultural dimensions. It heralds changes which will have far-reaching effects on our evolving formations of cultures and subcultures. Literacy itself is changing as a concept because of the impact of technology on writing and reading practices. In some ways, cyberlanguage can be perceived as providing a serious threat to educational 'standards'. In other ways it can be seen as an instrument of beneficial change, creating a new kind of language of communication, with WW connections.

Endnotes

1. Whilst the term cyberlanguage was 'coined' by the editors for the purpose of this book, a search of newspapers and magazines over the last ten years on the archives of the Reuters database [accessed 1998, November 4] indicates four previous usages—the first in June, 1996 and the last in January, 1998.
2. The term *cyborg* was first used by Manfred E. Clynes and Nathan S. Kline to describe their work on adapting organisms for life in space. Their article 'Cyborgs and Space' appeared in *Astronautics* in September, 1960, and is reprinted in *The cyborg handbook* (Gray, 1995).
3. Gibson's 'Burning Chrome' was first published in *Omni* in July, 1982.

The 'Cyberspace Seven' is referred to in the opening paragraph of the story:

I knew every chip in Bobby's simulator by heart; it looked like your workaday Ono-Sendai VII, the 'Cyberspace Seven', but I'd rebuilt it so many times that you'd have had a hard time finding a square millimeter of factory circuitry in all that silicon. (p. 72)

4. William J. Mitchell notes in *City of bits* that the word *cyberspace* 'does not have a respectable technical pedigree' and is 'detested by many old computer hands for the conceptual vulgarities that it has come to connote' (1995, p. 181).

5. See *The Jargon Dictionary* or *PCWebopedia* for definitions of these terms, and for additional examples of newly coined words.

6. Sue Butler, an editor of the *Macquarie Dictionary*, defines the digerati as people who comprise a professional clique of computer experts. She comments that the success of the digerati joke is that it not only conjures up the binary digits that are the atoms of cyberspace, but also the image of nimble fingers flying over the keys (*Sydney Morning Herald* April 5, 1997).

7. Further examples are given at *The Microsoft Lexicon or Microspeak made easier.*

8. The editors set up a website for *The Cyber Project* at http://www.mq.edu.au/Educ/cyberspeak/cyber1.htm for respondents to comment on a range of language matters including the origin and meaning of the term *cyberspace* and whether they considered the jargon of the Net acted as a barrier to their using technology. They were also invited to give examples of words and expressions they used to talk about the Net and the values and attitudes these suggested to them.

9. For further discussion of the undemocratic nature of the Net, see below, pp. 215-218.

10. Public records relating to Shakespeare's christening, marriage and burial, for example, contain the following spellings of his name: Shakspeare, Shakspere, Shaksper, Shakespeare, Shakespear, Shakesp, Shakp, Shackspeare and Shake-speare (Chambers & Williams, 1965).

11. A discussion of Japanese emoticons is included below at p. 195. For further examples of emoticons see *The Unofficial Smiley Dictionary.*

12. For an analysis of a transcript of chat room conversation, see Juliet Mar's chapter 8 below.

13. A detailed discussion of the conventions used in the construction of a web site is included in Anne Cranny-Francis' chapter 7 below.

14. The electronic literacies involved in reading these texts are discussed in Jennifer Thurston's chapter 4 below.

15. Further discussion of the changing nature of dictionaries is included in Scott Fitzgerald's chapter 3 below.

References

A'Herran, A. (1996). The landscape of technology: Conversations with the lost boys. In *Proceedings of the Style Council, 1996, 1997 and 1999.*

Bronson, B. H. (Ed.). (1966). *Rasselas, poems and selected prose*. New York: Holt, Rinehart and Winston.

Carlyle, T. (1858). *Chartism: Past and present.* London: Chapman and Hall.

Chambers, E. K., & Williams, C. (1965). *A short life of Shakepeare with sources*. Oxford: Clarendon Press.

Clynes, M. E., & Kline, N. S. (1995). Cyborgs and space. In C. H. Gray (Ed.), *The cyborg handbook.* London: Routledge.

Cole, A., Conlon, T., Jackson, S., & Welch, D. (1994). Information technology and gender: Problems and proposals. *Gender and Education, 6* (1), 77-85.

Delbridge, A., Bernard, J. R. L., Blair, D., Butler, S., Peters, P., & Yallop, C. (Eds.). (1997). *Macquarie Dictionary* (3rd ed.). Macquarie University: The Macquarie Library Pty. Ltd.

Gibbs, D., & Krause, K. (1997). Internet talk. *Australian Language Matters, 5* (3), 4-5.

Gibbs, D., & Krause, K. (1997). News from cyberspace. *Australian Style, 5* (2), 2-3.

Gibbs, D., & Krause, K. (1996). The Cyber Project. *Australian Style, 5* (1), 3.

Gibbs, D., & Krause, K. (1996). The Cyber Project. *English Today, 13* (2), 63.

Gibbs, D., & Krause, K. *The Cyber Project*. Available: http://www.mq.edu.au/Educ/cyberspeak/cyber1.htm [1998, December 5].

Gibson, W. (1994). An interview with William Gibson. Recorded by D. Josefsson in Stockholm, Sweden. Available: http://www.algonet.se/~danj/gibson1.html [1998, November 3].

Gibson, W. (1982). Burning Chrome. *Omni, 4* (10), 72-107.

Gibson, W. (1984). *Neuromancer.* New York: Ace Books.

Gray, C. H. (1995). (Ed.). *The cyborg handbook.* London: Routledge.

Mitchell, W. J. (1995). *City of bits*. Cambridge, MA: MIT Press.

Nicholson, P. (1996). From web 'master' to cyber virgin: Explorations of the Net. In L. Laskey & C. Beavis (Eds.), *Schooling and sexualities: Teaching for a positive sexuality.* Geelong: Deakin Centre for Education and Change.

Oxford English Dictionary. (1989). Prepared by J. A. Simpson & E. S. C.

Weiner. Oxford: Oxford University Press.

PCWebopedia. Available: http://www.webopedia.com/ [1998, November 3].

Senate Employment, Education and Training References Committee. (1998). *A class act: Inquiry into the status of the teaching profession.* Canberra: Commonwealth of Australia.

Spender, D. (1995). *Nattering on the Net: Women, power and cyberspace.* North Melbourne: Spinifex Press.

The Jargon Dictionary. Available: http://www.netmeg.net/jargon/terms/ [1998, November 3].

The Microsoft Lexicon or Microspeak made easier. Available: http://cinepad.com/mslex.htm [1998, November 3].

The Unofficial Smiley Dictionary. Available: http://www.queensu.ca/eegtti/eeg_286.html [1998, November 3].

Weiner, N. (1961). *Cybernetics, or control and communication in the animal and the machine* (2nd ed.). Cambridge, MA: MIT Press.

Chapter 2

Metaphor and meaning: Values in a virtual world

Donna Gibbs
Kerri-Lee Krause

it is from metaphor that we can best get hold of something fresh
Aristotle, *Rhetoric III*, 1410b

The Rev. Canon Chasuble, a character in Oscar Wilde's *The Importance of Being Earnest* (1895, 1998) with the distinction of being able to use language in extraordinary ways, has a strong predilection for metaphor: 'Were I fortunate enough to be Miss Prism's pupil I would hang upon her lips. (*Miss Prism glares.*) My metaphor was drawn from bees. Ahem!' (Act 2, p. 244). The Reverend Chasuble's response to Miss Prism's obviously censorious stare is a mumbled explanation and containment of the meaning of his metaphor. A century later the metaphors which abound and are so casually used to describe the electronic world are not always so well contained or understood by those who use them. The range of areas from which metaphors referring to the electronic world are selected, the patterns of metaphoric coinage, the functions they perform, and their values and implications for the nature and meanings of the world/s they construct are the subject of this chapter. The chapter is concerned not only with description of linguistic phenomena associated with information technology but also with the underlying sociological and cultural assumptions of which the language is symptomatic.

The range of metaphors used in cyberlanguage

The sources from which metaphors are drawn to talk about new and unfamiliar aspects of technology and its workings are various and diverse; they range in their representation from the homely to the violent, the ordinary to the miraculous, the vulgar to the visionary. Some metaphors make comparisons between relatively similar objects and contexts (e.g., the page of a book and the *page* of a computer screen) whilst others make less obvious connections (e.g., finding a piece of information and *getting a hit*; having your Internet usage tracked for commercial purposes and *getting a cookie*).

Popular sources for metaphoric ideas include the urban landscape (e.g., *superhighway*, *traffic, bus*); concepts of networks and convergence[1] (e.g., *Web*, *Net*, *networks*, *links*, *connections*); the office (e.g., *file, mailbox, bulletin board*); the home and domesticity (e.g., *homepage*, *cybernanny, trash*); animals (e.g., *mouse, spider, bugs, gopher*); machinery (e.g., *robots*, *avatars*, *download*, *search engine*); sexuality (e.g., *hot plugging, virgin, AIDS, SEX*[2]*); leisure activities* (e.g., *surfing, browsing, cruising*); violence and the underworld (e.g., *crash*, *abort, hotwired, lurking*); and disease and death[3] (e.g., *bug*, *virus*, *core cancer*, *blue screen of death*[4], *deadly embrace*). Many of these examples could be placed in different groupings, or in two or more groupings simultaneously—the labels are loosely chosen—and changes in nomenclature could also create different categories. Nevertheless, it is clear that the range of sources from which metaphors are drawn for use in the cyberworld is varied, considerable and often includes an element of surprise usually because the metaphor straddles such sharply contrasting contexts as in the examples of *getting a hit* or *getting a cookie* referred to above.

Patterns of metaphoric coinage

A common pattern of metaphorical coinage in the electronic world is for a metaphor to emerge from a particular source (e.g., the home, the office, the urban landscape) and then to become dominant for a period of time. This replicates patterns of metaphoric activity in other contexts but, again, it is the speed of their rise and fall in the electronic context which is noteworthy. When a metaphor gains dominance there is invariably a frenetic period of linguistic activity in the media and the metaphor is used repeatedly, usually in an increasing variety of contexts. Witty or humorous headlines are popular locations for spreading and familiarising these coinages. When the dominant metaphor is in the limelight it gives rise to new satellite metaphors drawn from the same or related sources which creates a metaphor cluster. Cyberlanguage is full of metaphor clusters —metaphors and their satellite images too numerous to document. A metaphor cluster can be seen in relation to other metaphor clusters which are linked to it by some form of association usually in terms of a narrowing or broadening of the concept. This creates a chain of images not unlike a network in its own right. Whether there is a causal relationship between these metaphor clusters or they are created independently is not always clear.

The superhighway metaphor

Consideration of the dominant metaphor of the *superhighway*, the values it carries, its spawning of related images, and its links with other related metaphor clusters provides a useful example of these processes in action. Senator Al Gore Jr. is credited with introducing the metaphor at a meeting of computer industry people in 1978 in homage to his father, Senator Albert Gore, who had helped establish the interstate highway system in the USA in the 1950s (Hale, 1996, p. 71). The superhighway metaphor has been pervasive over the last decade, though it has come in for a great deal of criticism[5] and may gradually be falling from favour. It carries ideas of the Net as the ultimate transport and communication system, superseding all other national and international linkages, a phenomenon that can take those who are visiting cyberspace to where they want to go, or have never before imagined they could go. Part of the appeal of this metaphor is that it links the known with the unknown; it makes the virtual world a clone of the 'real' world and so makes it seem more accessible.

The superhighway image also implies progress; some linguists, such as Lakoff and Johnson, go so far as to argue that most cognitive processes depend on metaphors derived from preconceptual experiences as infants, and that 'movement forwards' is associated in our minds with success (1980 as cited in Goatley, 1997, p. 6). The superhighway represents something which propels you forward and contains promise of success and fulfilment. As such it is a new expression of the American Dream. On the other hand, it has been pointed out that the superhighway is, in fact, 'paved according to the interests of government and big business' and does not represent progress but rather accords with other utopian Western narratives 'of progress and salvation through technology and transportation' (Druik, 1995, n.p.). For those who reject the highway's connection with progress or advancement, or for cultures for whom the highway has a low level of significance, the cultural associations of the notion of the superhighway can be excluding. Jane Kenway aptly notes further limitations of the metaphor: 'It says nothing about the direction, control and quality of traffic generally, nor anything about the different traffic activities in different lanes, nor about who controls the lights' (Kenway, 1995, p. 36).

The associations carried by the term *superhighway* are picked up in other metaphors used to refer to the Internet and its workings. In this context a metaphor such as *network* will be interpreted in the sense of a map of road-like connections which can take you places; *navigation* will help you find your way; *traffic* refers to the people travelling with you; and you need the power of *search engines* to get where you want to go. The extension of the metaphor to include the idea that information is the goal of the journey occurs in expressions such as *information superhighway* and *infobahn* (or *I-bahn*). This borrowing from the German 'autobahn' suggests not only a highway of, and to, seemingly unlimited information, but one associated with notoriously high speeds and exhilaration.

There are many metaphor clusters which can be seen to link up with the idea of the Net as a superhighway, though how intentionally these links have been, and are being, forged remains uncertain. Metaphor clusters centred around ideas of new territory or involving notions of a quest provide examples of these. New frontier images are quite common in discussions of the Net. Timothy Leary, for example, describes cyberspace as 'the only unconquered real estate of the twenty-first century, a virtual world at the electronic frontier inhabited by telematic nomads' (1995 as cited in Buick & Jevtic, 1995, p. 7). London reports John Perry Barlow, the hippy mystic, as saying cyberspace has a lot in common with the nineteenth century American West:

> It's vast, unmapped, culturally and legally ambiguous, hard to navigate and up for grabs. Large institutions already own the place, but most of the actual natives are solitary and independent, sometimes to the point of sociopathy. It is of course a perfect breeding ground for both outlaws and new ideas about liberty (London, 1995, n.p.).

Such new territories or spaces are associated with a need for establishing ground rules (e.g., *netiquette*, *netabuse, cybersquatters*), and ways of enforcing correct behaviour (e.g., *flaming, exile)* between regular 'inhabitants' of the Net—*netizens*. Quest images are also common—and carry with them associations of searching and journeying through a limitless world for that elusive piece of information or contact.

How metaphors function in cyberlanguage

Some analysts, according to David Crystal, consider metaphor 'to be the core of linguistic (and especially poetic) creativity' (Crystal, 1994, p. 70). The creation of metaphor involves an imaginative connection between objects or ideas and is at the heart of poetry, where it may serve to provide striking new ways of conceiving of experience, or it may draw attention to an idea or unify a set of ideas in previously unthought of or illuminating ways. In the electronic world metaphor is often used imaginatively and wittily, though many of its functions are more prosaic. Much that has to be defined or described in the electronic world is abstract, intangible and unseen. Hence, metaphor is an obvious resource for describing the contents and workings of the electronic world, or for making it possible to get hold of something fresh. It provides a succinct and efficient way to make meaning accessible, particularly to those with limited technical knowledge.

Familiarising the unfamiliar

Many of the metaphors of the *office* and the *home*, for example, serve the function of helping to familiarise the user with unfamiliar technical objects, commands or concepts. In this case the links between the objects or ideas being compared tend to be relatively logical: the logical place for storing your electronic *documents*, for example, is in your electronic *file*. When the connection requires a different kind of imaginative leap for the user, such as when Mac users are required to *dump* their discs in the *trash* to eject them from the machine, users become apprehensive fearing the contents of their discs will be deleted. Tim Rohrer points out this action requires users to act in ways that are 'counterintuitive' to their understanding of the DESKTOP metaphor which is fundamental to using the Apple Macintosh computer. He argues that human responses to metaphor choices pose a tremendous challenge for *interface* (note the metaphorical usage of a part of the human body, *face*, in this term) designers:

> I see not only a tension between the literal and magical qualities of metaphor, but a tension between the user's feelings that the computer is an extension of their bodies and believing that it is an 'other' sentient being with a consciousness of its own (and usually a malevolent consciousness at that). (Rohrer, 1995, n.p.)

Human beings regain a sense of control when they can use logic to help them find their way in a world where they may feel out of control and overwhelmed by new and mysterious demands. As Michalski argues 'relating objects in cyberspace to familiar objects from the physical world . . . quickly offers people a sense of place and sets expectations about what is possible and often about how to go about getting things done' (1997, n.p.).

Creating a sense of reality

A related function of some of the metaphorical language in use in the electronic context is the creation of the illusion that when you use the Internet you enter a 'real' world. In many ways, the virtual world is set up to reproduce the real world but makes it easier to get where you want to go and do what you want to do. The language used to navigate this world often encourages the perception that being online reproduces magically real experiences: you can actually *chat* with others in *chat rooms*, *visit* galleries and other sites, *access* a *global village*, *search* for new *buddies*, *shop* in the Internet's *mall,* and *post* your messages on the *bulletin board* by clicking a button, and without leaving your chair. At the same time, the metaphors available for talk about the Internet have built in concepts of things being bigger and better than in the real world—highways are *superhighways*, texts are *hypertexts*, seconds are *nanoseconds*, tech is *high tech*, media is *multimedia*, links are *hotlinks*; you get there faster, more easily, and seemingly at a fraction of the cost.

Expressing emotion through an impersonal medium

Communication on the Internet relies on the power of word and image to convey messages in an environment technically void of feeling. Metaphors can play a useful role in conveying strength of feeling or the seriousness of the issues involved. Images of war, violence, death and disease, for example, are often used to express strong emotion about aspects of Internet communication. The war metaphor is apparent in such phrases as *holy war* (of the kind between IBM PC users and Macintosh users, for example), and *flame war* (when an online discussion degenerates into a series of personal attacks). *Browser wars* (*Sydney Morning Herald*, 28/4/98) are on the rise as 'the Web's top tool vendors . . . tout custom-made . . . graphics tools' (p. 7c).

The weapons of war also feature strongly in extended metaphors of violence. For example, the image of firing a gun is apparent in *fire off* (to send out an email) and a *pistol* is 'a tool that makes it all too easy for you to shoot yourself in the foot' (*The Jargon Dictionary*). *Bulletproof* and *armour-plated* are highly prized qualities of computer programs and algorithms, while terms such as *kill file*, *killer poke* and *killer micro* connote destruction and ill intent. Destruction computer-style is also depicted by the term *bomb* (a general synonym for crash), which also appears in such phrases as *mail bomb* or *letterbomb* (an email message sent with the aim of crashing the recipient's mailserver or mailreader—a form of electronic harassment) and *logic bomb* (an error in logic leading to destruction of a program). Whilst associations of violence and destruction may eventually be lost or superseded through their usage in this new environment, the vein of destructive imagery identified here highlights what can be perceived as threatening and unattractive qualities of a world in the making.

Attracting attention

Metaphors are also commonly used in the electronic world to attract the attention of the user in what, after all, is a competitive market place. Metaphors which shock in their context, or which are sensual and provocative often serve to entice or engage the user's attention. The use of *hot* in a host of terms, such as *hotlist* (a list of frequently accessed WWW sites), *HotBot* (a search engine), *hot plugging* (the ability to add and remove devices to a computer while the computer is running) and *hot chat* ('a sexually explicit one-on-one' form of communication, according to *The Jargon Dictionary*) adds a strangely powerful sense of excitement and pleasure to the technology. Some metaphors contain more sexually explicit references: *teledildonics*, for example, describes sex in a computer-simulated virtual reality—especially computer-mediated sexual interaction; *rape* denotes the mass copying of files from another's web site or 'screwing someone or something violently . . . to destroy a program or information irrecoverably' (*The Jargon Dictionary*); whilst *screw* and *screwage* refer to 'user visible misbehaviour caused by a bug in the software' (*The Jargon Dictionary*).

In other cases rhetorical devices are combined with metaphorical usage to further increase the impact of the language. Wordplay is a favourite device for this purpose (e.g., *bytesexual* refers to hardware capable of computing data in different formats; *progasm* describes the euphoria experienced on the completion of a program or other computer-related project). Onomatopoeia is also commonly deployed for this purpose (e.g., *bletch*—a term of disgust used to describe a computer design or function; *gronking*—the action of disabling an individual's access to technology). The anaesthetising effect of the context of the technological world on this emotive language is a fascinating linguistic phenomenon worthy of further exploration.

Values in a virtual world

The values associated with metaphoric terms in discussions of the Internet reflect in part the shifting values of the user groups (e.g., chat room users, hackers, commercial interests, educators, researchers etc.) who create, select and give these images their meaning. It is a community always in the process of change or perpetually under reconstruction, to use a metaphor 'drawn from architecture'.

Metaphors used to talk about the Internet bring with them, initially at least, the values, attitudes and connotations of the contexts from which they are drawn. Hence, for example, *surfing the Net*, an expression used to describe the activity of visiting different Net sites according to interest or curiosity establishes this particular action as being something enjoyable, a rather free and easy activity which is not part of a work culture[6]. This has significant implications for the way the Internet is perceived by its various user groups, particularly educators. Yet there appears to be little understanding amongst users of the Internet or society at large, that language choices construct the social and cultural values of the Internet[7].

Perceptions of metaphor meanings

A further compounding factor in understanding the phenomenon of metaphors and the values they carry is that many metaphors simultaneously hold ambivalent meanings for different people and that perceptions of these meanings can change in a fairly short time span, as the discussion of the superhighway image above would indicate. The documentation of perceptions[8] gathered from responses to *The Cyber Project* are used here to provide further insights into this process.

When respondents to *The Cyber Project* were asked to identify ideas associated with terms such as the *Net*, the *Web* or *surfing the*

Net quite contradictory associations were suggested for the same item, though a core of common meanings seemed to predominate. In relation to the metaphor of the Net, for example, connotations of safety, security, linkage, connectedness and being 'drawn together' were inherent in many responses. On the other hand, a proportion of respondents saw the Net negatively as representing 'potential entrapment or imprisonment'. Similarly, the fishing net origin of the term was associated with a sense of being 'enclosed, locked in, limited, unable to move freely'. Different cultural associations can also influence interpretation of meanings—for example, the Buddhist image of the Net of Indra, a network of pearls in each of which all the other pearls of the net are reflected, an image which has particular meaning for some Net users (Cameron, 1995).

The Web was also perceived in contradictory ways by respondents to the Project. The image of 'spreading out', 'moving around the world' and facilitating communication was evident in some responses, whilst others emphasised the sense of belonging it gives: 'everything's related, part of a bigger whole—I'm part of a big picture'. Less attractive associations included the Web as a maze which confused and bewildered, and the spider-web image, in which the notion of entrapment was emphasised: the web was seen as 'sticky and likely to take captives', and embodying fatally attractive powers[9]. On the other hand, a positive spin is placed on the role of the spider and its web in some expressions using these terms: *Spiders,* for example, are useful and essential programs in a medium in which new information exceeds the usual manual indexing practices and the *WebCrawler* allows the user to travel anywhere on the Internet to gather relevant information. In contrast, Jon Casimir ascribes more ambiguous connotations to the Web: '...it is clear that the web is all things to all people. Like a mirror, it reflects your beliefs and interests' (*Sydney Morning Herald*, 2/5/98, p. 8).

Connotations listed for *surfing the Net* included relaxation and (possibly purposeless) enjoyment, youthful activity, having fun, exhilaration and danger. The term was seen as being linked with images which place emphasis on pleasurable activities such as *cruising* and *browsing* in a leisurely fashion. Some associated *browsing* with 'wandering', 'just looking around', 'relaxing' and 'not needing to think'. The actual activity of surfing the Net, according to statistics, is not exclusively taken up by the young; older age groups have responded equally well[10], and often happily talk of *surf-*

ing the Net and *getting a hit* as though born to the experience. Macquarie University in Sydney, NSW, has introduced a training course entitled 'Searching, not surfing, the Net' which may mark the beginning of a change in attitude. The new title seems to carry an element of disapproval for the laziness and lack of emphasis on serious business implied by 'surfing'.

New images and new meanings

Some researchers have called for changes to the kind of imagery being used in relation to the Net and have expressed the view that if only we could change our imagery we would be able to create a different kind of world which would prove more inviting and more productive. As noted in chapter one, Dale Spender has urged that metaphors of the village community be used to replace the current 'rev-head images of superhighways' arguing that such usage will make women feel and be less alienated (Spender, 1995, p. 166). Peter Russell, a physicist and philosopher, argues in his book *The Global Brain Awakes* that 'a global brain metaphor' has more to offer than the superhighway metaphor as he believes man's next evolutionary leap will be to advance to the point where minds are linked together to create a collective consciousness through an ever growing web of communication (1995 as cited in London, 1995, n.p.). Kevin Howley also makes a plea for moving away from the superhighway metaphor arguing that its connotations of linearity, transportation, progress and speed obscure the potential for emerging technologies to radically alter sociopolitical relations. He finds William Gibson's view of cyberspace as 'consensual hallucination'[11] an improvement but still problematic in its vague, illusory and decidedly pessimistic vision of the 'matrix'. He would like to see the metaphor of agricultural collaboration used to promote the new media environment 'in that it is a productive environment, an ongoing process of creating, using and sharing information, an electronic reaping and sowing' (Howley, 1996, n.p.).

Even the title of this book, 'Cyberlines: Languages and cultures of the Internet', can be interpreted as containing a view of the cyberworld as a place where individuals are linked into communities with their own histories and meanings, and implying that as a society we have a responsibility to ensure those meanings are made sensitively and inclusively.

However, attempts to encourage reconceptualisations of the virtual world are likely to be in vain as language is not normally responsive to legislation or to pleas by individuals. At the same time raising awareness and developing knowledge about the role of language in the construction of this world brings with it considerable benefits. It brings greater understanding about the nature of the world we are accessing. It helps us to understand how we are being positioned within that world both in relation to each other, and to the information which is provided. It teaches us about our society—what it is doing and where it is going. This is invaluable information for educators and for all those who surf the Internet, for whatever purpose.

Endnotes

1. For a discussion of discourses assembled around metaphors of convergence, and the market and liberal democracy, see Kenway (1995, pp. 38-39).
2. AIDS refers to A Infected Disk Syndrome (contracted as a result of practicing unsafe SEX). In hacker circles, the act of Software Exchange is abbreviated to the mnemonic SEX. SEX parties are described as a 'Good Thing, but unprotected SEX can propagate a virus' (*The Jargon Dictionary*).
3. Death metaphors tend to be used to signify the breakdown of a computer or the intentional sabotage of software programs. Paradoxically, the language suggests that to be without the technology —a lifeless entity in itself—is to be without life, for when one 'returns from the dead', one is said to regain access to the Net after a long absence.
4. The *PCWebopedia* recorded this as a new term in December, 1998 and defined it as 'an error that can appear on computers running Macintosh *Windows 95* or *Windows NT*. Jokingly called the *blue screen of death* because when the error occurs the screen turns blue, and the computer almost always freezes and requires rebooting'.
5. The superhighway metaphor has, for example, been criticised for being 'weak and tired' (Martin, 1995), 'cliched' (Hunt & Doherty, 1995), misleading, inaccurate and culturally exclusive (Adrian, 1995; Druick, 1995), and conceptually dangerous (Ackerman, 1994). For further discussion of the alienating impact of this metaphor, see below p. 212.
6. Other terms related to teenage surfing culture which were mentioned as part of this metaphor cluster include *bodysurf* code (a program written quickly in the heat of inspiration), *board* (often used as an abbreviation for circuit board) and *HotDog* (a professional web

editor).

7. Data collected from *The Cyber Project* (see above, Note 8, p. 27), and from preservice students in the Teacher Education Program at Macquarie University (see above pp. 24-25), along with analysis of language used by the media in reporting material related to the Internet, confirms the view that for many people there is a low level of awareness about the implications of language choices in this context.
8. The role of perceptions in the thinking processes and subsequent attitudes and behaviours of individuals is well supported by research (Kellogg, 1994; Neisser, 1976).
9. A new branch of psychological research has developed to address the chronic problems associated with Internet addiction. Experts in this growing field suggest that the Internet has become 'a destructive force, its remarkable benefits overshadowed by its potential to disrupt the lives of those who can't resist the lure of round-the-clock social opportunities, entertainment and information . . . Some smokers report that cravings to get on the Internet are even stronger than the urge to light up' (Potera, 1998, p. 66).
10. In November 1998, the Search Engine *Excite* reported on a study, Third Age Online, which found that 83% of 50 plus users of the Internet log on every day, the same percentage as that of under 50 users. (See the *Internet User Demographics, Attitudes* site).
11. For a fuller discussion of Gibson's views of cyberspace, see above p. 13 and below pp. 176-177.

References

Ackerman, M. S. (1994). Metaphors along the Information Highway. Available: http://www.ics.uci.edu/~ackerman/docs/diac94/diac.final.html [1998, December 5].

Adrian, R. (1995). Infobahn blues. Available: http://www.ctheory.com/a-infobahn_blues.html [1998, December 5].

Aristotle. (1924). *Rhetoric.* In W. D. Ross (Ed.), *Works*: Vol xi. (W. Rhys Roberts, Trans.). Oxford: Clarendon Press.

Buick, J., & Jevtic, Z. (1995). *Cyberspace for beginners.* Cambridge: Icon Books Ltd.

Cameron, C. (1995). Waterbird: A metaphor for the Net. Available: http://pespmc1.vub.ac.be/CYBSPACY/CCameron.html [1998, December 5].

Crystal, D. (1994). *The Cambridge Encyclopedia of Language.* Cambridge: Cambridge University Press.

Druick, Z. (1995). The information superhighway, or The politics of metaphor. Available: http://english-www.hss.cmu.edu:80/bs/18/Druck.html [1998, December 5].

Fiumara, G. C. (1995). *The metaphoric process*. London: Routledge.

Gibbs, D., & Krause, K. (1997). *The Cyber Project*. Available: http://www.mq.edu.au/Educ/cyberspeak/cyber1.htm [1998, December 5].

Goatley, A. (1997). *The language of metaphors*. London: Routledge.

Hale, C. (Ed.). (1996). *Wired style: Principles of English usage in the digital age*. San Francisco: Hardwired.

Howley, K. (1996). Electronic agrarianism: or Thomas Jefferson gets a modem. Available: http://pespmc1.vub.ac.be:80/BSPASY/Khowley.html [1998, December 5].

Hunt, K., & Doherty, M. (1995). Of ivory towers and infobahns. Available: http://www.december.com/cm/mag/1995/jan/lastlink.html [1998, December 5].

Internet User Demographics, Attitudes. Available: http://www.internet-magazine.com/hot/users.htm [1998, December 5].

Kellogg, R. T. (1994). *The psychology of writing*. New York: Oxford University Press.

Kenway, J. (1995). Reality bytes: Education, markets and the information superhighway. *Australian Education Researcher, 22* (1), 35-64.

London, S. (1995). Cyberspace and the new consciousness. Available: http://www.leary.com/news/NewMedia/London.html [1998, December 7].

Martin, G. (1995). Is the information superhighway a misnomer? Available: http://www.niehs.nih.gov:80/Connections/Archives/Arch95/Feb95/url.html [1998, December 5].

Michalski, J. (1997). Metaphors and the Net. Available: http://www.edventure.com/pods/physical.html [1998, December 5].

Neisser, U. (1976). *Cognition and reality: Principles and implications of cognitive psychology*. San Francisco: W. H. Freeman and Company.

PCWebopedia. Available: http://www.webopedia.com/ [1998, December 3].

Potera, C. (1998). Trapped in the web. *Psychology Today, 31* (2), 66-72.

Rohrer, T. (1995). Feelings stuck in a GUI web: Metaphors, image-schemata, and designing the human computer interface. Available: http://metaphor.uoregon.edu/gui4web.htm [1998, December 5].

Spender, D. (1995). *Nattering on the Net: Women, power and cyberspace*. North Melbourne: Spinifex Press.

The Jargon Dictionary. Available: http://www.netmeg.net/jargon/terms/ [1998, November 3].

Wilde, O. (1998). *The Importance of Being Earnest.* In *The complete plays.* London: Methuen. (Original work published in 1895).

Chapter 3

Re(de)fining dictionaries: From paper to pixel

Scott Fitzgerald

Naysaying the soothsayers

THE FUTURE OF THE BOOK
THE DEATH OF THE BOOK?
THE END OF THE BOOK

Headlines such as these have for some time been appearing in newspapers and magazines around the world, and have also been the subject of numerous academic books, journals and conferences. The more sensational articles depict a future in which the format of the book disappears, and is replaced totally by texts in such formats as CD-ROM and the Internet. These articles in the popular press have a rather fearful tenor, juxtaposing the warmth of the book with the cold, clinical nature of technology. The book format, which has enjoyed an exponential growth in popularity and accessibility since the Gutenberg Bible of 1453, does indeed face severe competition with these nascent technologies. The prediction of the future would seem to be nothing more than mere guesswork. While I can make no claims to be prescient on this matter, what I would like to do is to look at the effect of these technologies upon one genre of book—the dictionary.

The writing was off the wall, and onto ...

The currently dominant format of information storage, the book, has been with us since approximately 100 CE[1]. The invention of writing, in about 3500 BCE in Mesopotamia, and its use on clay tablets, was the start of the quantum leap in the information revolution, a revolution which has continued to this day. Of course, information had been recorded on natural and built structures before this, but with the flowering of pictography, and subsequently logography and orthography, and with the growth of civilisation, the revolution began.

By approximately 2000 BCE the Egyptians had begun to record information with a brush pen on papyrus, made from a plant found only in the Nile River Valley. Papyrus had the advantage of being a more manageable and portable material than clay tablets, an important point because the amount of information recorded was ever increasing. Papyrus was a finite resource, and the supply was soon exhausted. As always, technology advanced continually on, and parchment, a superior material to papyrus, began to be used around 1600 BCE, with sharp-tipped pens later replacing brush pens. Paper, as we know it today, was invented by the Chinese and exported around the world, later being manufactured in other countries, to become the absolutely dominant material by the tenth century.

The page is opened on the book

The next major development, in the second century, was the modern form of the book, hand-written at this stage of course. Its main predecessor, the papyrus roll, did last until the seventh century, but the book over time became the preferred format as a tool in the information revolution. The real explosion in the development of the book came as the metal type press was invented, pioneered by Johannes Gutenberg and others in the late fifteenth century. These early printing presses were hand-powered, and incredibly successful, resulting in an unprecedented number of new texts—it is estimated that there were more books printed in the last thirty years of the fifteenth century than there had been in the preceding nine hundred years (Kilgour, 1998, p. 85). The achievement of these early presses was dwarfed by the technical innovation, in the nineteenth century, of machine-powered printing presses, and, in our century, of offset printing.

Importantly, particularly in view of contemporary concern for the fate of the book, it should be remembered that the early formats, the clay tablet, papyrus roll and book, were not successive. All of these formats experienced a period in which they overlapped, by up to 2000 years.

The continuing sophistication of printing technology brought associated benefits for society. Literacy has continued to increase, in line with the increase in information available. Initially books were for the privileged classes, but as books have become more plentiful and cheaper, and with the institution of public libraries (in the middle of the nineteenth century in England and the United States), the reading public has grown. Printed matter was not limited to books — newspapers began to be published in the early seventeenth century, and periodicals a short time later. In addition to this increased printed matter was the flourishing of education, with more schools and an increasing number of universities. Demand for texts was driven by better technology, more availability, and a growing base of consumers. As the number of texts increased, and the number of readers, there was an associated growth in the need for a particular type of book: the dictionary.

A brief history of lexicography

The dictionary has also had a long history, its content, appearance and philosophies evolving into the various types of dictionaries (such as general, or unabridged, learners', bilingual, specialist subject and so on) that are used today. The early dictionaries used in England in the Middle Ages were nothing more than glossaries, giving word equivalents to enable the English to learn words in Latin and French, a reflection of the troubled and fighting birth of the English language. English was regarded as a vernacular, those other languages being the prestige varieties. English was a cobbled together language that had absorbed words and influences from not only Latin and French, but also Celtic, Germanic and Norse languages.

In the late sixteenth century various countries began to form language academies, with the intention of keeping their languages 'pure'. Examples of these academies were the Accademia della Crusca in Italy, founded in 1582, and in France the Académie Française, founded in 1625[2]. There were plans to establish an academy in England at that time, and there were later attempts, none of which came to fruition. However, what did occur was the continued acceptance of English in England, to the point that it became not only the language of popular choice, but also the language of officialdom. A standard English was in use in the fourteenth century. A flow-on from this acceptance was the use of English in literature, and the publication of dictionaries to support this literary activity. The importance of this is that the language was *validated* by its use in these endeavours. The first dictionary of English alone was Robert Cawdrey's *A Table Alphabeticall*[3], published in 1604. This was a collection of approximately 2500 headwords[4], with many being defined by synonyms rather than actual definitions. Another difference between this dictionary and those that came later was that the headwords were all hard words, that is words considered unknown to those English people without the benefit of a Classical education. Many of these words were Anglicised versions of Greek and Latin words.

Dictionaries continued to evolve, with the art and craft of lexicography ever improving. The books defined an increasing number of words, with definitions that were more than simply synonyms, and compilations that were more than simply collections of hard words. Of the many dictionaries published, several stand out for their innovation, providing the bridge between the past and the present. Nathan Bailey's *Universal Etymological Dictionary* of 1721 used diagrams, provided etymological details and illustrative phrases, and showed the syllabification of the headwords. Samuel Johnson's *Dictionary of the English Language* of 1755 used citations from literary works to illustrate a word's usage, and Noah Webster's *An American Dictionary of the English Language* blazed a trail for dictionaries of regional varieties of English after its publication in 1828. The *Oxford English Dictionary* published between 1884 and 1928, a mammoth twelve-volume dictionary based on historical principles, provided the story, lexicographically, of the English language.

Lexicography and the computer

All modern dictionaries have benefited from the trail-blazing achievements of these and other works. However, there is one invaluable tool we have to add to the ideas of the pioneers — the computer. Lexicographers have made increasing use of computers since the mid-1960s, when a database system was first used by the editors of the *Random House Dictionary of the English Language*. In the latter years of the 1960s dictionaries began to be typeset using computers. In the time since then computers have enabled the compilation of huge dictionary databases and language corpora, enabling lexicographers to analyse and extract data far more rapidly than they had previously, in addition to being able to more precisely fashion a query using that data. The dictionary user has benefited over this time through the publication of improved dictionaries, with a wider range of titles and perhaps a better picture of the language due to the evidence obtained from the corpora.

While these have been no small achievements, recent technological developments can even more directly benefit the dictionary user. CD-ROMs and the Internet both became viable commercial formats in the early 1990s. A CD-ROM is at the moment able to contain on one disk the same amount of text held in between 500 and 1000 novels. With the invention of graphical user interface browser software in 1993, the Internet, or to be more precise the World Wide Web (WWW) has experienced a remarkably rapid growth rate. It is estimated that by the year 2000 there will be one billion users of the WWW worldwide (Nielsen, 1995, p. 167). What, then, will be the effect of these formats upon the dictionary? Following are some possibilities, in no order of importance.

Space — the elimination of frontiers

One of the more frustrating limitations of the book format when compiling a dictionary is the finiteness of space. So-called unabridged dictionaries (also known as general dictionaries), which attempt to give the user the most overall picture of the landscape of a language, are in no way unabridged. Given that these dictionaries usually contain just over 100,000 headwords, and that there is still no firm idea of the number of words actually contained in a language (estimates at the size of the English lexicon have been put at over four million words (Landau, 1989, p. 17)), no dictionary can be truly unabridged. These dictionaries are not only limited by space in what can be printed between the covers, but also by what is a manageable physical size of these covers. A dictionary of large proportions would buckle under its own weight, and equally importantly, the cost of such a dictionary to the user would be prohibitive.

Therefore, with each new edition of a dictionary the finiteness of space dictates a selection process. What headwords do the editors include? In the case of an unabridged dictionary, what archaic or obsolete words or senses of words have to be deleted to make way for new words and new senses? The selection of what stays and what goes is usually a lively source of debate, sometimes heated, and always there is regret. There are only so many ways a book can be tweaked so that the regret can be minimised[5]. The new digital formats eliminate this problem. There is of course, as mentioned earlier, a finiteness to the CD-ROM, but it is far less restrictive than the book, and it should also be remembered that the amount of data held on a disk is sure to increase as the technology matures. A dictionary published on the Internet has even fewer spatial limitations, being only limited by the amount of disk storage space held by the server of the publisher, which is easily and relatively cheaply upgradeable.

It would still be an ambitious pursuit, to say the least, for a dictionary to contain all of a language, but the elimination of spatial restrictions will enable dictionaries to more accurately and fully record a language. All manner of neologisms could be included, from the mainstream to the esoteric. This would be without paying the price of losing any of the historical nature of a dictionary, so that the digitised dictionary will be not only a more functional tool for the user, but also a better reflection of the language.

Words and phrases everywhere, and all of them are linked

In addition to being able to provide more headwords, the editors could also provide more information within each entry. Some dictionaries currently provide usage notes, which give advice on common problems with certain lexical items (for example, the difference between *affect* and *effect*). In an electronic dictionary the number of usage notes could be increased, perhaps to the point where the dictionary acquires much of the role of another type of book, the style guide.

Links could be provided to a thesaurus, and also, if there were more than one style of dictionary available, the different definitions of the same words could be hyperlinked. The use of hyperlinks would solve the difficulty of tailoring a dictionary for a particular age group, or level of proficiency. If a user felt a definition inadequate for their needs they could simply uplink to a more suitable definition.

The ability to hyperlink, both internally and externally, provides numerous advantages for the user. Within the dictionary hyperlinks could be used to explain the meaning of difficult words in a given definition, in the tradition of the hard words dictionaries of the past. In this way, the meaning of a word may be more quickly assimilated. Whether this was in the form of another window opening with the meaning of the difficult word, or whether it was another method, such as a *mouseover*[6], the user would be able to quickly and conveniently satisfy their lexical enquiry.

Another helpful feature would be the ability to provide hyperlinks from every record or location within the dictionary to the information that is contained within the book form of the dictionary, in the preliminary pages. This is the part of the book form of the dictionary which few people read, which is a matter of some regret, as contained here are the instructions to be able to more fully understand and use the content. There are guides to grammar and pronunciation, the style of the dictionary (that is, the explanatory notes on the construction of the entries), and often also small essays on various aspects of the language. Any way in which the user can be alerted to this part of the dictionary is something to be pursued with some vigour.

External links to other parts of a website, or indeed to other websites, could be very helpful in a dictionary containing encyclopedic material. The dictionary would provide a dictionary-style definition, providing the briefest of information, and also a link to a complete encyclopedic entry. This of course further blurs the distinction between the dictionary and the encyclopedia, and begs the question of the future of the two styles of book—will they simply be more closely related, or will there evolve a new hybrid style?

Etymology exploded

As previously mentioned, the ability to hyperlink to the explanatory matter of the dictionary opens new frontiers for the user, as does the elimination of spatial restraint. Another possible new frontier for some users, and in which the lessening of space restrictions and hyperlinking is a boon, is in the area of etymology. This, in the book form, is an area which is heavily condensed, or packed, and, as a result, etymology is perhaps a widely neglected component of a dictionary. This is a pity, as the etymology of words provides a fascinating insight into the history of not only a language, but also of a society. Given that space is not a limiting factor in the new dictionary, etymology may assume a new image. There are numerous ways of accomplishing this, and it is also important to remember that in all areas a dictionary will no longer be a static database, it becomes, through the aid of technology, a fluid and flexible database, with the user able to navigate all of the data in any number of ways. Thus the condensed nature could be sought by those who are used to that representation of etymology, or a user could choose to tailor the dictionary to unpack the etymology, by linking to a more discursive form. Another option could be to represent the etymology graphically. Perhaps the various words that are the antecedents of the headword could be located on something akin to a family tree, much like the tree of Indo-European languages that are found as an appendix in many larger general dictionaries. Another option would be to use the notion of a timeline, locating the antecedents temporally. Any of these, or indeed any other ideas that a lexicographer may have, would add to the functionality of the dictionary, and open the mine of information that is currently in the book form of dictionaries to more people.

Multimedia

The notion of graphic representation is a reminder of the other great advantage of the digital dictionary over the print version—the ability to make a multimedia dictionary. Put simply, a dictionary can be given graphics and sound. Graphics are of course not a recent innovation, they have been a feature of some print dictionaries since the mid-nineteenth century, and since that time there have been numerous dictionaries employing either drawings or photographs to accompany and enhance the definition of words. In this, the new dictionary faces similar issues to those of print dictionaries, regardless of the fact that there are no spatial restraints. The illustration in a dictionary is not merely decoration: it is there to aid the user's comprehension of a headword or definition. Secondly, there is the matter of the cost of the acquisition of the illustrations. Even if it were physically possible in a print dictionary, the cost of acquisition, that is the cost of employing an illustrator or photographer, or of purchasing existing graphics, and of course the added printing costs, limits the amount of illustration. Indeed, even if it were possible, both physically and fiscally, it should be remembered that the role of an illustration in a dictionary is to depict 'unusual or unfamiliar things' (Landau, 1989, p. 112). It is also dependent upon the type of dictionary: 'The more elementary or pedagogical the work is, the more useful are illustrations' (p. 115).

While on the topic of graphics, a related subject is that of the appearance of the dictionary on the computer screen. The notion of flexibility again comes into play, as, in the case of a dictionary on the WWW, the user can alter such things as font colour, type and size, as well as the colour of the background of the screen. Most online dictionaries allow the user to search for a word, and then present the user with the hits, in the form of links, from the database that the search term matches. Upon clicking a link, the user is taken directly to the entry in isolation. What would be a helpful option would be to be taken to a complete page, just as you would if you were looking up a word in a print dictionary. This is not an act of Luddism—it can be interesting, sometimes serendipitous, to see what surrounds a particular headword.

In addition to the greater capacity to display graphics, the ability to employ multimedia in the new dictionary provides at least one other quantum leap in user-friendliness—spoken pronunciation. In print dictionaries pronunciation is often represented by the use of the International Phonetic Alphabet (IPA), in which a combination of regular and altered alphabetic characters phonetically represent the sound of words, or by a systematic method of respelling the headwords, using the standard letters of the alphabet, sometimes with diacritical marks. Both are useful methods, but again there is the matter of accessibility, as they do require a degree of decoding. A preferable method would be that of providing the actual sound of the words using links, and in both CD-ROM and Internet dictionaries this facility can be provided. While this will be of some benefit in general dictionaries, particularly in such areas as difficult words, and those which are words borrowed from another language, the real benefits will be for dictionaries for children and learners, and for bilingual/multilingual dictionaries.

The dictionary for now

An associated benefit of publishing a dictionary on the WWW is the immediacy of electronic media. As previously mentioned, dictionaries will be far more lexically contemporary, as there will no longer be a period of years between editions as there is in print dictionaries. There will be more frequent updates, resulting in an extremely well-tended database.

Other benefits of this immediacy will be provided through the enthusiastically and widely used communications system of electronic mail, or email. The publishers of dictionaries will be able to send out, via a mailing list, newsletters and the like informing the users of new additions or developments. The users will also be able to email the dictionary editors, and this is the exciting part of the relationship for both parties involved. A regrettable fact is that sometimes errors do creep into the data, and as dictionaries are not a text that is, as a rule, read from cover to cover, they can go unnoticed for some time. With a large base of users, such errors can be picked up, the editors alerted by email, and the errors duly corrected.

Access to the lexicographical citadel

Another exciting use of email is to allow the user to contribute to the content of the dictionary[7]. The evidence of the existence of a word, its spelling, meaning and part of speech, is through citations or examples of the word in actual use. These are collected by a specialist team of readers employed only for this purpose, or through the tireless and eagle-eyed efforts of lexicographers, or specialists in the various subject areas the dictionary covers. Citations are taken from novels, textbooks, journals, magazines, newspapers, spoken texts, indeed from all media, and all genres. The base of users would vastly multiply the number of word watchers that a dictionary publisher has at its disposal. Ideally there would be a citation form as part of the dictionary website, showing the user exactly how to record a citation. Not only would this increase the number of citations, it would also be of help in some areas of evidentiary impoverishment. A prime example of this could be the contribution to the recording of regional varieties of a language[8].

The search for meaning ... and spelling, subject, crossword solutions, ...

A print dictionary can be a daunting text, often due to its size, or perhaps the complexity of a language, and the needs of a user can be many. It can be difficult for the user to formulate a query in such a way as to give them an entry point into the dictionary. Publishing a dictionary electronically can make dictionaries far less formidable, through the search capacity of computers, and through the use of markup languages.

In McLean's chapter 5 in this collection, problems faced by users searching for information in the vastness that is the WWW are discussed. While dictionary databases in no way approach the vastness of the Web, they are quite large, and the query of a user can be sometimes difficult to fashion. They may of course know exactly what they wish to find, and exactly how that lexical item is spelt, but as stated earlier, digital dictionaries can be extremely flexible, designed in such a way that the user can tailor the dictionary for their particular usage.

Spelling, as mentioned above, can sometimes be a problem. How is a user to look up an unknown word and yet be expected to spell it correctly? Systems to aid this have been in place for some time in electronic publishing. 'Wildcard' searches, in which the user places a character, such as **?** or *, to stand for unknown characters, is an excellent method. Another is to allow 'fuzzy spelling' searches, in which the user makes a best guess at the correct spelling, with common spelling errors or close approximations of the correct spelling built into the dictionary search engine. The benefit of systems such as these is that the user still finds the information they seek, and, hopefully, they are alerted to the correct spelling in their future usage of that word.

Another boon in the search for information in the digital format is the markup language, which facilitates the structuring and presentation of information[9]. Dictionary data is sorted not only into fields such as headwords and definitions, but others such as pronunciation, etymology, and labels, be they restrictive (the labelling of taboo words for example), regional or field (special areas such as Astronomy, Metallurgy, Cricket). Because of this structure of the data, searches can be restricted to specified fields. This ability to search on an atom of dictionary data means that not only is the data more accessible, allowing the user to find what they need from only a small or partial query, but it also allows the user to filter the data. Rather than conducting a haphazard read-through of a printed dictionary, a user could, if they wanted to, research a particular subject area for instance, search on a specialised subject label, be given all the terms with that label, and by following links located within those entries, both to encylopedic information and to external websites, become armed with a good knowledge of that particular area.

Tailored searches such as this are limited only by the level of complexity of the underlying markup language. The ability to conduct searches in this way makes the dictionary a less formidable, but no less authoritative publication, and gives the dictionary user a valuable tool that lexicographers have enjoyed for some time.

The cash ceiling?

The cost of publishing a dictionary was alluded to earlier, and if there is one restriction that remains to any advancement, it is money. Most print dictionaries of the world are commercial publishing ventures, and it is estimated that the annual cost of running even a small dictionary staff is in excess of US$100,000 (Landau, 1989, p. 291). This is not including such things as the cost of computing equipment and the costs of the production of each publication (design, typesetting, paper, ink, printing, etc.). Although a dictionary in electronic form, whether CD-ROM or online, is cheaper to produce than that in book form, the cost of staffing does not fall. The user must also outlay quite a large amount simply to own a computer and associated equipment, and also in the case of online content they must pay fees to an Internet Service Provider. Add to this the extreme youth of the media, and the future is again unclear. There will certainly be growth, and costs will come down, but financial matters will continue to influence not only growth, but also content, and the implementation of new ideas and technologies.

Conclusion

Dictionaries are a storehouse, not only of our language, but also of our culture, in that our words are a reflection of our culture. They are documents that tell much about the society who speaks the language — about its history, politics, social structures, leisure activities, religions, and much more. By comparing the dictionaries of different countries we can see the different world views of those countries, or cultures. The next generation of digital dictionaries will, by its advantages over the book form, enable lexicographers to more faithfully and fully record language, and the user to better investigate it.

The reference book is well served by the unlimited structural possibilities of digitisation. As Philip Gove, the eminent American lexicographer wrote in 1970, 'dictionaries of the future—of the next century—will be much better than those of the twentieth century' (as cited in Ilson, 1986, p. 123), and we will long leave behind Samuel Johnson's notion of a lexicographer as 'a writer of dictionaries; a harmless drudge, that busies himself in tracing the original and detailing the significance of words'[10]. Rather lexicography will be an exciting record of the continuing advances of the information revolution.

Endnotes

1. I have used the convention of Common Era rather than the culturally loaded BC and AD, with BCE (Before Common Era) replacing BC, and CE (Common Era) replacing AD.
2. The French desire to maintain the purity of their language is still quite strong. In 1977 it was made law that where a French word existed, an English loan word could not be used in official documents. For a discussion of ways the French have resisted English-based character sets see below, chapter 9.
3. The title of Cawdrey's book is a pointer to the fact that arranging the words in alphabetical order was something of an innovation and a selling point. Other dictionaries had grouped words together in semantic concepts, in the manner of a thesaurus.
4. A headword is a word or expression in a dictionary which begins an entry, and is usually printed in a bold typeface. An alternative term is lemma.
5. In the case of the third edition of the *Macquarie Dictionary*, published in 1997, it was found that the book could accommodate 500 more pages than the second edition, while keeping the thickness of the book the same size, by using paper normally used to publish Bibles.
6. A mouseover is a small program written in the computer language Java, in which a small text box appears as the cursor is dragged over a particular part of the text on a screen.
7. An example of this is KiD (*Kids' Internet Dictionary*), a website at which children from around the world contribute words and their own definitions, and notes on their usage.
8. This is particularly relevant to Australia, where both the country and its dictionaries are young. There has been work done on regionalisms by linguists, but there is far more to be done, and far more to be included in Australian dictionaries.
9. The language SGML (standard general markup language) structures data, while HTML (hypertext markup language) dictates the way in which the structured data is presented on the screen.
10. This is the definition of 'lexicographer' as it appears in Johnson's Dictionary.

References

Atkins, B. T. S. (1996). Bilingual dictionaries past, present and future. In M. Gellerstam (Ed.), *Euralex '96 Proceedings: Papers submitted to the Seventh EURALEX International Congress on Lexicography in Göteborg, Sweden: Part II* (pp. 515-546).

Atkins, B. T. S., & Zampolli, A. (Eds.). (1994). *Computational approaches to the lexicon*. Oxford: Oxford University Press.

Australian National Dictionary Centre - Schools Dictionary Project. Available: http://www.anu.edu.au/ANDC/Schools [1998, September 15].

Carr, M. (1997). Internet dictionaries and lexicography. *International Journal of Lexicography*, *10* (3), 209-230.

Crystal, D. (1995). *The Cambridge Encyclopedia of the English Language*. Cambridge: Cambridge University Press.

Ilson, R. (Ed.). (1986). *Lexicography: An emerging international profession*. Manchester: Manchester University Press.

KiD Kids' Internet Dictionary. Available: http://macdict.dict.mq.edu.au:5780/mackidnet [1998, September 10].

Kilgour, F. G. (1998). *The evolution of the book*. New York: Oxford University Press.

Landau, S. I. (1989). *Dictionaries: The art and craft of lexicography*. Cambridge: Cambridge University Press.

MacquarieNet. Available: http://www.macnet.mq.edu.au [1998, September 15].

Nielsen, J. (1995). *Multimedia and hypertext: The internet and beyond*. Cambridge, MA: Academic Press.

Nunberg, G. (Ed.). (1996). *The future of the book*. Berkeley: University of California Press.

OneLook Dictionaries. Available: http://www.onelook.com/ [1998, September 15].

PCWebopedia. Available: http://www.webopedia.internet.com/ [1998, September 15].

WordNet. Available: http://www.cogsci.princeton.edu/~wn/about/ [1998, September 15].

Wordsmyth English Dictionary-Thesaurus. Available: http://www.lightlink.com/bobp/wedt/wedt-artfl.html [1998, September 15].

Part 2

The New Literacies

Chapter 4

Screenreading: Challenges of the new literacy

Jennifer Thurstun

Introduction

The technology of the late twentieth century is radically altering the nature of literacy. Courseware, training materials, books, journals, magazines, newspapers and letters are all being supplemented and sometimes replaced by electronic text and multimedia information. Considering the enormity of the impact on our habits of learning, accessing information and communicating, surprisingly little attention has been given to the challenges facing the reader, who is expected, often with little or no training, to deal with electronically presented information.

Technology and literacy

Technology has always been closely associated with literacy—from the development of the alphabet, written script, the printing press, the ballpoint pen, film and television, ultimately to the computer, the Internet and the World Wide Web[1]. Each new development has influenced our understanding of literacy and literacy practices, and computers are perhaps the most revolutionary of all the more recent developments. Some consider computers to have interrupted our normal understandings and practices of literacy (Bigum & Green, 1993). More accepting attitudes (see Corbel, 1997) see literacy as an endless process of extending one's repertoire of text types and genres, and computer literacy as an extension of that repertoire. There is little doubt, however, that the new technology is changing the nature of how people read and acquire information and that this transition is not without its difficulties.

Although the ability to read is fundamental to the ability to use a computer and the Internet effectively, it is doubtful that the print reading skills to which most of us are accustomed are adequate for efficient screen reading (or, from another point of view, that the reading skills fostered by frequent computer use are the kind of skills that support effective print reading). Indeed, much of the skill required for accessing online information requires an ability to understand icons and hieroglyphics and to navigate between graphic displays, video and sound rather than the actual reading of text. Text, however, remains, despite determined efforts to reduce it when in online form. The basic problems for the reader of online materials, apart from perceptual difficulties, seem to spring from the lack of a traditional schema (the text structure that allows a reader to make assumptions and predictions about a text), which leaves the reader with problems for navigating an effective way through electronic text and with searching for specific information. These are skills which are often assumed rather than taught.

The new medium relies on both old and new skills and understandings. Kress (1995, p. 1) suggests that it is 'taking us both backwards and forwards into a new era of iconic forms of communication, backwards and forwards into hieroglyphics'. He considers that this move to icons is related to an increasing awareness of the problems of using language alone as a form of communication in heterogeneous and multicultural societies. It also seems to be a development imposed by the nature of the technology itself. Corbel (1997) points out that with scrolling (which he believes impedes online reading) designers went even further back in history than the development of print for a metaphor. He considers that classic print literacy may be pushed aside as new text types and forms of communication gain power. He counted 126 actions available from the menu and window borders surrounding *Word 6.0*. About half of these are terms familiar from print, but many others have no print equivalent.

Technology is providing enormously exciting possibilities for the presentation of information, but the difficulties encountered when reading and interpreting information presented on the new medium are perhaps given insufficient attention both by writers of online material and by those who require users to obtain information via the computer screen. Bigum and Green (1993) stress the lack of critique in the presentation of information via the new technologies and the need for critical thought on the implications of these innovations for education and literacy. They also remind us that new information technologies in education are driven largely by commercial rather than educational interests. In some ways, the information superhighway is 'a solution in search of a problem' (Kenway,

1995, p. 40) and education, for example, is seen as a promising application. The so-called experts in educational software are often also marketing directors. Some degree of caution is therefore appropriate as we launch into the era of electronic literacy— we need to be sure that it works for us, not vice versa.

Differences between e-texts and p-texts

Electronic texts (e-texts) differ in quite radical ways from print texts (p-texts), and it appears that some of these differences create difficulties for the reader. The differences have definite implications for the way we work with e-texts and skills we need to acquire in order to work with them well. To summarise some of these differences briefly:

- e-texts are flexible and can be altered or added to by the user (particularly with hypertext in which users create a version of the text as they go), whereas p-texts are fixed and permanent;
- e-texts draw on a range of meaning systems (print, icons, illustrations, sound and movies can be fully integrated into the text) whereas p-texts use a much more limited range of meaning systems;
- in e-texts, there is usually a smaller proportion of print to images than in p-texts;
- interaction with e-texts is overt, with p-texts it is private and less obvious. One can choose pathways in e-texts, change them, add to them, delete them—quite a different relationship to that of p-texts which involves selection, reflection and creation of meaning;
- e-texts permit easy collaboration whereas p-texts are more amenable to individual work;
- in e-texts the reader needs to follow links, understand the way links are signalled and find ways of going to a previous location. P-texts, on the other hand, provide the reader with the more familiar features of page numbers, table of contents, index, chapter divisions, headings; and
- search techniques for e-texts are new skills to be learned (by category, search word, theme), whereas p-texts use the features mentioned above.

Considering the differences between these two systems, the reader of electronic texts needs to develop new skills and understandings in order to deal effectively with electronically presented information. The following sections will address some of the challenges facing the reader and outline steps that are being taken in an attempt to enhance screen readability.

Challenges for the reader

Difficulties relating to navigation and searching seem to emerge as the major challenges to the reader of electronic texts. These are partly due to the lack of familiar text structures or schemas, and the problems are compounded by the perceptual difficulties of screen reading. Completely new habits and skills are required in order to deal effectively with electronically presented information.

Perceptual difficulties

Some of the basic difficulties with reading e-texts may relate to perceptual difficulties and consequent disorientation. Landauer (1996) claims that reading text from a computer screen is perceptually difficult and slower than with paper, slow reading being compounded by about 10% if print is right-justified (Trollip & Sales, 1986 as cited in Landauer, 1996). Nielsen (1997b) states that reading from computer screens is about 25% slower than from paper and that users say they feel unpleasant when reading online text. Some of these problems and readers' preferences for obtaining information from print rather than the computer screen may be related to the difference in image quality. Limited screen space also creates difficulties for establishing sufficient context, and scrolling, which users seem to dislike, results in disorientation with long texts (the reader can 'jump' to the next window rather than scroll, but this is another learning process and does not solve the problem of disorientation).

Disappearance of schema

The structure of a text has been considered vital in enabling understanding, and linguists and discourse analysts have identified many structural patterns used by writers. Readers depend on these patterns to identify a text's genre, anticipate its development and integrate its parts. The order in which readers see information is an important part of this schema. According to Charney (1994), hypertext violates standard assumptions of what texts are like, proliferating the possible sequences and leaving the user without the help of traditional structures or discourse cues. She claims that, by giving readers greater control over the information they read and the sequence they read it in, hypertext places considerable pressure on the reader who needs to locate necessary information and relate it to other facts in the network. Users can become overwhelmed by the choices among links and the difficulties of maneuvering through the structure. They can lose track of where they are and read a lot of irrelevant material. Charney believes that, although hypertext designers have recognised the navigational difficulties, they have not considered deeper implications for the reading process. Tuman (1992) refers to the hyperchaos of poorly implemented hypertext with too many links and confusing structure. He underlines the reader's need for a firm sense of direction and purpose, a sense of being an information-seeker rather than a print reader (and is led to question whether critical and aesthetic reading and writing will give way to information retrieval and report generation).

There is some evidence that linear format and paper-based information result in better comprehension than hypertext-based information. McKnight, Dillon and Richardson (1991) refer to a number of studies that seem to support this, including their own, in which information on wine was presented in four different forms (paper, word processor, HyperTIES or HyperCard). Comprehension tasks were designed to reflect a range of retrieval strategies for locating information, and subjects were found to be significantly more accurate with paper and word processor versions than with hypertexts. The authors consider that the familiar, linear structure supported performance and that, although hypertext may be better than paper for locating specific information contained within a text, when readers have a less specific idea of what they are looking for, paper has definite advantages.

Disorientation

Electronic literacy places an increased burden on the reader who can manipulate the text and is often responsible for constructing her/his own pathway through information. The author of electronic texts seems to lose importance and identity, simply providing the general context within which a reader moves, and handing over control of the information to the reader. Tuman (1992, p. 65) views this optimistically, stating that, 'The deaths of the author and the text so boldly announced by postmodern critics and so clearly visible in the conditions of online literacy itself are offset by the renewed life of the reader'. With hypertext, individual works lose their distinctive boundaries (as part of a larger database) and the searching and eventual reading are driven by the user. The online text is a database from which readers are intended to construct paths to meet their specific and individual needs. The virtues of this renewed life, however, are not always very apparent.

Perhaps the major challenge for the reader of electronic prose is 'getting a sense of the text'. The reader must adapt to texts that lack fixed boundaries, that can be expanded or condensed, and to the possibilities of jumping between nonconsecutive sections. One must be able to decode icons and understand the visual maps developed by software designers.

> In a world defined by a single literature rather than a multitude of texts, reading becomes essentially a means of finding one's way — one moves, not ever deeper into a single text in quest of some world-altering hermeneutic understanding, but playfully between texts, from side to side as it were. (Tuman, 1992, p. 62)

Readers of e-texts can lose sight of where they are in a text, can find themselves unable to get back to where they want to be, and have trouble locating required information. Landauer (1996) claims that there have been nine scientifically satisfactory studies comparing online and print texts. In most cases, users found information more quickly and successfully using print than electronic form, and this result was more significant for hypertext documents.

It is easy to see when you are finding unwanted text, but almost impossible to tell when you are missing items you want—and the skill of searching electronic texts for required information is not one that seems easily learnt. Landauer (1996) refers to a case study (Blair & Manon, 1985) of a legal text search system, in which lawyers kept sending professional searchers back until they believed they had found at least 70% of the relevant information. They had actually retrieved less than 20%. On a slightly different but related tack, Borgman (1986 as cited in Landauer, 1996) found that after a day's instruction, only a quarter of the students at Stanford University could use the library's online catalogue system, and most of these were engineers who reported that they rarely used the library.

The frequently expressed view that hypertext mirrors the mind and relates to human thinking (reflected by the Cartesian view of mind) requires serious questioning. According to Smith (1994, p. 269), 'It's a model that describes well what the early technology could do but not what the user's mind does, or at least not much of what a mind does'. She asks whether hypertext systems can support complex human knowing which incorporates, along with orderly, logical abilities, more anarchistic elements like doubt, contradiction, intuition, recollection, forgetfulness, denial, partial awareness and tacit knowledge.

Cognitive abilities are only one factor that might contribute to efficient hypertext use, and it seems that even individuals with well developed cognitive abilities of the required kind have difficulties dealing with complex hypertexts. Castelli, Colazzo and Molinari (1998) have looked at the effect of such cognitive abilities (i.e., intellectual efficiency, analytical capacity and flexibility, synthetic capacity, abstract reasoning and cognitive field-independence) on disorientation in hypertext. They found that subjects with low analytical flexibility tended to confuse synthesis procedures. They also had problems with logical inference and experienced extreme difficulty handling hypertext. They became disoriented, careless and unmotivated, making superficial analyses of information and jumping frequently between links without logical or spatial coherence. Slightly better cognitive performers spent a great deal of time trying to understand context (possibly because they were aware of disorientation) but processed information inadequately and often wandered aimlessly through the maps, concentrating on navigation rather than the search for and acquisition of information. Subjects whose spatial abilities were better than their general cognitive efficiency showed fewer navigational hesitations but, as information accumulated, performance became less coherent and cognitive overload led to loss of control over the information acquired. Subjects with good analytical and synthetic capacities, and an ability to apply abstract thought and logical inference, but who were weak in spatial orientation, were quite competent hypertext performers. There was, however, some fall-off in efficiency due to the complexity of the hypertext. The best cognitive performers had well integrated analytical and synthetic skills and were considered potentially good hypertext performers, moving efficiently through the context, using their cognitive abilities to control it and optimise the acquisition of information. Even these subjects, however, required a limited number of clearly connected paths and a limited number of links to prevent logical and conceptual overload.

This study (Castelli et al., 1998) also found interesting results regarding gender, suggesting that females performed significantly better than males both on cognitive tests and the hypertext[2]. Males had a greater ability to control spatial dimensions, and devoted more time to spatial exploration of the hypertext whereas females devoted more time and attention to the texts, concentrating more on the problem and showing less evidence of distraction. Males however performed better in navigation (assessed by analysing the moves made by subjects).

The phenomenon of disorientation in hypertext is obviously extremely complex, involving many more variables than cognitive factors and gender — how, for example, are cultural factors or the semiotic systems of different first languages involved? It may be, as Nielsen (1998) suggests, that current web design is grossly inadequate for the support of navigation and other user needs. But even if hypertext thinking were simply a skill in handling certain text structures, of teaching a 'hypertext philosophy', Dobrin (1994, p. 315) pinpoints the difficulty of teaching and learning this skill and way of thinking:

> Skill in handling text structures is what teaching literacy attempts to impart. With hypertext, we have yet to determine precisely what skills are needed or how they can be taught, mostly because hypertext structures themselves are not well developed and the technical capabilities of the machines are not well established.

Readers of electronic text face real problems regarding effective navigation, but it seems to be generally considered that they will work the problems out for themselves without specific teaching and skill development. Charney (1994) challenges the assumption by hypertext designers that readers know the sequence of information that is best for them. She refers to evidence that readers are not good at assessing the adequacy of the information they find or whether important information remains that they have not reached. Kieras (1985 as cited in Charney, 1994) found that readers tend to stop reading before discovering crucial details, and that participants reading and following traditional linear instructions were more successful at completing a task than those dealing with the non-linear, hypertext structures. Studies by Reinking and Schreiner (1985 as cited in Charney, 1994) suggest that when readers are responsible for selecting what text to read, they often omit significant information because they cannot find it, are unaware that it is there, or do not think it is important: 'For the reader, the consequences of whimsically following links into disparate texts or text segments may be to obstruct or hinder the more conventional but durable processes of systematically integrating new information with old' (p. 259). In short, in order to effectively extract meaning from what is read, one needs systematic patterns of information, and hypertext often fails to provide these.

Associative literacy and the need for new habits of thought

Faced with the differences between p-texts and e-texts and the challenges of hypertext, users of computers need to adopt new reading skills and even new habits of thought. Although the transfer of skills from paper-based texts can be useful to a certain degree, with skilled writers using word processing more effectively (Corbel, 1997), the old skills may ultimately get in the way of effective work with electronic texts. Linear, printed text supports critical thinking in which the text is considered holistically, where reading involves looking at what is 'written between the lines', considering what is absent as well as what is present, thinking of purpose and audience as well as assumptions implicit in the writing. Hypertext, in contrast, supports associative thinking, encouraging the reader to move between initially unrelated pieces of information, linking separate, interconnected concepts in ways that are not linear. As Tuman (1992) suggests, there seems to be a move away from critical literacy to the associative thinking of the new literacy.

This trend can, perhaps, be illustrated by an online publication of Jane Austen's *Pride and Prejudice* (n.d.) (see Figure 4.1). The reader can peruse the whole novel online, chapter by chapter (if s/he is not unduly bothered by the perceptual difficulties of screen reading and the need for scrolling or 'jumping'). Each paragraph of each chapter is dotted with highlighted links for almost every character and place mentioned. The reader can click on these links to be taken to information about characters, family trees, maps, historical information about the places and cross-linkings to other references to the same item within the novel. Each link can lead to another link which provides further information and, unless there is a clear sense of purpose, can lead the reader further away from the original text. If the reader has a thorough linear grasp of the novel before accessing the hypertext version, this linking is obviously of great potential interest and value. If, however, the reader depends more exclusively on the hypertext version, the temptation to click on highlighted words could give the reader a wealth of associated information but distract attention from the original work, leaving her/him with reduced chances of considering the novel itself in a holistic, critical manner.

Figure 4.1 Excerpt from Austen's *Pride and Prejudice* online

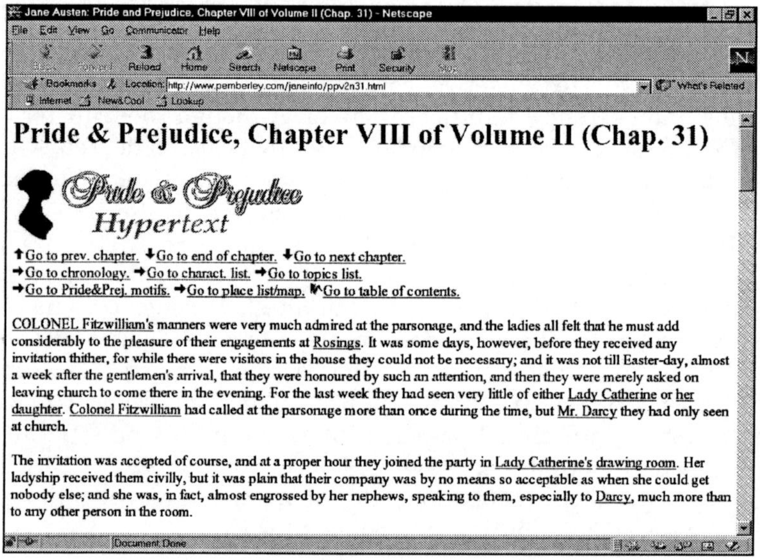

Jane Austen: Pride and Prejudice, Chapter VIII of Volume II (Chap. 31) - Netscape

http://www.pemberley.com/janeinfo/ppv2n31.html

Pride & Prejudice, Chapter VIII of Volume II (Chap. 31)

Pride & Prejudice Hypertext

Go to prev. chapter. Go to end of chapter. Go to next chapter.
Go to chronology. Go to charact. list. Go to topics list.
Go to Pride&Prej. motifs. Go to place list/map. Go to table of contents.

COLONEL Fitzwilliam's manners were very much admired at the parsonage, and the ladies all felt that he must add considerably to the pleasure of their engagements at Rosings. It was some days, however, before they received any invitation thither, for while there were visitors in the house they could not be necessary; and it was not till Easter-day, almost a week after the gentlemen's arrival, that they were honoured by such an attention, and then they were merely asked on leaving church to come there in the evening. For the last week they had seen very little of either Lady Catherine or her daughter. Colonel Fitzwilliam had called at the parsonage more than once during the time, but Mr. Darcy they had only seen at church.

The invitation was accepted of course, and at a proper hour they joined the party in Lady Catherine's drawing room. Her ladyship received them civilly, but it was plain that their company was by no means so acceptable as when she could get nobody else; and she was, in fact, almost engrossed by her nephews, speaking to them, especially to Darcy, much more than to any other person in the room.

Document: Done

Source: http://www.pemberley.com/janeinfo/ppv2n31.html

Tuman (1992) considers that the hypertext environment may be being used as a crib for literary texts, overriding first hand understanding and providing an easy path through complex literature rather than supporting aesthetic reading. A set of poems or a piece of literature with a linear sequence established by the author can become a computer database, a system providing readers with a range of historical, literary, textual and biographical materials to enrich their reading. There is no denying the possibilities of hypertext—arduous searching of a library for secondary sources can be substituted by the pressing of keys to connect text with other materials. However there is a justified sense of concern that interest in the secondary sources may become a substitute for engagement with the primary source. There are also questions about whether the system inhibits the play of imagination.

The hypertexts referred to above are intended for the study of what was originally a printed, literary text. Most hypertext documents, however, do not refer to a linear background text, and instead rely on processes of association and linking. If the reader is concerned (and of course, she/he may not be—the Internet lends itself to flitting around information and serendipitously lighting upon treasures) about losing sight of the original reason for accessing the information, or about gaining a superficial rather than considered understanding of material, new skills are needed. The valuable skills for this new literacy pertain to navigation and searching. Computer users and hypertext audiences in particular require new habits of thought to perceive coherence in patterns and links, and to create their own patterns and links—to think associatively. They also need to be able to decode the icons and other signs encountered, to be able to predict the consequences of acting on the symbol system, and to understand how to send commands (for example to save, print and send documents).

Acknowledging the difficulties

Writers of online material are not unaware of the problems experienced by readers when dealing with text on the screen. The most significant response has been to dramatically decrease the amount of text presented, but other suggestions for enhancing screen readability are also being put forward, despite a certain conservativeness noticed among users, who appear reluctant to deal with yet further changes.

Disappearance of text

Those who design online materials accept that readers have little patience with dense written text on screen and seem to take pride in using as few words as possible. This is not surprising, considering the substantial numbers of studies indicating the ability of readers to find and understand information more quickly and successfully using print. There is also the kind of reaction observed by Bigum (1998)—that students attempting to discover how software works generally tend to ignore any printed information on the screen and try to work it out by trial and error, only resorting to text information on the screen or in a printed manual after much frustration.

A'Herran (1997) considers that one of the most important skills of the online writer is to reduce text while retaining meaning. She refers to the textual impoverishment of the Internet, indicating that when writing an online version of printed text, she starts with a full prose version on screen which, in the final version, may be reduced to ten dot points. According to Nielsen (1997a) halving the word count increases readability by about 58%. Corbel (1997) confirms this change in proportion of print to images when comparing print text with electronic text. He considers that this proportion varies between text types and genres, but an increasing proportion of image to print can be expected in electronic texts, with web documents becoming increasingly complex mixes of text, image, sound and video. Bolter (1996) states that multimedia applications and other cyberspace programs use text as grudgingly and sparingly as possible, relying for rhetorical effect principally on video and graphics, secondarily on sound. Words are used as captions for graphics or to identify buttons (where words function as a magic formula, the clicking of which calls forth another graphic or video). Text, confined to boxes, tends to be used only to communicate what cannot be easily pictured. The attitude to text can be summed up in Bolter's (1996, p. 106) claim that:

> Multimedia designers consider it an admission of failure to clutter the screen with blocks of text. The worst criticism one can make of a multimedia system is to call it a mere "page turner", a set of texts that the user examines one after another—in other words, the electronic equivalent of a book.

Although educational multimedia uses text more than business applications, the strategy is still to displace text, even when teaching literature. Bolter (1996) provides the example of *Ulysses*, an IBM application for teaching English literature. He describes how the student can click on words to obtain dictionary definitions, historical explanations and critical interpretations. Whenever possible, the linked material is video or audio rather than alphabetic text. Although the program is based on Tennyson's poem, it tends to pull the user away from the actual text to visual or aural experiences, with video windows opening up to compete with the text of the poem (which does remain in a window which can always be accessed) for the reader's attention.

Although the Internet is more text based than multimedia, email and newsgroups (the most widely used Internet applications) also show signs of breaking away from text with icons and emoticons. As the Internet evolves, synchronous and asynchronous video are likely to replace email for many purposes (Bolter, 1996). It is quite likely that electronic graphic presentation will take over increasing amounts of the communicative work in our culture which has traditionally been done by the alphabet.

Suggestions for enhancing screen readability

Apart from efforts to reduce the amount of text on screen while retaining meaning, enhancement of screen readability is likely to come about through higher resolution screens and new approaches to the way information is presented. Some perceptual problems may be solved in the future by high resolution (300dpi) screens which, according to Nielsen (1997a), have been found to have as good readability as paper. But these screens are currently too expensive, and resolution is only one of the problems that needs addressing.

A study by Morkes and Nielsen (1998) suggests a number of means by which the writer can make online texts more readable. They claim, on the basis of this study, that halving the word count improves readability by 58%, that use of a scannable layout with bulleted lists improves readability by 47%, that use of objective rather than subjective language improved it by 27%, and that by combining all of these (concise text, scannable layout, objective language), readability was improved by 124%.

Nielsen (1997b) also insists that, since readers scan information rather than reading word for word, writers should endeavour to make text short without sacrificing depth of content. This, he claims, can be done by splitting information into multiple nodes with hypertext links. Extra information is available through links that need not be used by readers who do not want it. To address the problem of lack of schema, Nielsen (1996) proposes that the so-called 'inverted pyramid' style should be used. This follows journalistic style in which an article starts by telling the reader the conclusion, continues by providing supporting information and ends by giving background. This, it is suggested, allows the reader to stop reading at any time and still get the idea of the article. The advantages of this format may, however, be culturally relative, considering the way text structures and expectations of text structures differ from one culture to another.

Nielsen (1998) sees a need for considerable changes in web design but expresses disappointment that hypertext readers appear to be conservative, to be unwilling to change the habits they have learnt in order to learn other possibly more helpful approaches. When he tested what he considered advanced homepage concepts, users reacted with comments such as 'I don't have time to learn special conventions for your site' or 'Just give it to us plain and simple, using interaction techniques we already know from other sites'. User reluctance to learn yet another approach may act as a barrier to the creation of better ways of presenting information on the World Wide Web—one is reminded of our attachment to the anachronistic QWERTY keyboard and our refusal to change to superior innovations. Nielsen considers, however, that modest advances in web design should be attempted with new sites following most conventions while pushing a small number of new ideas.

Possible advantages and disadvantages of the new literacy

It is considered by some that the new literacy may provide an advantage or liberation for those who have had difficulty acquiring the old print literacy. Online text tends to be provided in brief chunks, often using dot points. Robinson and Versluis (1985 as cited in Bigum, 1988, p. 33) suggest that 'the presentation of prose in short semantic units . . . . could assist not only the less able reader but also the more able reader'. This is the model that seems to be promoted in the new literacy, and one wonders about the implications that a style of this type might have on our understanding of the paragraph.

According to Bigum (1988), much computer screen reading requires the rapid comprehension typical of computer games in which the user shoots objects on the screen. He considers that, while the computer may provide a context for reading for some children who have been uninclined to read printed text, the reading skills developed by computers may not be sufficient to support the reading of printed text. In short, there is concern at what might be lost.

One must also consider who is most likely to be exposed to the new literacy. Those most likely to benefit may already be the 'information rich' while the 'information poor' may find that the new literacy produces yet another layer of inequality. A study by the Australian Council for Educational Research (McGaw, Long, Morgan, & Rosier, 1989 as cited in Freebody, 1993) shows that print literacy is affected by the socioeconomic background of the student as measured by father's occupation and number of books in the home. If socioeconomic class and the availability of material and human resources in schools and homes affect the literacy levels of less advantaged students, it is reasonable to suspect that this disadvantage is likely to be compounded, in terms of literacy, with the new medium. Zeni (1994) refers to studies by Gomez and Jessup (n.d.) which show that access to technology varies by students' race, gender, social class and language background. Lankshear and Knobel (1995) confirm that several Australian reports have found similar differences between the technology rich and poor to those noted in the US and Britain. LeBlanc (1994) notes that middle class parents seem deeply convinced of the value of computer-based learning, considering computer expertise essential for their children's future. As the big computer companies compete for the computer market, they play on these assumptions. Homes and schools which are short of money are less able to purchase and update equipment and software or to obtain technical support.

Conclusion

The new literacy associated with computers, the Internet and the World Wide Web is still in its infancy. The momentous shift being made by readers and writers from the intimate, familiar, well-signposted world of print, to the public, mutable and rapidly changing, evolving world of computer literacy is exciting but also presents considerable possibilities of frustration and anxiety, and the need to develop entirely new habits of thinking, reading and writing. The present conventions for web design and the presentation of electronic text still leave much room for improvement, and writers and designers who are aware of the difficulties experienced by readers are attempting to increase screen readability and improve web design. The computer may be extremely forgiving and infinitely patient, permitting any amount of experimentation, however human beings are not. It would therefore seem essential that, before the present conventions become 'fossilised', a great deal of clear thought should be given to the problems involved in screen reading and systems for improving readability and ease of access to information via the new technology.

Endnotes

1. An interesting survey of this development can be found in chapter 3.
2. Females produced lower scores on spatial relations, but the

researchers consider that the superior performance of females may have resulted from their greater logical efficiency along with closer attention to the verbal elements of tasks.

References

A'Herran, A. (1997) (forthcoming). Lite Text. *Proceedings of the Style Council 1996, 1997 and 1998.*

Bigum, C. (1988). *Readin', writin' and computin'.* Waurn Ponds, Vic: Deakin University Press.

Bigum, C., & Green, B. (1993). Technologizing literacy: Or interrupting the dream of reason. In A. Luke & P. Gilbert (Eds.), *Literacy in contexts.* (pp. 4-28). Sydney: Allen & Unwin.

Bolter, J. D. (1996). Virtual reality and the redefinition of self. In L. Strate, R. Jacobson, & S. Gibson (Eds.), *Communication and cyberspace – social interaction in an electronic environment* (pp. 105-120). New Jersey: Hampton Press.

Castelli, C., Colazzo, L., & Molinari, A. (1998). Cognitive variables and patterns of hypertext performances: Lessons learned for educational hypermedia construction. *Journal of Educational Multimedia and Hypermedia,* 7 (2/3), 177-206.

Charney, D. (1994). The effect of hypertext on processes of reading and writing. In C. Selfe & S. Hilligoss (Eds.), *Literacy and Computers.* New York: The Modern Language Association of America.

Chou, C., & Lin, H. (1988). The effect of navigation map types and cognitive styles on learners' performance in a computer-networked hypertext learning system. *Journal of Educational Multimedia and Hypermedia, 7* (2/3), 151-176.

Corbel, C. (1997). *Computer literacies: Working effectively with electronic texts.* Sydney: NCELTR.

Costanzo, W. (1994). Reading, writing and thinking in an age of electronic literacy. In C. Selfe & S. Hilligoss (Eds.), *Literacy and computers.* New York: The Modern Language Association of America.

Dobrin, D. (1994). Hype and hypertext. In C. Selfe & S. Hilligoss (Eds.), *Literacy and computers.* New York: The Modern Language Association of America.

Dougherty, D. (1997). Don't forget to write: Graphics may get attention but good writing rewards it. *Web Review.* Available: http://webreview.com/iwr/static/97/10/10/imho/index.html [1998, October 27].

Freebody, P. (1993). Social class and reading. In A. Luke & P. Gilbert (Eds.), *Literacy in contexts* (pp. 68-84). Sydney: Allen & Unwin.

Gibson, S. (1996). Pedagogy and hypertext. In L. Strate, R. Jacobson, & S.

Gibson (Eds.), *Communication and cyberspace – social interaction in an electronic environment* (pp. 243-260). New Jersey: Hampton Press.

Kenway, J. (1995). Reality bytes: Education, markets and the information superhighway. *Australian Educational Researcher, 22* (1), 35-65.

Kress, G. (1995). Preface. In C. Preston (Ed.), *21st Century A-Z literacy handbook*. London: Project Miranda.

Landauer, T. (1996). *The trouble with computers*. Massachussets, MA: The MIT Press.

Lankshear, C., & Knobel, M. (1995). Literacies, texts and difference in the electronic age. *Critical Forum, 4* (2), 3-33.

LeBlanc, P. (1994). The politics of literacy and technology in secondary school classrooms. In C. Selfe & S. Hilligoss (Eds.), *Literacy and computers*. New York: The Modern Language Association of America.

Lee, J. (1996). Charting the codes of cyberspace: A rhetoric of electronic mail. In L. Strate, R. Jacobson, & S. Gibson (Eds.), *Communication and cyberspace – social interaction in an electronic environment* (pp. 275-296). New Jersey: Hampton Press.

McKnight, C., Dillon, A., & Richardson, J. (1991). *Hypertext in context*. Cambridge: Cambridge University Press.

Morkes, J., & Nielsen, J. (1998). *Concise, scannable and objective: How to write for the Web*. Available: http://www.useit.com/papers/webwriting/writing.html [1998, July 6].

Nielsen, J. (1996). *Inverted pyramids in cyberspace*. Available: http://www.useit.com/alertbox/9606.html [1998, October 27].

Nielsen, J. (1997a). *How users read on the web*. Available: http://www.useit.com/alertbox/9710a.html [1998, October 27].

Nielsen, J. (1997b). *Be succinct! (Writing for the web)*. Available: http://www.useit.com/alertbox/9703b.html [1998, October 27].

Nielsen, J. (1998). *Conservatism of web users*. Available: http://www.useit.com/alertbox/980322.html [1998, October 27].

Pride and Prejudice Hypertext. Available: http://www.pemberley.com/janeinfo/ppv2n31.html [1998, October 27].

Selfe, C., & Hilligoss, S. (Eds.). (1994). *Literacy and computers*. New York: The Modern Language Association of America.

Smith, C. (1994). Hypertextual thinking. In C. Selfe & S. Hilligoss (Eds.), *Literacy and computers*. New York: The Modern Language Association of America.

Strate, L., Jacobson, R., & Gibson, S. (Eds.). (1996). *Communication and cyberspace – Social interaction in an electronic environment.* New Jersey: Hampton Press.

Thomas, H. (1997). The new literacy?: The challenges of hypertextual discourse. *Computer Assisted Language Learning, 10* (5), 479-489.

Tuman, M. (1992). *Word Perfect: Literacy in the computer age*. London: Falmer Press.

Zeni, J. (1994). Literacy, technology and teacher education. In C. Selfe & S. Hilligoss (Eds.), *Literacy and computers*. New York: The Modern Language Association of America.

Chapter 5

Cyberseeking: Language and the quest for information

Juliet McLean

The quest for knowledge is as old as the origin of human consciousness and is fundamental to human development and the achievement of self-actualization. Developing minds, from infancy to maturity, depend on ever widening sources of information for knowledge to understand themselves and the ways of the world and the society in which they find themselves.

From library land to cybersearching

There is a dramatic shift in the vocabulary of information access in the digital age compared with pre-electronic times which corresponds with changes in, and extension of, access to a new population of information users. Because of the electronic form of delivery, the language of information science or informatics has largely superseded the language of libraries and library science when it comes to information searching on the Web. Much of the more esoteric language is confined to the technical pages and literature about electronic searching for professionals but some of the general language drift emerges on front pages of search engines and directories. Although the rapidly changing vocabulary used to describe the apparatus of information searching in the electronic context makes definition elusive, a table of rough equivalencies can be drawn up, with such examples as indicated in Table 5.1.

Conceptions about the role and function of libraries are part of the change from library to cybersearching. Libraries were, and to some extent still are, conceived of as repositories of knowledge in the form of collections of publications and documents which can be retrieved by persons who have the need to know about their contents. The client group of a particular library, be it educational, commercial, professional or public, is in fact, by its membership or patronage, given certain rights of access, and has certain responsibilities in return for the privilege of access which can be revoked if these responsibilities are not fulfilled.

Table 5.1 A comparison of terminology used in library searches and that used in cybersearches

Terminology used in library searches	Terminology used in cybersearches
catalogue	database
look up	search, find, find it, go get it!
filed as, or retrievable by	tags, metatags
subject headings	descriptors
publisher	originator
author	names, people, creator
items found	hits
see also	more like this
index	word list
phrase	string or chain
how often up-dated	freshness
match	relevancy (often expressed as a %)
abstract	summary
title page	heading

The library paraphernalia of catalogues, indexes, abstracts and thesauruses has only ever been dimly understood by the majority of library users. There are many use and user studies in the library and Information Science literature, both from the functional standpoint of examining overt behaviour of library users and user-centred studies focusing more directly on the mind of the user (Budd, 1995). In one such study, conducted by Kuhlthau, Turock, George and Belvin (1990), the authors concluded that, since uncertainty is the natural state of a user at the start of a search, librarians must be aware that they are in fact facilitators of a learning process. Despite the reluctance of many library users to ask for assistance in locating particular books or information, there has been a tacit understanding that the librarian is somehow keeper of, and guide to, the contents of the library. When a library user commences an information search there is generally the idea that the answer will be in a book, periodical or some other form of publication and that a particular author or body of authors will be responsible for that information. The authority of the author is assumed to be traceable and verifiable.

Substitute the cyberworld of information seeking and the predominant characteristic is anonymity. Although a great deal of cybersearching goes on in libraries, a vast and rapidly growing amount goes on at home and in non-institutionalised venues[1]. In their study of children's use of electronic technologies in the home, Downes and Redacliff (1997) note that the home market in Australia will soon represent 20% of total sales of PCs and that this will increase to 35% in the near future. Publications in the form of every kind of homepage and website proliferate but the average user has little conception of looking for authorship or evidence of the responsibility for the information therein. Many search engines do not in fact search by the author field specifically and if the name does not occur within the first 100 words of a webpage it will not be retrieved. Despite the fact that the Internet empowers individuals who have the skills to create a homepage with the privilege of authorship and publication, the effect of publishing on the Web is often to de-personalise information and text.

Another characteristic of cybersearching is that the user of information on the Internet, unless operating within the framework of institutional policy, is free of limitations, other than that of the cost of equipment and connection, in the amount and type of information accessed. There are legal restrictions on what can be done with that information in terms of copyright and defamation laws, but the individual is uniquely free of accountability in respect of what is accessed in the public domain.

If the cybersearcher is typically private, independent and anonymous, there is a sense in which the cyber quest unites and identifies its participants. Searching on the Net is a numbers game: information frequently sought is therefore highlighted at the top of retrieval lists. Many webpages have built in counters to record the numbers of visitors to the site. Some of the search engines deliberately exploit the numbers game by making a feature of sites most visited. *Hotbot*, for example, operating out of the USA, has a 'TOP 40' feature which exploits the celebrity factor in its promotion of these sites, in much the same way as music record charts or bestsellers' lists. This may be not a bad thing if *HotBot* users are searching categories such as Entertainment, but when applied to News sites in the *HotBot Guide to News Online* (1998) it might be considered a manipulative form of marketing news.

Broadcast network browsers using Push Technology[2], which encourage users to specify, or *personalise* their areas of interest and then subsequently push information across the screen whilst other sites are being viewed or when other applications such as word processing are being used, could be considered aggressive or intrusive. An idea of the 'Push' and 'Pull' principle is given in this extract from the homepage of the *Push Council* (1998):

> Let's start with the big picture first. If you think of conventional web surfing as 'pulling', 'pushing' is just the opposite. You 'pull' information from different websites by searching for topics that interest you. With 'push', the Internet finds you and delivers information based upon what interests you.

Examples are the news banner headlines that flash across the screen if a product such as *PointCast* has been downloaded and integrated with a web browser. This is illustrated in Figure 5.1 below.

Figure 5.1 PointCast homepage 'Help' screen

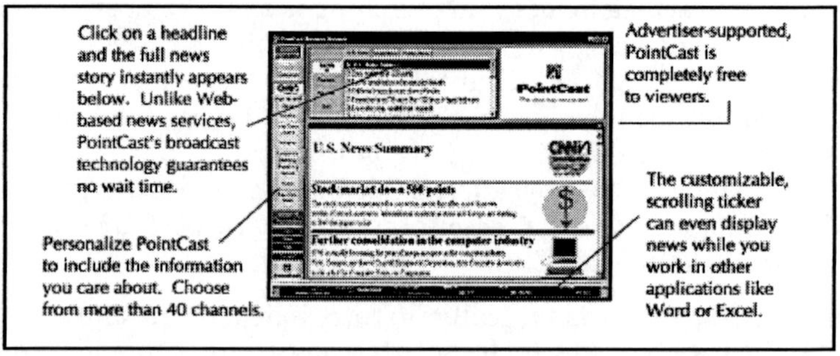

Source: http://www.pointcast.com/products/pcn/index.html?home

For would-be cybersouls, a visit to *GeoCities Neighborhoods* (1998) is instructive in demonstrating the nature of much of the disembodied communication on the Web. Anyone who thinks that cyberseeking is lonely will find that there is much virtual companionship in these 'cities'. *Geocities* consists of personal homepages organised into groupings and communities of interest, which have little to do with research for hard information. As with any community, a familiar language develops among the *cognoscenti*. The names of these communities and streets within this site are borrowed from real geographic locations, as with *Paris: Left Bank,* but the content is largely creative. For example, a search for James Joyce, in the *GeoCities:Paris* (1998) site, the neighbourhood for 'romance, poetry and the arts' (see Figure 5. 2), does not tell the cyberseeker much about the writer, as this homepage dedicated to 'useless facts', reveals:

Figure 5.2 A graphic excerpt from the *Paris: Left Bank* site

Source: http://www.geocities.com/Paris/

The following information is provided when one conducts a search for James Joyce in the site referred to in Figure 5.2 above:

> Physicist Murray Gell-Mann named the sub-atomic particles known as quarks for a random line in James Joyce, "Three quarks for Muster Mark!" (http://www.geocities.com/Paris/4633/useless.html)

Concern for the ways in which learners are inducted into the knowledge pathways offered by electronic information searching is increasingly evident and an important educational mission. Although the educational journey towards independent learning is often represented in sequential terms progressing from the intimacy of parent and home learning, to the guidance of teachers with selected texts and materials, to the independence of information searching and research, these widely different contexts for learning may all be occurring concurrently in a child's life. Educators may construct scenarios in which students move through stages or processes to acquire the skills to use resources such as the Internet as a source of information but the fact is that, with or without instruction, they are using the Internet and, in many cases, at a very young age.

One of the consequences of web searching is the lack of inbuilt guidance for the young or inexperienced in their information searching. There are directories, web guides and specialist search services, often integrated with commercial or subscription services, and there are numerous advertisements, but there is no guiding light especially for young Internet users, beyond the work of certain directories, e.g., *Yahooligans* (1998) and *Magellan Internet Guide* 'green light' sites (1998), to point the way to appropriate sources of information according to level of knowledge, experience, or age of user. Equally, users of all ages with little previous experience of information searching in other contexts, are making the Internet a virtual home resource centre but frequently without much experience of evaluating information and dealing with misinformation.

Information providers on the Internet are entirely without a code of responsibility, legal or otherwise, to construct pathways which make the information pages on their websites accessible or digestible. Search engines, which are after all businesses, provide the major point of entry for information searching on the Net. They have commercial pressures to attract users in numbers and are not primarily motivated by quality in terms of educational provision. The implication is, therefore, that major responsibilities rest with educators to ensure that pathways to skilled information seeking are established.

Many abstracts that accompany search results on search engines such as *Lycos* (1998) are composed automatically from the databank retrieved by spiders and robots. It is interesting that the names of the major Internet browsers, such as *Netscape Navigator* and *Internet Explorer* imply some concept of personal guidance through uncharted waters when, in fact, search engines work on the basis of automatic scanning and indexing. Exploration, including nautical adventure and discovery, is a common metaphor for information searching on the Web, but sometimes mining for gold dust might be more appropriate.

The nature of automatic keyword indexing of the webpages and documents which are scanned by the spiders and robots of search engines ('what tangled webs we weave…') is little understood by the majority of information seekers. Each search engine has its own mechanism or formula for deciding which sites are indexed, and how often, and there is great variation in these aspects of their operations. Dedicated web watchers would do well to consult Danny Sullivan's *Search Engine Watch* (1998), a table of ratings of performance on a variety of features, to establish how a search engine functions. Searchers do not always understand that these automatic indexing mechanisms can be manipulated by creators of webpages to induce the retrieval of pages by the constant repetition of keywords in titles or first 100 words (despite the counter mechanisms of some search engines to combat this 'spamming'). The apparent ease with which 'hits' are obtained by simple keyword searching belies the difficulty of getting precise, accurate information at the level required by the searcher.

Evidence for lack of user understanding, including users in the tertiary education environment, of electronic search and retrieval mechanisms in general is to be found in research studies conducted in Universities both in Australia and in the USA. Hildreth (1997), studying the use of Online Public Access Catalogues (OPACs) at the University of Oklahoma, draws the conclusions that:

- users of this online catalogue search more often by keyword searches than any other search;
- their keyword searches fail more often than not; and
- a majority of users do not understand how the system processes their keyword searches.

In some ways changes in access vocabulary have made it easier for people who were never comfortable with the institutional aspects of libraries to feel an ownership of information searching on the Web. The fact that there is no obvious personal scrutiny of requests or expectation of acquaintance with the procedures for looking up information seems to be liberating to many. The anonymity of searching on home browsers becomes an assumed right and individuals both in the workplace and in schools can be dismayed to find that in networked services it is perfectly possible to track which Internet sites are visited and how often. Even with the home browser privacy is not completely assured. Although it is claimed that individual searchers cannot be personally identified, live web search replay on services such as MetaCrawler's *MetaSpy Exposed* (1998) makes interesting, if voyeuristic, viewing of other people's searches. These examples of searches in progress recorded on September 6, 1998 (1.35pm) were copied to the word processor and are illustrated in Figure 5.3.

Also cookies on computers and servers obviously garner data relevant to information providers about users of their sites, especially product information sites. Cookies placed on computers by information providers appear on the notepad and can be checked but not edited by the user. A cookie file screen display is exemplified in Figure 5.4.

Examples of the ways in which cookies may be used are evident in the banner advertising for products and 'pals' that appear on search engine screens and the announcements and publicity for Internet services.

Figure 5.3 Results of *MetaSpy Exposed* searches in progress (September 6, 1998, 1.35pm)

metaspy
exposed

fantasy football; buffy naked hack; +picture +post; Efferox XR; appz; calculator roms; winston-salem police department; upskirt; endora; alpha and sex

Figure 5.4 An example of a cookie file notepad screen display

Netscape HTTP Cookie File
http://www.netscape.com/newsref/std/cookie_spec.html
This is a generated file! Do not edit.

Initially the facility to search using natural language, rather than prescribed subject headings or thesaurus terminology, gives the cyberseeker a sense of ease with the medium and with that a sense of confidence. The language employed by the search engines also gives the cyberseeker a sense of individual power *(e.g., power search, personalize, wizard*). The individual feels in control of the process even if the results of the searching do not justify this confidence.

One of the attractions and challenges for students in the cyberworld is that in presentation this world appears forever new in the language employed to describe functions (e.g., *cool sites* one day *hot topics* the next), by contrast with the certainties and traditions of the pre-electronic world of information gathering. The more transient, mechanistic world of computers, in which the technology moves at breathtaking speed and the information searcher has to be constantly up-dating knowledge, vocabulary and skills, now predominates. The language of information-seeking in the cyberworld has changed with the ethos. The essentially scholarly, womb-like aura of libraries aptly described by David Lodge (1965, p. 44) in *The*

British Museum is falling down, where tradition and protocol seemed to perpetuate a world of permanence and stability, has been left behind:

> The dome looked down on the scholars, and the scholars looked down on their books; and the scholars loved their books, stroking the pages with soft pale fingers. The pages responded to the fingers' touch, and yielded their knowledge gladly to the scholars, who collected it in little boxes of file-cards.

Search engines, to be competitive in the electronic world, need to be importing not only new refinements in computer-assisted search techniques but also new 'hot' language to describe what they are doing. Use of the imperative in instructions, such as *Show, Go get it! Find it* and the words in logos such as *Smart, Active, Power, Wired, Hot, Electric Wizard, HotMetal*, have an energising and empowering effect. They also offer a challenge to the searcher to be innovative and capable in using the technology.

Keywords, concept building or Boolean searching

Most users embarking on a search would fall into one of two categories: they either engage in a particular question or *query* search, or are looking to extend knowledge of a subject through a *browse* search. Sometimes one kind of search merges or extends into another by the powers of suggestion and serendipity but there are appropriate strategies for each kind of search. The user must always ask 'What do I already know about this subject?' and 'What do I want to find out?' It is a discipline for the user to be aware of the level of their prior subject knowledge; to know whether introductory material is required or whether the enquiry is at a level of general or specialist knowledge.

In respect of *query* searching, the user is working generally from a known element in the search, such as a name, part of a website title, a generic subject keyword or descriptive words. The mental process that translates those known elements into a query to search for the unknown is little understood. Simple keyword searches for subjects such as *fly fishing* or *scuba diving* might seem to be straight forward enough until the number of hits convinces users with experience to refine their subject. By entering the words *scuba diving* 112,250 hits were produced using the *Excite* search engine (1998). However, by simply selecting to add the words *snorkeling* and *dives* from a list of 12 words, and by selecting to search UK sites only, this total was reduced to 2,383 hits. If British spelling of *snorkelling* is entered, the hit rate is slightly higher (2,525). Similarly *fly fishing* produced 626,340 hits, but adding the words *flyfishing* and *trout* and searching only UK sites reduced this to 23,790 hits. Further refinement using the 'select words to add to your search', or using the option to select sites 'more like this' would obviously help the user to get closer to a specific area of interest to these searches. Addition of the words *resorts* and *cornwall* would be helpful to a potential inquiry about diving in the UK (top five results highly relevant), whilst adding *scotland* and then subsequently *ireland* would convince the searcher to make Ireland the destination for a fishing trip.

For several years Universities, information brokers, harvest services and research organisations have experimented with retrieval protocols based on the use of metadata (data about data). Metadata, as developed by the Dublin Core (1997) for example, allows retrieval by searching on 15 fields of particular information such as author (creator), title, publisher (originator), subject descriptors, language, rights, format, date. This is relevant especially for precise document retrieval and is of much interest to academic users of the Internet (and therefore to the library world), who have had their tool for document transmission highjacked by popular and commercial users. Increasingly search engines will offer users a search mode which supports the use of metadata, although currently several search engines (e.g., *Excite*) have declared that they will not support the use of the metatags which identify these search fields because of the increased possibility of deliberate spamming by website information providers. Use of metadata may be an added burden for the average Web user, unused to thinking in terms of the search field ('Do I want to retrieve text *by* or *about* a certain author?'). For more precise retrieval, however, there may be some relief in being able to search directly on the subject, author or title fields to retrieve only particular documents tagged in that way.

Some of the features of search engines have the facility to extend the cyberseeker's definition of a subject, in such a way as to develop the searcher's linguistic resources and powers of thought by suggesting word groups or associated concepts for further refinement of the search query. The word mapping facility provided by the *Alta Vista* (US site, 1998) search engine, backed by a thesaurus maintained by the retained history of previous searches, is a case in point. If the searcher clicks on 'Refine', words associated with each element of the search phrase are given. By introducing new word categories and synonyms that can be included or excluded in the search, then by either listing or graphically mapping the results, the searcher is helped to define the subject of the search in much greater precision. This facility is particularly helpful in breaking down a parochial view or implication of a word usage (e.g., *aborigine* used as though there are only Australian aborigines), particularly in the context of a search engine operating out of the USA and searching documents originating from all over the world.

The search engine *Excite*, referred to above, has the facility to refine the search by the 'select words to add to your search' feature. The *Excite Search Wizard* (1997) notes inform us that:

> The words suggested at search time are statistically derived from the words and concepts resident in our 50 million URL index. We accomplish this by clustering the body of words contained in our index and identifying relationships between the words. For each word or group of words you enter into a search box, we have a pool of hundreds of related words from which we can derive the ten words most closely related to the one(s) you've entered.

The results achieved searching with *Excite*, a UK based organisation, make an interesting comparison from the language point of view with those achieved using the American English *Alta Vista* search engine, even when both are asked to search 'the entire Web'. Using a search example consisting of the words *kenneth branagh film, Excite* suggested the following words to 'add to your search': *filmmaking cannes critics cinematography screenplay documentaries basinger gilliam showbiz*. Using the search words *kenneth branagh movie*, another list was produced in a different linguistic register, including: *karloff twists drab flicks pacino goldwyn vies idiotic cannes actors*. The fact that *movie* and *film* are virtual synonyms is not born out in any similarity in the context of webpages in which they appear. These two searches were repeated using the USA *Alta Vista* site with the 'Refine' facility. In fact, by requiring or excluding words suggested by both lists, very similar results could be achieved so that the effects of the accidental selection of the initial search term of *movie* or *film* could be overcome.

The automatic word map facility also demonstrates the hierarchical nature of language constructs in relation to knowledge classification which is so important to successful information searching.

Searchers are introduced to some principles of functional modern language use by means of the words suggested to include or exclude. These principles may then be applied to other searches. Some useful precepts may include using concrete nouns as plurals rather than in the singular form (e.g., *rocks* rather than *rock,* unless a particular rock such as Uluru is wanted, but if geological information is required, use *minerals*). If an academic overview of a subject is required, abstractions such as *prejudice* or *racism* achieve better results than phrases or strings of words meaning the same thing, for example *discrimination +race* or *discrimination based on race*, because these are the words that academics use when writing about these subjects. If the searcher is more interested in tracking down examples of biased writing or propaganda, the more concrete expressions such as *racial*, *coloured,* or *ethnic* will produce better results. Levels of technical or specialist language will result in hits using a similar level of specificity. This is evident in searches using medical terminology. Use of the vocabulary in the register of the type of article the searcher wishes to retrieve is advisable. Searching for articles published by the Federal Bureau of Investigation will not be retrieved by using the acronym FBI. Conversely, journalism or commentary about this Bureau's activities is more likely to be found by using the acronym.

In the Simple Search mode, *Alta Vista* searching has the added advantage of being able to search for phrases by enclosing words in inverted commas and indicating that the search must include or exclude terms by the use of + or - modifiers before a search term. This achieves a similar precision of search results to the use of the 'require' or 'exclude' offered in the 'Refine' facility on *Alta Vista*. By using these operators a search for the film script of the popular movie *Titanic* can be found directly, as described by Skipworth (1998). A simple search for *titanic* produces a mountain of results (528,490 hits) including every version of the story from newspaper articles, earlier films and heaps of irrelevant advertising for products such as steel and pornographic sites. A precise result will be achieved adding terms to indicate that the movie script is required, the name of the director (both enclosed in inverted commas to ensure searching by phrase rather than by the separate words), and by using the + modifier to indicate that all these terms must be included in the search result:

+titanic +"movie script" +"james cameron"

Use of the - operator (exclude) is equally effective in constructing some searches. If, for example, a searcher wished to find information on the original families arriving on *The Mayflower*, and knowing that this ship has lent its name to a score of enterprises in the USA, the precaution of searching on some terms and excluding others would be advisable:

+mayflower +puritans -restaurants

Boolean searching

Boolean searching[3], a facility offered by some, but not all search engines, is based on the application of formal logic and precise search syntax to the construction of searches. Table 5. 2 indicates the major search engines which use Boolean search features and those which do not.

Table 5.2 Search engines using/not using Boolean search features, as of June 1998

Boolean search allowed	Boolean search not allowed
Alta Vista	InfoSeek
Excite	Open Text
WebCrawler	Lycos
HotBot	Northern Lights
Yahoo/Magellan	

The use of Boolean logic is a search strategy which should be taught if students are to use it successfully in any context. The sense of the Boolean AND is not the same as natural (conversational) language would imply (i.e., 'cats and dogs' meaning both, not just what they have in common), and diagrammatic representation (Venn diagrams) is necessary to explain the logical function of operators AND, OR, NOT, NEAR. Whilst concept building using word strings or the 'Refine' type of computer assisted search will increase accuracy of results beyond simple keyword searching, for a precise definition of a complex search requirement Boolean searching offers a considerable advantage to those capable of using it.

The further question that searchers need to ask themselves beyond, 'What do I want to find out?' and 'What do I already know?' is 'What is the logical relationship between the words which are used to describe or are associated with this subject?' Professional online information searchers familiar with using structured, or thesaurus vocabulary for database searching are well versed in the art of Boolean searching. Most amateur newcomers to searching on the Web, however, find the use of formal logical constructs difficult and many do not read the help notes provided by the search engines. Generally the expectation is that the operators of Boolean logic (AND, OR, NOT, NEAR) are used in the same way by each search engine, but this is not the case.

A study conducted at the University of Newcastle looked at users' application of search terminology on the basis of 1000 searches from two such devices, *WebCrawler's Search Voyeur* (1997) and *Magellan's Search Voyeur* (1997)[4]. Table 5.3 is reproduced from the study by Keily (1997, p. 206).

Table 5.3 Results of Keily's (1997) study of the use of search terminology

Search Type	Magellan Voyeur	WebCrawler Search Ticker
Single word	318	331
2 words or more	437	391
Phrase using " "	89	101
Boolean	124*	122#
String/question	32	55
Total	1000	1000

#75 of these used uppercase Boolean operators as NOT required in the Help
*69 used uppercase Boolean operators, as recommended in Help

Some of the key points of Keily's (1997) analysis are summarised below:

- By far the majority of searches were those consisting of one or more keywords, simply typed without using 'advanced' syntax described in the 'Help' for each search engine.
- Many of the searches included under string/question consisted of natural language, without the use of inverted commas to specify an exact phrase, e.g., *German Shepherd puppies for sale*, and included upper case letters which would have narrowed the search.
- There were four questions asked by *WebCrawler* users and one question asked of *Magellan* that were fully expressed questions, e.g., *Where can I see pictures of lions.*
- It was noted that some people do read the 'Help' or search tips provided by the search engine administrators, but that many

are under the impression that similar syntax is used for all search engines.

- Similar numbers of users for each search engine used similar syntax for phrase and Boolean searches.

Keily (1997, p. 207) notes that:

> Around 10% of *WebCrawler* users and 9% of *Magellan* users enclose phrases in inverted commas, as per the instructions in the Help. A number of these also use initial upper case letters to narrow the search. Some 12% of *WebCrawler* users and *Magellan* users used Boolean operators in their search strategies but only 0.5% of them used a combination of Boolean operators and phrases. It appears that some *Magellan* users had not noticed that the Help specifies that Boolean operators must be entered in UPPERCASE. Of the 124 users who used Boolean syntax, only 69 used uppercase operators. *WebCrawler* on the other hand, states in its Help that "we've capitalised the search operators in this chart, but it is not necessary to do so when you type a search" yet 75 of the 122 searches used uppercase Boolean operators. However, as the operators are case insensitive this would not have affected their search results, unlike those *Magellan* users who did not follow the instructions in the Help. [italics added]

This study, based on a random sample of Internet searches, reveals that users need assistance to improve their searching techniques and to increase their satisfaction with the experience of searching on the Internet.

What is the question?

Questioning is the basis for information literacy—the ability to interpret information and extract or create new meaning, to solve problems and to make decisions based on reliable evidence and a thorough understanding. Questions enable us to search for pertinent information and convert data into information and information into insight. Questions also enable us to interpret information and take us beyond interpretation by supporting synthesis and the development of new understandings.

The primary difficulty and the biggest area for educational input into training and developing skilful information searching in any context, but particularly with reference to Internet searching, is to help users to develop strategies to think about the question they are attempting to research, or to formulate a question from a given topic or area of interest. Many searchers, adults and students alike, approach the query window of the search engine as though it were a dictionary; that is they put the word in and expect to get a definitive answer. More useful than any amount of explanation of technical matters about the Internet, is the time spent analysing, or 'brainstorming' concepts implicit in questions.

An example of this process of brainstorming or mapping a subject which is to be researched would be looking at the implications and arguments surrounding a morally contentious issue such as euthanasia. Whilst a Simple Search on *Alta Vista* (Australian site) using the term *euthanasia* produced a usable and varied list of results, it illustrated the need for establishing a broad understanding of the issues and aspects of the subject before undertaking an Internet search. A preliminary word map outlining the dimensions of the topic (moral, religious, humanitarian, medical, political, human rights, legal, psychological), the contexts for the debate (national laws, international and United Nations statements, professional codes of ethics, provision of palliative care, acute situations of protracted suffering, effects on relatives and carers), the main bodies actively involved in pro- and anti- arguments, and the current slogans or catch phrases (e.g., *right to die, freedom of choice, assisted suicide, sanctity of life*) would be of great assistance before beginning to search on this topic. Using a variety of search terminology, very different results were retrieved ranging from sites pertaining to recent cases and legislative events in Australia to views of world churches and faiths, humanist viewpoints and United Nations charter, professional groups, medical and sufferers' views and views expressed by the lunatic fringe.

1. Using *Alta Vista* Advanced Search, searching the Web on:

   euthanasia AND *morality* OR *"freedom of choice"*

   the top 10 results out of 4,091 hits included three religious sites (Seventh-day Adventist, Bahai and Uniting Church), a Canadian Senate Committee Report, two pro and contrary debates, one Australian Democrats' senate speech, one humanist viewpoint, one plea for euthanasia and one Church of Euthanasia (plus a Unabomber manifesto) site.
2. Using *Alta Vista* Advanced Search, searching the Web on:

   euthanasia AND *"right to die"*

   the top 10 results out of 3,086 hits included one religious site (Seventh-day Adventist), three anti-euthanasia sites from hospice physicians, a *Quadrant* article and a Right to Life site (Ohio), two pro-euthanasia sites from Ithaca College and a rights' organisation arguing the case for assisted suicide for AIDS and other sufferers, two sites adopting a neutral stance (psycom.net/bookstore and a news service 'futures' report) and one Canadian Senate Committee Report.

These two lists were complementary with only one common site, showing that a variation of terminology is essential for a balanced view.

3. Using the *LookSmart* directory category search, searching Australian sites only:

   euthanasia from Australia

   the top 10 of 16 matches were all different from the above and included a newspaper report from the *Age* following the world's first legally assisted suicide, two Queensland *Right to Life* reports, The Northern Territory *Rights of the Terminally Ill* Act, the ALP position and the Australian Democrats' party policy, one resource list, one site providing key definitions, the Australian Medical Association list and a moderated forum on the issue.

4. Using the *Alta Vista* search engine linked to the *LookSmart* directory to search the entire Web:

   euthanasia AND *right to die*

   the top 10 of 1,161,700 matches included three United Nations hits for the same report on Euthanasia and the United Nations Universal Declaration of Human Rights, one Catholic Information Network report, two hits for a report on euthanasia and physician assisted suicide, a comparative report of the American Society of Clinical Oncology, a letter from Pope John Paul II on the subject and two further reports from the New Advent Catholic website on this letter. Again no cross matches appeared on these lists and the difference in retrieval between using a local directory versus an international search was clearly evident. The *LookSmart* directory list was, however, a good starting point in the Australian context.

From this example of subject research it is clear that arguments and evidence can be accumulated on all sides of the debate. More challenging issues may, however, lie in the area of belief and value systems and these issues can certainly be informed by knowledge and facts but are rarely shaped by them.

It is particularly important in the educative process for students to learn to develop the skills to ask the 'telling questions' McKenzie (1997b) writes about in his electronic journal *From Now On*. These are the questions which lead students to develop true understanding and insights about a subject:

> Telling questions lead us (like a smart bomb) right to the target. They are built with such precision that they provide sorting and sifting during the gathering or discovery process. They focus the investigation so that we gather only the very specific evidence and information we require, only those facts which "cast light upon" or illuminate the main question at hand. (McKenzie, 1997b, n.p.)

The example on McKenzie's website is of a study of violent crime in USA cities. McKenzie suggests the strategy of asking just two 'telling questions' to structure the inquiry:

> How many crimes in each city per 100,000 population?
>
> How have the numbers changed since 1985? 1990?

Using the *Alta Vista* Advanced Search and Boolean logic he searched on the following terms to produce a list of 25 useful information sources:

> "violent crime rate" AND Boston

Focussing the enquiry by pin-pointing central and significant questions greatly assists the selection of useful search terminology.

Implications for educators

The ability to ask the fundamental relationship questions is a product of 'deep reading' and 'deep thinking' about a subject. Sven Birkerts in *The Gutenberg Elegies* (1994) maintains that it is contemplative, probing and reflective reading which lies at the heart of the search for truth and therefore at the heart of the educational mission. This is the antidote to what McKenzie (1997a) calls 'mind candy' arising particularly from the World Wide Web and more recent developments in the news and entertainment world, where we see 'difficult and troubling content simplified and sweetened for general consumption' (n.p.). Is the World Wide Web an information tool or a 'mind candy kafe'? Deep reading is the antithesis of the information grazing and browsing which is often encouraged by information searching on the Web and by the amassing of large quantities of data. It depends on reflective thinking, analysing and probing of text and is probably a product of dealing with fewer rather than more sources of information.

How is skilful questioning taught? This question leads into an area of thinking about thinking, or metacognition. Metacognitive processes are not subject specific (Sewell, 1990). They cut across domains and include activities such as planning, self-monitoring and learning how to learn. Sewell comments that, 'It is within the general context of metacognition that the potential of computer-based empowering environments resides, i.e., in their ability to stimulate reflection on the nature of one's own thinking' (p. 20).

A full battery of questioning techniques and competencies is developed over time and with experience but will include elaborating techniques, defining and clarifying questions, hypothetical and strategic questions, divergent and convergent questions, probing, inventive and planning questions (McKenzie, 1997c). Research on student-generated questions is relevant to an understanding of how questioning techniques can be developed as an aid to comprehension and interaction with text. The InSight project (Williamson, 1996) explored a variety of strategies for questioning, and Gillespie (1990) looked at student questioning as a technique to improve literacy at elementary school levels. In examining how student-generated questions can be taught and how students can be taught to ask higher level questions, Gillespie's (p. 256) conclusions were that:

- if students are to ask good questions, they must receive instruction; and
- in order to teach students to generate questions the teacher must understand the types of questions, teach students the types, teach students how to generate questions, and teach them to transfer the material to content area subjects.

Combined with the use of an established information skills model such as that outlined by the New South Wales Department of School Education (Dawson & Kallenberger, 1989), or Eisenberg (1998), appropriate questions can be introduced according to steps in the information process: planning, defining, locating, selecting, synthesising, presenting, evaluating. As applied to making effective use of the Internet in the classroom, guides such as the publication *Computer based technologies in the English Key Learning Area* (1997) are of relevance. Work on progressive abstraction in relation to language awareness, reflected in the National Curriculum (England and Wales), examined by Cameron (1993) in *Degrees of knowing,* gives some indication of the groundwork necessary to develop good understanding of conceptual language and its relationship to experiential language.

Computer assisted searching mechanisms are extremely helpful in aiding searchers towards helpful search outcomes. They are employed more and more, both in the context of devices such as the *Alta Vista* 'Refine' button and the word banks that lie behind *Excite* and *HotBot* assisted searching, demonstrating that the computer can certainly help users to think more precisely about their search terminology and the nature of their search. In the end, however, the machine cannot make value decisions or decide on the logical interplay between the linguistic elements involved: that is the computer cannot think or decide which is the best question to ask about a subject. Deeper subject knowledge contributes greatly to the process of information retrieval but is short-circuited or frustrated without information skills. Skilful questioning, not the glitz of infomechanics, is the basis of the *power* or *empowerment* that comes to the individual with the mastery of the techniques of information searching. It requires both linguistic and logical skills, and as Socrates knew, lies at the heart of true learning.

Endnotes

1. Home ownership of computers in Australian capital cities is approaching 50% (Australian Bureau of Statistics,1996) and in some affluent communities over 85% of children have computer access at home. Figures are higher in Canada where 36% of all homes have computers and 18% use the Internet (*CNET NEWS.COM*; Nov 28, 1997). Martin (1997) predicts that the number of Internet users in America (40 million) will only continue to approach the total population and cites Bill Gates' belief that this statistic will eventually be 90% of the total population.
2. The term 'Push Technology' includes a wide spectrum of products and services. Generally it refers to a system in which the user receives information or applications automatically from a network server (Dragan, 1997). One category of network products is intended for use on a corporate network. The second category consists of services that broadcast general-interest content over the Internet; some of these services, including *PointCast* and *Back Web*, allow the user to download client details and subscribe to the product and information services free.

3. The term *Boolean* is derived from Boolean algebra (named after mathematician George Boole, 1815-1864) by which logical propositions are denoted by symbols and can be acted on by abstract mathematical operators that correspond to the laws of logic. Boolean algebra is of prime importance to the study of pure mathematics and to the design of modern computers.
4. Search terms were copied and pasted into word processor documents and then classified by the following headings: single word, two or more words in a meaningful sequence, phrase searching (words enclosed in inverted commas), Boolean searching, and searches posed in the form of a question or in a string of words which included a verb and/or preposition. The results of this exercise were then considered in relation to tentative conclusions drawn concerning the extent to which users had read the 'Help' of the particular engine they were using to the search instructions and advice offered in the 'Help' of both search engines.

REFERENCES

Alta Vista (Australian site). Available: http://www.altavista.yellowpages.com.au [1998, June 30].

Alta Vista (US site). Available: http://altavista.digital.com [1998, June 29].

Birkerts, S. (1994). *The Gutenberg elegies.* New York: Fawcett Colombine.

Budd, J. M. (1995). User-centered thinking: Lessons from reader centered theory. *RQ, 34* (4), 487-497.

Cameron, L. (1993). Degrees of knowing: An exploration of progressive abstraction in language awareness work. *Language Awareness, 2* (1), 3-13.

CNET NEWS.COM. (November 28, 1997. 2.00pm). Available: http://www.news.com/News/Item/0,4,16848,00.html [1998, July 3].

Dawson, M., & Kallenberger, N. (Eds.). (1989). *Information skills in the school.* Sydney: New South Wales Department of School Education.

Downes, T., & Redacliff, C. (1997). *Children's use of electronic technologies in the home: Stage 3 preliminary report.* Available: http://www.notebooksystems.com/LinkSite/DownesStg3rep.html [1998, July 3].

Dragan, R. V. (1997). Coming soon: The push desktop. *PC Magazine Online.* Available: http://www8.zdnet.com/pcmag/features/pushserv/sbdesk.htm [1998, July 5].

Dublin Core Elements. (1997, November 2). Available: http://purl.org/metadata/dublin_core_elements [1998, July 2].

Eisenberg, M. (1998). The Big6 model of information problem-solving. In *Teaching technology and information skills.* Available: http://big6.syr.edu/overview/index.html [1998, July 8].

Excite (UK site). Available: http://www.excite.co.uk [1998, June 29].

Excite Search Wizard. (1997). Available: www.excite.co.uk/info/suggest.dcg [1998, July 2].

GeoCities Neighborhoods. (1998). Available: http://www.geocities.com [1998, September 6].

GeoCities: Paris. (1998). Available: http://www.geocities.com/Paris/ [1998, September 6].

Gillespie, C. (1990). Questions about student-generated questions. *Journal of Reading, 34* (4), 250-257.

Hildreth, C. (1997). The use and understanding of keyword searching in a university online catalog. *Information Technology and Libraries, 16* (2), 52-62.

HotBot Guide to News Online. (1998). Available: http://www.wire.com/newsbot/ [1998, December 18]

HotBot. (1998). Available: http://www.hotbot.com [1998, December 21].

Keily, L. (1997). Improving resource discovery on the Internet: The user perspective. In D. I. Raitt, P. Blake, & B. Jeapes (Eds.), *Proceedings of the 21st International Online Information Meeting* (pp. 205-212). Oxford: Learned Information Europe Limited.

Kuhlthau, C. C., Turock, B. J., George, M. W., & Belvin, R. J. (1990). Validating a model of the search process: A comparison of academic, public and school library users. *Library and Information Science Research, 12*, 53-93.

Lodge, D. (1965). *The British Museum is falling down.* Harmondsworth: Penguin.

LookSmart. (1998). Available: http://www.looksmart.com.au [1998, June 30].

Lycos. Available: http://www.lycosuk.co.uk [1998, June 30].

McKenzie, J. (1997a). Deep reading and deep thinking in an age of info-glut, info-garbage, info-glitz and info-glimmer. *From Now On: The Educational Technology Journal, 6* (6). Available: http://fromnowon.org/mar97/deep.html [1998, June 30].

McKenzie, J. (1997b). Telling questions. *From Now On: The Educational Technology Journal, 7* (1). Available: http://www.fromnowon.org/sept97/telling.html [1998, September 6].

McKenzie, J. (1997c). A questioning toolkit. *From Now On: The Educational Technology Journal, 7* (6). Available: http://www.fromnowon/nov97/toolkit.html [1998, June 30].

Magellan Internet Guide. (1998). Green light sites. Available: http://www.mckinley.com [1998, June 30].

Magellan Search Voyeur. (1997). Available: http://voyeur.mckinley.com/cgi-bin/voyeur.cgi [1998, June 30].

Martin, A. C. (1997). Predicting the future of computer technology. Available: http://www.enteract.com/~tjmartin/main/research/research.shtml [1998, July 3].

MetaSpy Exposed. (1998). Available: http://www.metaspy.com/Spy/ [1998, September 6].

New South Wales Department of Education and Training, Curriculum Support Directorate. (1997). *Computer based technologies in the English KLA: Enhancing student learning.* Sydney: New South Wales Department of Education and Training.

Push Council: Push 101 - what is push? (1998). Available: http://iatek.bitshop.com/push/rart1.htm [1998, September 9].

Sewell, D. F. (1990). *New tools for new minds: A cognitive perspective of the use of computers with young children.* New York: St. Martin's Press.

Skipworth, P. (1998). *Global Web Directory.* Available: http:www.globalwebdir.com.au [1998, June 30].

Sullivan, D. (1998). *Search Engine Watch.* Available: http://searchenginewatch.com [1998, June 30].

WebCrawler Search Voyeur. (1997). Available: http://webcrawler.com/Games/SearchTicker.html [1998, June 30].

Williamson, R. A. (1996). InSight-strategies for questioning. *The State of Reading, 3* (1), 35-38.

Yahooligans. (1998). Available: http://www.yahooligans.com [1998, June 30].

Chapter 6

Negotiating the Web: Language, critical literacies and learning

Ross Todd

This chapter provides a conceptual discussion of the information and critical literacies that underpin effective connecting to, interacting with, and utilising of World Wide Web information. While the context of this discussion is about high school students using the Internet to access information as part of their assignment research tasks, the theoretical framework is drawn from Information Science. In particular it draws on input from the fields of cognitive information processing, information seeking behaviour, information access and retrieval, and information utilisation. It presents an analysis of a series of classroom scenarios—real ones—where students have been asked to locate and use information from the World Wide Web as part of their classroom activities and research assignments. This research makes clear a number of principles of relevance to all information seekers in a range of different contexts beyond schooling, and these will be elucidated.

Background

The disciplinary field of Information Science is concerned with the flow of information in society from its generation to its ultimate use by people. It is particularly interested in what information is, how it is represented, how people interact with it, interpret it, use it and transform it, all as a part of daily living and getting on with life. Laurence Heilprin (1989), a noted American information scientist has characterised the emergence of the *information society* in two phases, each with a distinctive persona and locus of scholarly concern. The first phase, labelled the *Age of Information*, describes the exponential growth, organisation and global distribution of information. Heilprin asserts that during this phase, the generation, processing, provision and use of information has emerged as the predominant human activity, and much scholarly energy has been spent in developing laws, theories, generalisations, policies and speculations about these. However, he identifies a fundamental shift in our thinking about the information society, labelled as the *Age of the Mind* where the emerging focus appears to have shifted from the phenomenon of information itself to understanding people as human information processors; and how this understanding can inform the effective organisation and provision of information to society.

In a similar vein, Wersig (1990), a Dutch information scientist, urges us to shift our thinking about the information society from information occupations, information technology and information products, to 'immaterial human needs, including the processing of information' (p.185). Concerned about the 'rubbish' explosion that has occurred as a result of the dramatic increase of large stores of 'senseless data' and 'useless literature', and concerned about the present day illiteracy levels, he calls for a 'back to knowledge' movement and an information culture founded on understanding the relationship of information, people, senses, space and time (p. 197). The need for this people-centred orientation is further encapsulated in Baran and Davis' notion of how people deal with information:

> Each day we are exposed to vast quantities of sensory information; we take in only a small fraction of it, process and use an even smaller fraction, and then we finally store a tiny fraction of this in long-term memory. According to some cognitive theorists, we are not so much information handlers as information avoiders . . . Very little of what goes on around us ever reaches our consciousness and most of this is soon forgotten. (Baran & Davis, 1995, p. 267)

The development of the World Wide Web as a major mechanism of information access, characterised by both the quantity of information it makes available and its magnitude as a global information infrastructure, brings to the forefront the need for scholars to understand how people connect with it, interact with it, and make sense of and actually utilise the information that it so easily provides. In its short life, the World Wide Web has generated significant comment about its major transformative role in society. Social impacts of e-business, e-commerce, e-marketing, e-shopping, e-mail, e-gambling, and e-tainment, to name a few, are already being identified.

It is in the arena of education and learning, however, that the transformative promises of the World Wide Web are most prominent. Through access to its vast stores of information, there are promises that the Web will, for instance, stimulate students' development of reasoning, problem solving, and decision making; foster their creativity; encourage them to engage in *deep learning* rather than *surface learning* (Trigwell, Prosser, & Taylor, 1994); encourage greater intrinsic and spontaneous interest in learning tasks; help them develop *optimising* rather than *satisficing* search strategies (Harrison & Pelletier, 1995; Kaye, 1995); and promote more cooperative and interactive classroom behaviour. These are significant claims, and at present, substantially unsupported. Our understanding of how students interact with the World Wide Web, how they negotiate its vast stores of information, how they make sense of this information and make use of it in their learning, is indeed limited. Some commentators argue that it does not matter; others claim that the inevitability of technological development means that 'if you are not part of the steamroller, you are part of the road'.

This chapter contends and demonstrates that it does matter. The World Wide Web represents a dramatic change in the nature of our information environment, particularly in terms of how information is structured, provided and accessed, notwithstanding the volume of information available at any one time. Historically, our information environment could be characterised as print-based, linear, contained, controlled, and structured. The World Wide Web challenges these notions. Computer technology enables the traditional linear flow of information to be replaced by a hyperlinked structure enabling multiple pathways of moving through the information, with the possibility of following, even creating, linkages as ideas evolve. The complexity of the World Wide Web's information organisation and linkages, at times poorly organised and often with limited advance organisers that are familiar to us in print environments, is compounded by the integration of different media—sound, text, video, animation, graphics. This is particularly the case where much of the integration of different media is no more than bells and whistles to show a designer's flair or ability to use a particular authoring package. The potential of information noise and information overload is real.

The complexity of the World Wide Web is also shown in the nature of the information itself that it provides. Burbules (1997) describes the World Wide Web as an indiscriminate and ambiguous mix of five types of information, where the quality, importance and reliability of information is difficult to determine. These types are:

- *Information:* the factual, clearly sourced information that bears all the traditional hallmarks of reliability and quality;
- *Misinformation:* information that is judged to be false, out of date, or incomplete in a misleading way, or that seeks deliberately to misinform and manipulate opinions and ideas;
- *Malinformation:* potentially dangerous or damaging information; inappropriate information; information people feel uncomfortable with in openly accessible circulation;
- *Messed up information:* information that might be useful and appropriate but is poorly organised, sloppily designed and presented, or where navigating the multiple layers of hyperlinks creates notions of being 'lost in space'; and
- *Useless information:* information that appears to serve little informing purpose (recognising of course that one person's trash is another person's treasure).

For school students this undifferentiated mix of information contrasts with the typical school information environment—the school library. Here information resources are carefully selected, often within budget constraints, to serve clear purposes within the mission and curriculum offerings of the schools. There is some control over the quality and reliability of the information provided to ensure it meets learning objectives. On the other hand, the World Wide Web, as an information source, is unconstrained and uncontrolled. The indicators of credibility found in traditional print sources in school libraries, such as authors' credentials, prefaces and introductions providing context and ideological stance, direct sourcing of information, and the presence of a bibliography, are often not present in World Wide Web information. Common features include the invisibility of web authors, the problem of unknown authorship, the absence of indicators of the origins of information, arguments sourced in unreliable information, the intrusive inclusion of advertising, and indiscriminate links.

The nature of on-screen presentation of the information also adds to the complexity of this information environment. Everything on the World Wide Web looks authentic as an official publication. There is the plausible presentation of false and/or misleading information such that the boundaries between rumour, gossip, and what is credible and authentic, are blurred. In addition, the nature of searching and accessing information through one of many search engines available means that often the document retrieved may stand without a functional context. In many sites, information just sits there, without any background or contextual statements, or without any links to other sites which may help place it in a meaningful context[1].

For students, the complexity of this information environment is often not apparent. From my own research (McNicholas & Todd, 1996), there is evidence to suggest that the seductiveness of computer technology and the captivating media hype is contributing to an expectation of students that every answer is on the World Wide Web and is an effortless button click away. Understanding how students interact with this information and make sense of it is thus a crucial aspect of learning, and a crucial part of the scholarly focus on the Age of the Mind. Kehoe (1993, p. 11) sums up the essential dilemma:

> Access to vast amounts of information is not the whole answer. The power to discover the right information quickly and easily, to separate nice to know from need to know information is essential if superhighway users do not drown in electronic junk information . . . An information flood does not necessarily mean that people become informed.

The development of information and critical literacies

The key challenge confronting education in the wake of the Web revolution and the enormous volume of information it provides is empowering learners to be creative, critical and constructive users of its information. This chapter posits that in order to address this challenge, we need to develop learners' information and critical literacies: developing the skills needed so that they are able to successfully access and look critically at information to meet their learning needs; to question and challenge the ambiguous world of ideas made available; to understand and analyse the ways information works to empower some and exclude others; and to have the capability of managing and effectively utilising the quantities of information they confront. The development of information and critical literacies is fundamental to assisting learners in making decisions about, for example, what information to believe, what to doubt, what to pay attention to, what to be concerned with, and what to reject. At a more specific level, these literacies enable students to make evaluations of websites, and to ask important questions such as: What is this site trying to do? What is this site trying to do to me? Whose interests are being served here? What is the text trying to say? What are the possible meanings of this text? What do I already know about this information and how does this relate to it? How does this relate to other sites on the World Wide Web, and sources of information other than the World Wide Web? What are some alternative or opposing views, and where might I find them? How does this site help me construct an alternative position? What do I do with this site now? Who can I talk to about this site? Which voices are silent here? What actions can/should/will I take? (modified from Freebody & Luke, 1990).

The development of information and critical literacies embraces three overlapping cognitive and behavioural dimensions—connecting to, interacting with, and utilising information—that are fundamental to information seeking and information processing. These dimensions are about knowing how and knowing what, that is, *procedural knowledge* and *declarative knowledge* (Gaines, 1987; Gordon, 1992). These dimensions are active thinking and reasoning processes oriented to action. However, they will only be realised in the classroom when explicit and systematic learning activities are designed and implemented on a daily basis in all curriculum areas. These activities need to centre on the following processes:

- *Connecting with the world of information*: questioning the task, identifying and defining what needs to be known, creating search terms, developing search strategies, understanding the structure of the information base, implementing searching strategies to interrogate the database, compiling a hitlist of located sources.
- *Interacting with the world of information*: knowing the indicators of quality information, questioning the relevance of the located resources, challenging, confirming or disconfirming the validity of the information, evaluating the appropriateness of the sources, filtering out unsuitable information, dealing with the threat of information overload, analysing the information to identify important and needed components, interpreting the information against frames of reference, understanding the ideas, organising the salient ideas into some meaningful structure to create a synthesis, critiquing multiple viewpoints and opposing ideas, reflecting on and evaluating the information process and the information product.
- *Utilising the world of information*: taking action; applying the

information to construct an answer to the question, solving the gap in previous understanding, finding help, getting direction and being able to move on, making decisions and implementing solutions, developing new applications.

The research evidence

There is considerable research evidence available to suggest that developing students' information handling skills contributes to their ability to negotiate their information environment. While it is not the intention of this chapter to provide a full review of this evidence, some is presented here to illustrate the claim. To date, five research studies undertaken by the author and colleagues have been documented (Lamb & Todd, 1993; McNicholas & Todd, 1996; Sivanesarajah, McNicholas & Todd, 1993; Todd, 1995; Todd, Lamb & McNicholas, 1993), and others are in progress. In addition, replication and extension of these studies have been undertaken (Hawkes, 1997; Jones, 1996). These studies, using both quantitative and qualitative methodologies, have involved secondary school students at different grade levels and subject areas, and have employed a range of data collection techniques, such as standardised questionnaires, surveys, focus group discussions, individual interviews, hypothetical writing tasks, research assignments, diary logs, and subject examinations and scores. These aspects are elaborated in each of the individual papers.

Common to all of these studies is the explicit and systematic attention given to developing a range of information and critical literacies. The conceptual model underpinning this is the Information Process developed by the Department of School Education in New South Wales (1988). This model presents a sequenced process, neither unidirectional nor linear, which focusses on developing the skills of defining information, locating information, selecting information, organising information, presenting information and evaluating information. A person who is information literate demonstrates competence with these skills. Table 6. 1 presents a synthesis of this research undertaken by the author and colleagues which identifies some of the improvements and benefits of explicitly developing information handling skills as part of teaching activities.

Table 6.1 Integrated information skills development: Key findings

Factors improved by explicit teaching of information handling skills	Benefits of teaching information handling skills[2]
Perception of self as a learner	• increased active participation and enhanced questioning techniques. • using information process as mechanism for self-analysis and diagnosis of learning process • enhanced self-esteem and confidence as a learner • greater sense of self-control • independence and willingness to learn from mistakes • more positive attitudes towards self as a learner
Learning Process	• use of information process as mechanism for charting learning progress • improved understanding of subject content in a shorter time • improved scores on class tests and formal exams • more accepting of learning as a challenge and managing difficult learning tasks • providing a structured process for organising ideas • more effective managing of the quantity of information
Perception of information	• more global view of information • more lateral information seeking • greater valuing of own knowledge
Learning outcomes	• development of reflective thinking; improved manipulation of and assessment of information • improved ability to remember • increased concentration • some transfer of learning • more active exchange of ideas
Learning environment	• atmosphere of respect • greater collaboration amongst peers • thought given to identifying information needs • greater interest and motivation

In essence, the evidence presented in this research program suggests that an integrated information skills program does have a positive impact on students' academic mastery and the development of information problem solving strategies using a range of information skills. It also has an impact on their attitudes to school life, their self-esteem, and their own confidence to take charge of their learning. Ongoing cumulative research will continue to test the validity of these generalisations.

However, some key questions remain. Given that the World Wide Web is poised to be a major information source for teaching and learning, what are the information and critical literacies essential for negotiating this global electronic environment? How can students' interactions with the World Wide Web be made more meaningful and productive? What are the learning barriers they face when negotiating the World Wide Web?

World Wide Web scenarios

The scenarios documented here seek to unpack some of the key issues that shape effective searching of the World Wide Web. While seemingly simple in task definition, purpose and outcome, they highlight the complexities faced by students while using the World Wide Web as part of their classwork.

Scenario 1

A mixed ability class of 32 Year 7 students studying General Science in a Sydney suburban high school were posed the following question 'How do birds sing?'. This question was part of a preparatory lesson in using the World Wide Web. The students were asked to write down the term(s) they would use to search the Web to develop their answer to the question. The class was familiar with using the online library catalogue and putting in subject terms to locate resources. The students, whose experiences with searching the World Wide Web ranged from 'I have no idea how to do it', to 'I have never done it but I think I know how', to 'I use it all of the time for my assignments at home', to 'I play for hours at home', provided the following responses, shown in Table 6. 2. Most students provided more than one term, and the attempt to understand why they did this could be summed up simply. They wanted an expedient range of options if the first search term proved unsuccessful.

Table 6.2 Search terms and frequency

Search term	Number of responses
bird	5
birds	12
birds singing	15
bird's song	4
singing birds	9
birds - songs	2
birds that sing	1
birds and singing	5
how birds sing	2
how do birds sing	1
songs - birds	2
bird's voice box	1
warbling birds	1
birds and sounds	2
tweet tweet	1
sounds - birds	5
ornithology	2
tweeting	0

When these terms are actually keyed into the search box of a search engine such as *Alta Vista*, the number of hits varies considerably, as shown in Table 6. 3.

Table 6.3 Search terms and hit rates

Search term	Number of hits (*Alta Vista*) (1998, September 20)
bird	1,730,650
birds	1,304,860
birds singing	648,119
bird's song	253,185
singing birds	648,089
birds - songs	584,393
birds that sing	735,737
birds and singing	648,119
how birds sing	1,287,430
how do birds sing	1,287,430
songs - birds	958,288
bird's voice box	576,555
warbling birds	512,460
tweet tweet	4,612
birds and sounds	1,337,670
sounds - birds	1,356,275
ornithology	49,180
tweeting	313

This activity illustrates that language, expressed as search terms, does matter. World Wide Web English is not the English of an expert in ornithology, and is not necessarily the English of a novice who is expected to interrogate an expert system. For example, in the above illustration, 'birdsong' appears to be an accepted biologist's term for tweeting. Neither term was identified by the students. The terms that a student decides to input to search the system, based on existing knowledge and understanding of the words in the task, may not be the most appropriate terms that the system uses to retrieve relevant documents. While students are familiar with using school library catalogues, which tend to use a controlled vocabulary for searching, and require them to translate their chosen terms into the language used by the system, the World Wide Web poses additional complexity. The search engines available to access World Wide Web documents all have different approaches to deciding what a document is about, that is, its 'aboutness'. To know what are the best search terms to recall a document set that is highly precise and relevant to the task at hand is a complex issue. In essence, the student has to know how each search engine has established its aboutness[3].

The approaches to aboutness used by the different search engines varies considerably, as does the extent to which human indexers, as opposed to automatic indexing, are used. Approaches include: simply allowing plain text searching in the hope that the search term or phrase finds a match in the text; identifying broad concepts and creating concept trees; a cast-of-characters approach whereby the predominant ideas, names, and places are listed, often determined by automatic frequency counts where the most frequently occurring word becomes the subject of the document; an appeal-to-unity approach to identify the unifying concept that explains the presence of the rest and leaves no questions unanswered; a figure-round approach to identify the idea occupying the centre of attention or that gives the impression of dominance; and approaches based on linguistic analysis, particularly the thematic organisation of text (Todd, 1995). There is no agreement on approaches used by search engines, although there is increasing effort on the part of search engine developers to explicate a specifiable procedure for deciding aboutness.

Clearly this points to the importance of developing explicit and systematic teaching and learning strategies that enable students to connect effectively with the World Wide Web. These should include strategies that enable students to understand the impact of using different search terms and different search engines on the set of documents retrieved. A hit-and-miss approach to searching might produce satisfactory results in the long term, but there are real productivity issues at stake here, including: the cognitive load involved in identifying a relevant set of documents; the cost of connect time; the time involved in searching; the anxieties associated with fruitless searching; and the pressure of meeting assignment deadlines. The second scenario documented here, provides evidence that these productivity issues are indeed important.

Scenario 2

The second scenario outlined here sought to examine more systematically how students made use of World Wide Web information in the process of completing research assignments, and to identify learning barriers and difficulties. As part of an action research project, the study also sought to identify specific information and critical literacies needed for effective searching, and to implement and evaluate these. The case study took place at a secondary Catholic College for girls in Sydney during 1996 (McNicholas & Todd, 1996).

The study involved one classroom teacher and two senior classes, one Geography and one Religious Education class comprising a total of 42 students. The research tasks were set by the classroom teacher and designed without consulting the teacher-librarian, this serving to represent common practice. Each class comprised two randomly selected groups. Group A used information sources considered traditional at the school, that is print texts, multimedia and electronic indexes and full text services. Group B primarily accessed the World Wide Web from any of fifty possible sites around the College using *Netscape* as the browser with any number of search engine choices, and unconstrained by any electronic censorship. Group B students had open access to the World Wide Web at all times throughout the course of the study. The tasks were initially set with a firm timeline that reflected the program for both subjects. The research was planned using naturalistic observation of the students and teacher, recording their experiences and impressions of 'traditional' versus new information sources while documenting the process and the product outcome.

Prior to beginning their tasks, both groups of students were asked to record their search plans making comment on what information was to be to looked for and where they expected to find it. In addition a process diary was used by each student to make comment about their impressions and perceptions of the sites visited and judgements about the quality and usefulness of the information gathered.

The learning process was tracked in depth from the time the students were given the research tasks, to the time the tasks were assessed by the classroom teacher. An action research framework underpinned the process. This involved five phases, namely identifying, planning, acting, observing, and reflecting. The research process involved careful observations of and discussions with the students during their work; it involved articulating problems, barriers, concerns; then planning and implementing appropriate teaching and learning strategies based on an information literacy framework to address the concerns; and finally, evaluating and reflecting on the processes with a view to ongoing planning, classroom action, and evaluation. Table 6. 4 identifies a range of learning dilemmas experienced by students in the study. It also indicates the information literacy-based requirements of the tasks and associated teaching and learning strategies used to meet these requirements. Issues emerging from the study are also noted.

Table 6.4. Learning dilemmas, information literacy actions and emergent issues

Learning dilemmas	Information literacy-based requirements and associated teaching and learning strategies	Emerging issues
superficial analysis/diagnosis of the learning task; indiscriminate choice of search terms; inability to construct appropriate and effective search strategies	**defining information** brainstorming and concept mapping of key ideas of task; activities to identify narrower, broader, related and alternative search terms	tasks need to be designed with an understanding of metacognitive processes; colloquial English is not Net English; perceptions of a topic's 'aboutness' were too narrow/fuzzy
not a clear understanding of search engines; using only one search engine; expectation that answer will be provided - a one-stop shop for information	**locating information** explore help screens for each search engine and analyse differences in constructing search designs; test search designs on different engines and	sloppy searches are expensive, both in terms of learner time and effort, and online cost; extreme frustration of poorly designed approaches to searching negates positive aspects of the Net;

Table 6.4 continued over page

	compare outputs; guided search activities; one-to-one assistance	perceptions of what the Net is impede the use/ exacerbate frustrations
real difficulty in judging the quality of the information found at the various web-sites; not a clear understanding of selection criteria	**selecting information** understanding the range of on-screen cues to assist quality of judgement; structured activities to compare sources; organised sharing to collaborate on site searches	students need to confront and learn to deal with the diversity of the Net; is the pre-selection and provision of a limited number of 'good sites' realistic or legal?; who determines what is a 'good site'?
copying large slabs of information seen as legitimate	**organising information** activities to foster skills of sorting ideas; comparing and contrasting different sites for the same content; comparing website information with resources in the library; synthesis activities; understanding how to construct an argument using ideas from different sources; developing note-taking skills e.g., concept mapping	time management is a critical factor; required skills can not be assumed; tasks that encourage regurgitation receive regurgitations; prioritise the probable success rate of any source to a given task
indiscriminate dumping to print; cutting and pasting seen as the solution; group collaboration leading to identical presentation	**presenting information** using different forms of information; presenting information in different forms	imposed formats restrict responses; self-imposed barriers limit productivity; visual literacy is understressed
students have no role in the process of evaluation; time frustrations mean little reflection on process or output	**assessing output** review and comment on completed product; redesign the task	mechanisms for feedback on process and product are necessary

(Modified from Todd & McNicholas, 1997, pp. 370-371)

The learning dilemmas identified in Table 6.4 were conceptualised through the process of data analysis, particularly in relation to student comments. These comments included: 'I don't know what to search for'; 'I'm lost'; 'I know there's information in here but I can't seem to find it'; 'I can't work out if the info's good or not'; 'I can't find any useful information'; 'I get so much useless information'; 'The Internet's great—a one stop shop for information'; 'it doesn't encourage you to use your brain'; and 'it's so easy to cut and paste'. These learning dilemmas lead to a consideration of the design of research tasks, understanding search engines and designing searches, information quality, and productivity issues. Each is briefly discussed, highlighting explicit strategies for dealing with them.

Design of research tasks

A major barrier to effective searching is a poorly designed research task. This problem, one that classroom teachers must resolve, compounds the difficulties as students engage in the search, analysis and synthesis processes. In setting research tasks, classroom teachers should be asking important questions such as: Is it a meaningful task? Does it really matter if the students ever know? Is the research task connected to current learning? What information and critical skills are required to successfully complete the task? Do the students have these skills to complete the task, and if not, how will they develop them? Does the research task encourage students to present their own ideas and arguments, or copy others?

It is not only about having a clear sense of the expectations that a research task places on students, but also ensuring that they have the appropriate intellectual scaffolding to confidently and responsibly manage the flood of Web information they are likely to encounter. Web searchers need to be able to answer questions such as: What is this site about? Is the site's purpose clearly indicated? Can I trust this site? Where can I go for alternative perspectives and views? —and other questions enumerated above (see pp. 107-108 for a more extensive list of questions modified from Freebody and Luke (1990)).

Search engines and designing search strings

When beginning their web searches, students typically do not attempt to differentiate between search engines, tending to search the one that the system opens as default. However, getting the best information for the purpose at hand often requires quite complex decisions about search engines. This involves understanding how the many search engines work, knowing which search engine is best for the topic at hand, what types of information the search engines access, and how to interrogate the different databases with search terms.

Search engines vary considerably in terms of what they collect, how they collect it, how they index the content, how they establish quality control, how they create the abstract, how the search terms should be entered, and how they decide and rank the list[4]. Choice of search engine and search terms clearly impact on the nature and quality of the output. Some search engines like *Alta Vista* index every word, thus creating high recall, low relevance listings of websites. Some have human selection of sites to be included in the database while others automatically gather anything and everything. Some access a range of text types while others limit this; similarly, some function more as directories and specialist subject guides rather than comprehensive databases. Some have abstracts that are created automatically through the selection of the first 25 words of the document, while others provide a precis of the whole site created by people. The range of Boolean operators used to combine search terms into a search string vary with each search engine. The search engines also have different types of searches, approaches to refining the search output, and approaches to ranking the matches.

Searchers need a range of skills to be able to effectively interact with the Web, and our research shows that searching it without these skills has created uncertainties and frustrations, and impacted on search time and overall productivity (McNicholas & Todd, 1996). Teaching and learning activities might include helping students to: analyse their research task for alternative, narrower, broader and/or related search terms; realise that Net English is not necessarily the same as classroom English; test and examine the impact of a range of search terms for a topic; work through guided searching activities where the process is understood and output discussed; use search engine help screens; and test the output by combining a range of Boolean operators.

Information quality

Judging the quality and utility of information for the required task can be a major barrier for students. Students traditionally work in a school environment where library resources are assumed to be 'good' by their mere presence in the collection. The assumption that all information is 'good' has been carried over to the Web, an inappropriate assumption in this ambiguous virtual world. It is clear that an important skill for successfully using the Web is being able to make judgements about the quality of the information accessed. It is important to provide opportunities for students to evaluate sites through identifying on-screen cues of quality. This could be achieved by helping them to understand the typical text types available at the *edu, com, org, gov* domains and by encouraging students to critique websites by asking such questions as: Who is sponsoring this page? Can I verify the legitimacy of the organisation? Who is the author, and what are the author's credentials? Can the facts be verified (e.g., by consulting a bibliography which has been included)? Is the site free of grammatical and typographical errors? Are there dates when the document was written, revised, and placed on the Web? Are sources of data in graphs and charts provided? Is the page completed or under construction? Are the biases stated or readily identified? Is the advertising separated from the content? Developing skills of critically evaluating websites is fundamental to accessing quality information[5].

Productivity

Poorly developed search skills which result in the collection of huge volumes of information often lead to prolonged and frustrating search processes for students. This impacts both on students' productivity as well as on time-cost efficiencies of being online on the Net. Searching takes a long time, and when a site is located that looks appropriate, it is accepted often without careful evaluation because of the time pressures. Abilities to analyse and synthesise information, and to construct a personal answer that demonstrates understanding of the ideas are likely to be poorly developed. There is a tendency to scroll through pages to find the answer, and to cut and paste the relevant paragraph without adapting it for the requirements of the task.

Underpinning effective utilisation of web information, as with any information, is knowing what to do with it, knowing how to apply it to construct an answer. This is a complex process, and involves skills of analysing, synthesising and organising information, developing arguments, working with evidence, as well as a range of competencies relating to presenting the information in a variety of ways.

Conclusion

Effective searching of the Web is a complex reasoning and decision-making process. The notion of getting appropriate information at the right time for the right purpose is not a matter of being in front of a computer terminal, clicking a search button and hoping for some vicarious, miraculous, answer-producing experience to take place. It is a complex and compounding interplay of choices about existing knowledge and human cognition, what is needed to be known, the language of knowing, the language of the Net, and the nature of the electronic interface. The emerging evidence suggests that web searchers who are equipped with the intellectual scaffolding that enables them to make these reasoned choices will be effective and successful searchers. This intellectual scaffolding centres on competencies related to being competent information handlers, who are able to identify their information needs, and locate, access and utilise information resources effectively. In the world of the Web, this also means that they have the ability to be creative, responsible, critical and constructive users of its information. In our information rich environment and information intense economy, this intellectual scaffolding is not just an essential learning process, it is increasingly vital for life and survival.

Endnotes

1. The nature and problems of searching the Net are described in chapter 5 above.
2. For elaboration of the nature and extent of these benefits see Lamb and Todd (1993), Todd (1995) and Todd et al., (1993).
3. See chapter 5 for an exploration of the language of search terms.
4. A detailed account of search engines and search strategies is provided in chapter 5 above.
5. Critical evaluation of a particular website is the subject of chapter 7 below.

References

Baran, S., & Davis, D. (1995). *Mass communication theory: Foundations, ferment, and future*. Los Angeles, CA: Wadsworth.

Burbules, N. (1997). Struggling with the World Wide Web. *Campus Review, August: 13-19, 19*, 20-22.

Freebody, P., & Luke, A. (1990). Literacies programs: Debate and demands in cultural context. *Prospect, 5*, 7-16.

Gaines, B. (1987). An overview of knowledge-acquisition and transfer. *International Journal of Man-Machine Studies, 26*, 453-472.

Gordon, S. (1992). Implications of cognitive theory for knowledge acquisition. In R. Hoffman (Ed.), *The psychology of expertise: Cognitive research and experimental AI* (pp. 99-120). New York: Springer-Verlag.

Harrison, E., & Pelletier, M. (1995). A paradigm for strategic decision success. *Management Decision, 33* (7), 53-59.

Hawkes, J. (1997). Views from the top: The information skills process and senior students. *Scan, 16* (3), 47-52.

Heilprin, L. (1989). Foundations of information science reexamined. *Annual Review of Information Science and Technology, 24*, 343-372.

Jones, E. (1996). The value of research assignments. *Scan, 15* (3), 45-48.

Kaye, D. (1995). The importance of information. *Library Management, 16* (5), 6-15.

Kehoe, L. (1993, November 30). Casting the net worldwide. *Financial Times,* p. 1.

Kuhlthau, C. (1989). Information search process: A summary of research and implications for school library media programs. *School Library Media Quarterly, Fall*, 19-25.

Kuhlthau, C. (1993). *Seeking meaning: A process approach to library and information services.* Norwood, NJ: Ablex.

Lamb, E., & Todd, R. (1993). Philosophy, information skills and partners in learning. *Orana, 29* (3), 150-160.

McNicholas, C., & Todd, R. (1996). New kids on the box: Is it worth the investment? *Scan, 15* (4), 40-42.

New South Wales Department of School Education. (1988). *Information skills in the school.* Sydney: New South Wales Department of School Education.

Sivanesarajah, Y., McNicholas, C., & Todd, R. (1993). Making sense of Science: An information skills approach. *Science Education News, 42*, 25-27.

Spender, D. (1995). *Nattering on the Net: Women, power and cyberspace.* Melbourne: Spinifex.

Todd, R. (1995). Integrated information skills instruction: Does it make a difference? *School Library Media Quarterly, 23* (2), 133-139.

Todd, R. (1996). Independent learning and information literacy: An essential partnership for learning. In M. Nimon (Ed.), *Learning resourcefully: Challenges for teacher librarians in the information age. (Library Challenges Series Number Nine)* (pp. 3-18). Adelaide: Auslib Press.

Todd, R., Lamb, E., & McNicholas, C. (1993). Information skills and learning: Some research findings. *Access, 7* (1), 14-16.

Todd, R., & McNicholas, C. (1997, January). Electronic information and learning organisations. In *Information Online & On Disc 97. Proceedings of the Eighth Australasian Information Online & On Disc Conference and Exhibition. Sydney Convention and Exhibition Centre, Sydney Australia* (pp. 363-373). Sydney: Information Science Section, Australian Library and Information Association.

Trigwell, K., Prosser, K., & Taylor, P. (1994). Qualitative differences in approaches to teaching first year university Science. *Higher Education*, *27* (1), 75-84.

Wersig, G. (1990). The changing role of knowledge in an information society. In *The information environment: A world view. Studies in honour of Professor A. I. Mikhailov* (pp. 185-198). North-Holland: Elsevier Science Publishers.

Chapter 7

Connexions

Anne Cranny-Francis

We are immersed in a textual and social environment in which multimodality is the norm. The literary literacy of the first half of the twentieth century is no longer sufficient to deal with this new world. And that is not just because the technologies to which we now have access—as readers and/or writers—have enabled an expansion of semiotic potentials (verbal, visual, aural); it is also, and perhaps more importantly, because the political and sociocultural practices in which that earlier literacy is embedded and which it reproduces are no longer so clearly dominant. The literary literacy of early twentieth century western societies was a literacy which had been developed to position the middle class as the dominant social group, and which, more or less implicitly, positioned 'the masculine' and 'the European' (or sometimes more explicitly 'the English') as categories associated with power and control. The story of Matthew Arnold's role in the development of the corresponding (literary) literacy is too well known to need explication here, but the history of twentieth century literacy is the history of his highly-politicised legacy (Eagleton, 1983; Willinsky, 1991). His concern was to raise the conceptual capacity of the English middle class to such a high standard that they were capable and qualified to perform a leading role in society; a role produced by the technological, economic and political changes enacted by that middle class. Arnold did not question their right to rule, just their ability to rule with the ethical and intellectual sophistication he judged necessary.

We no longer live in that world. Or at least, we live in a modified version of that world. The voices which were silenced relatively easily in the late nineteenth century are now heard, if not always listened to. Accordingly, the literacy which is necessary to this new world is one which registers many different voices, not the one voice. This literacy may nevertheless position one voice more prominently than others; may accord one particular voice more influence, more 'objectivity', more rationality and judgement than others. As Donna Haraway writes of the development of scientific methodology in

Modest_Witness@Second_Millennium, 'women might watch a demonstration; they could not witness it'. Similarly the (working-class) '[t]echnicians, who were physically present [at an experiment], were also epistemologically invisible persons in the experimental way of life' just as 'women were invisible in both the physical and epistemological senses' (Haraway, 1997, p. 27). In the late twentieth century, working-class, female, non-Anglo, and non-European subjects (and others) are seizing the role of witness—and the meaning-making resources of their society are consequently being deployed in new ways to accommodate those new voices. This means not only that textual strategies are being used differently, but also that they are being read differently. Nevertheless, conservative social forces— the remnants of earlier, more repressive modes of thought and practice and the inertial lag of our major social institutions—work to maintain the social order which suppressed those different voices. And one of the major means by which this conservative practice operates is through the literacy practices of the society.

This chapter addresses some of the literacy demands placed on us, as writers and readers, by contemporary modes of communication and information management. These demands are, as might be anticipated, a mix of the old and the new— the old which makes it possible for us to access and understand these texts, the new which is partly a consequence of changes in technology and partly the result of social and cultural changes. The term which most articulates this new literacy is *'CONNECT'*—the word which, when hit, begins the process of connection to the Internet, and which, at the same time, recalls the unrelenting intertextuality of contemporary (postmodern, multimodal, multimedia) texts. It also raises the issue of who connects what to whom—that is, the question of authority in which is embedded the notion of 'author'— as well as how we relate, or connect, to/with these texts. Each of these areas is a research project in its own right, of course, but I hope here to open up some of the relevant questions and some of the possible solutions.

I also want to explore the popular use of the rhizome as a metaphoric image for the Internet and its sites. Here the notion of CONNECT is given its most anarchic representation, with the Internet being seen as a space of democracy and freedom most like the Earth of the 23rd century *Star Trek* adventures. And like the *Star Trek* Earth it sometimes forgets (and positions users/readers to forget) that this space is dominated by one society and its cultures.

CONNECT I: Reading a website

1. An anecdotal story about a website

Once upon a time there was a large public institution, the employees of which wanted an assessment of how well their website was operating. So they called in a media consultant who just happened to have, in the past, worked closely with a computer specialist and a cultural theorist who specialised in critical reading. The three of them worked together to analyse the website: the media consultant consulted the audience; the computer specialist explored the internal links and buttons on the site; and the cultural theorist explored the kinds of meanings or readings and the reading/subject positions generated by the site.

When the media consultant presented the report to the workers at the large public institution, the response was overwhelmingly positive. The audience surveys and interviews told the workers lots of interesting and useful things about how the users thought and felt about the site. The study of links told them a great deal about how the users navigate the site. And the study of the actual website text told them not only how readers were being positioned by the site, but also how the workers themselves thought and felt about their own institution.

So the workers at the large public institution realised that the first step they had to take to produce the kind of website they wanted for their institution was to work out what they actually thought and felt about their institution and about the changes to it produced by the new technology. Which might seem an obvious exercise in self-awareness, but is not one which large public institutions necessarily encourage or want to pay for. The consultancy report generated this self-reflexive exercise among workers, who actually got to say what they thought and felt about their institution, the new technology, and the ways it positioned them as social subjects.

2. In which the cultural theorist explains to her colleagues how she analysed the text of the site

Websites are such a new and different genre of text that we may feel we do not have the skills to analyse how a particular text is operating as a meaning-making site. Websites include verbal text, visual text, and, increasingly, aural text. We read, see, and hear the meanings of the site, and the meanings are produced by not only the separate elements of verbal, visual and aural text, but also the interrelationship of the three.

In the past, information storage and retrieval was mostly a verbal task, with visual text operating as a kind of illustrative prompt. More recently, the relationship between visual and verbal text has changed, with much more information carried by the visual text, to which the verbal text operates as a complement or sometimes as a prompt. The reasons for this change in our use of different semiotic (meaning-making) systems no doubt lies with the development of visual technologies, such as photography, film and television and their impact on us as social subjects. While we make the technologies, they also make us. We create their material form and they modify our embodied being.

So we have generated these semiotic practices and their texts and they (re)constitute us as meaning-making social subjects. We have learned these semiotic practices over a long period of time, during which their meanings have changed, particularly as the (inter)relationship between semiotic systems changes. The literacy which enables us to generate meanings from these texts has, therefore, developed over this time. It is not simply a new, and completely different, literacy, though its final effect may be to produce a new kind of social subject. Rather it is a literacy based on familiar literacies, rearticulated or reworked for, by and in a new technology and new sociocultural context. We know this to be the case, otherwise no-one could read these sites.

So we can explore the meanings of a website using principles drawn from more familiar literacy practices—practices originally used to read the texts which are the basis of our 'new' Information Technology (IT) literacy. It should also be noted that these familiar reading practices are currently being modified by the new literacy —just as painting was transformed by the development of photography in the nineteenth century even though photographic composition was originally formulated by reference to visual (literacy) conventions derived from, among other practices, painting. The separate pages of the website, then, can be analysed using principles formulated for the analysis of specific semiotic systems (e.g., what does the use of a particular set of words or image or sound mean?), of composition (e.g., what kinds of meanings are generated by arranging textual elements in a particular configuration?), and of multimedia texts (e.g., what meanings are produced by the interrelation of the many different meanings of the site?), as well as concepts drawn from a specific study of this new genre of text (e.g., what does it mean if links in the verbal text are indicated by underlining specific words or by the colour red rather than by the default colour, blue?).

With the website analysed by our three explorers, the principles of composition used for analysis were those developed by Gunther Kress and Theo van Leeuwen in their book, *Reading Images.* The layout of the site was examined by reference to their layout diagram shown in Figure 7.1 below:

Figure 7. 1 Based on 'The dimensions of visual space' (Kress & van Leeuwen, 1996, p. 208)

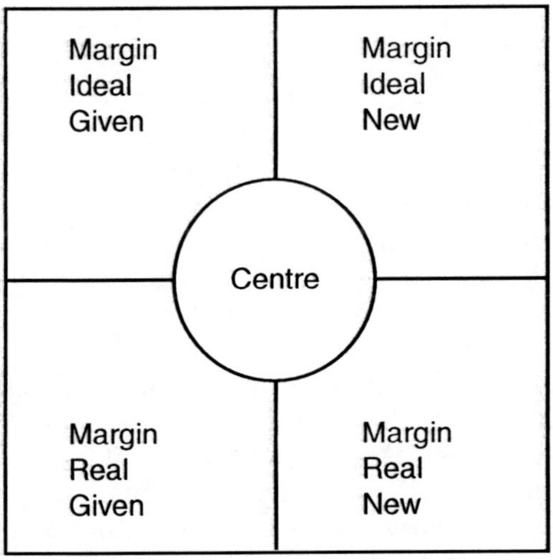

In this diagram Kress and van Leeuwen assign particular significances to the four quarters of the grid, as well as to the central position. The centre is identified, fairly obviously, as a point of focus for the composition. The meanings they assign to the parameters Real v. Ideal and Given v. New require more explanation. Kress and van Leeuwen (1996, pp. 193-194) gloss the terms, 'Real' and 'Ideal':

> For something to be ideal means that it is presented as the idealized or generalized essence of the information, hence also as its, ostensibly,

most salient part. The Real is then opposed to this in that it presents more specific information (e.g., details), more 'down-to-earth' information (e.g., photographs as documentary evidence, or maps or charts), or more practical information (e.g., practical consequences, directions for action). This is of course no less ideological.

The terms, 'Given' and 'New' are glossed as follows:

> For something to be Given means that it is something the viewer already knows, as a familiar and agreed-upon point of departure for the message. For something to be New means that it is presented as something which is not yet known, or perhaps not yet agreed upon by the viewer, hence as something to which the viewer must pay special attention . . . The structure is ideological in the sense that it may not correspond to what is the case either for the producer or for the consumer of the image or layout: the important point is that the information is presented as *though* it had that status or value for the reader, and that readers have to read it within that structure, even if that valuation may then be rejected by a particular reader. (Kress & van Leeuwen, 1996, p. 187)

In these terms the website of the public institution under review was quite conventional, with the 'generalized essence of the information' contained on the site appearing at the top of the page, and with the actual uses of or places in which to find this information appearing in the bottom half. Furthermore, a lot of the information with which the user was familiar in another mode appears on the left side, with information about new services and facilities spread from the centre to the right side. Of particular interest, however, were the icons used to identify the institution. One appeared in the left side of the page and was in the form of a large, relief (grey on white), realist graphic, which was used as background to much of the text on left to centre. Its meaning seemed to be: this is the traditional, canonical form of this institution. In the top right-hand side of the page was a pared-down, stylised, miniaturised, red version of this icon, the most obvious reading of which was: this is the new institution, less elitist than may have once been the case (pared-down), which has undergone something of a paradigm change in its relationship with clients (stylised), and which uses IT extensively (miniaturised). The use of the colour 'red' on this site is interesting. It is used also for the slogans which announce the mission of this electronic version of the institution. From one perspective the dominant use of three colours—black, white, red—recalls the print technology which was the basis of the traditional form of the institution. From another perspective, use of the colour red picks up the multiple associations of this colour within most Western cultures—red as desire, as warmth, as fire, as danger, as flashy. So the icon of the new (IT version of the) institution articulates the paradigmatic change that generated the development of the site—along with the fears and expectations which attend such changes.

Between the two icons was a verbal description of the facilities of the institution, with a number of small photographic images which served as illustration to the verbal text. In this verbal text the links were indicated not by the conventional (default) blue but by underlining, a graphic reference to the print-based technology which was the recent past of this institution. Its use can be read as a concession to users, who might be unfamiliar with the technology of the website but whose print-based, verbal literacy is high. And it was also a concession to staff whose commitment to that print-based literacy was still very high. From that viewpoint it might also be read as something of a refusal by the staff of this new technology and the literacies it demands. So the central section of the page mobilises the resources of the print-based literacy which has been the focus of the institution in the past—a move which may work for some users as a bridge into the new technology and new literacies, but which also operates as a resistance strategy against the new.

The homepage could, therefore, be read as a map of the conflicting attitudes to the new technology and new literacies which exist not only in outside users but within the institution itself. Arguably an institutional effort to deal with this conflict and to resolve it in favour of the new would result in a homepage which articulates that resolution through its (transformed) use of iconography and graphics. And the staff of the institution agreed with this assessment.

3. In which the critical reader thinks about the homepage and other linked pages on the website

This analysis of the homepage depended on a reading of the configuration or composition of the iconography, graphics and verbal text used on the page, not only on the verbal text. For the website it appears 'the medium is the message'. The meaning of the icons on the homepage (discussed earlier) was: canonical version of the institution as the Given or assumed, IT version of the institution as the New. If the institution wishes to establish the IT version as familiar and accepted, one strategy suggested by the design analysis is to move the IT icon to the left, so that it is read as Given. This may be adopted for other linked pages, if not for the homepage. This is a matter of judgement, of course. It may be that users require a phase-in process, in which their ambivalence and unfamiliarity with the technology and its literacy is mediated by the current design. Yet, it might also be argued that this design works against user acceptance of their immersion in the new technology/literacy.

The pages linked to the homepage reinforced the ambivalence conveyed by the homepage. For example, the page which announced and explained an archive of images which was held physically at the institution and was now available on the website was verbally dense and contained not one image. This page might be read (or ignored) by some users as boring and monotonous, but the implications of its composition are more important than this. By basing the use/reading of this page on verbal literacy—conveying all the information about the visual archive verbally—the site calls into question the value of visual literacy. It seems to say: visual texts are only valuable and useful once they have been translated into verbal text. This again positions users within an older print-based literacy and articulates a great ambivalence (distrust? fear?) about the new technology and its multimedia literacy.

When one of the archival pages was accessed, the story was repeated. The page contained a visual image (Centre), beneath which was printed basic catalogue information. The visual image itself was very interesting, and users could view it in closeup by clicking on the image. The catalogue data included a physical description of the image, its date of production, the names of its creator and its printer, and provided some links to associated subject materials in the library catalogue, along with a 'Summary' of the image. This data enabled users to contextualise the image and so to speculate about its sociocultural significance: What kinds of attitudes and values did it articulate? What was the nature of its audience — popular or elite? How would that image challenge or reinforce popular attitudes? This task of speculation was not, however, assisted by the 'Summary' which contained a rather enigmatic reference to the image as being satiric and parodic, without actually specifying how this satire or parody would have been read by viewers at the time of production of the image. Other notable omissions in the presentation of the image were its context of publication: for example, whether this image was used as an illustration to a book, magazine or newspaper and, if so, what sort of book, magazine or newspaper it was (what were its fundamental assumptions, as articulated by author or editor?). This was an important issue with this particular image because of its inherent racism, which was simultaneously presented as anti-racism. In other words, this was an extremely complex image which captured the complexity of attitudes to race at the time of its production. In our current context, then, the 'Summary' has the crucial function of explaining the kinds of meanings which might have originally been made from the image, and also the current institution's attitude to those meanings.

The assumption that the institution does have an attitude to its collection is an essential basis for its construction of both the collection itself and its description of the collection. The arguments about objectivity have surely been comprehensively deconstructed at this point. In the context of the literacies operating here, the admission that the institution has an ideology (albeit one which is constantly in the process of change) enables the user to make crucial distinctions between data, information and knowledge which are frequently obscured in the use of information technology.

In this particular example the 130 year-old image could be read in different ways—including racist by omission and racist by commission. The 'Summary' did not enable the user to distinguish the institution's attitude, though the subject-area links (including one to 'Race Discrimination') suggests an awareness of racist issues in relation to the image. One implication which might be drawn from this is that the institution is also racist by omission— because it did not comment directly on the racism on which the visual was based, nor did it provide information about the original context of publication which might have clarified the use of the image. The argument against this reading of the situation might be that the institution provides data and/or information, leaving the user to formulate this into knowledge. However, this claim takes no account of the principles of selection involved in the collection and presentation of data and of the contextualising material which enables that data to be transformed into information—all of which encodes or assumes particular values and attitudes. It also fails to consider the tendency among IT users to regard information accessed via the Internet as knowledge. Since this major public institution is centrally concerned with issues of information and knowledge, it might be expected to address explicitly and self-consciously the nature of knowledge, the distinction between information and knowledge, and specifically the sociocultural character and role of the information presented on its own site. Not to do so implies that the site colludes in this conflation of information and knowledge and so with the unexamined, unself-conscious assimilation of institutional ideology and the individual subject positions it offers.

So, on these two linked website pages there are a number of interesting anomalies. Firstly, there is a page about images which has no images, and which therefore challenges the value of the visual literacy it otherwise champions. Secondly, there is a page focussed on an image which presents that image without effectively contextualising it; that is, a page which fails to effectively interrelate the verbal and visual text on the page. In both cases, the page does not effectively utilise the multimedia/multimodal literacy which characterises information technology, and the effect of this goes beyond the content of the individual page. Since the page effectively constructs the institution for the user, the elisions and absences which characterise the website characterise the institution.

4. In which the (rather long-winded) critical reader describes the literacy skills used to analyse the website

Analysing the site involved a combination of critical reading practices, some of which are relatively new. Nevertheless, many are familiar practices, developed for the consumption and analysis of texts in a range of media. As noted earlier, familiar reading practices provide the context for the construction of new reading practices, which subsequently act back on the familiar practices modifying them for the current age.

i. verbal text

Allucquère Rosanne Stone writes in *The War of Desire and Technology at the Close of the Mechanical Age* that 'entry to the world of virtual community requires high levels of skills in the English language and a high level of technical proficiency, but this annoying fact usually passes unremarked' (Stone, 1995, p. 181). In the website analysis the concern over technical proficiency is the undeclared, but nevertheless articulated, anxiety (the repressed) of the website. Verbal literacy, however, was a given; in fact, as analysis of the page about the visual archive demonstrated, high verbal literacy was not only assumed among users, but also prioritised on the site. In this sense, then, the site seems not to ignore the demand for high verbal proficiency which Stone identifies as necessary for the use of IT, but which the focus on visual literacy in much writing about IT seems to ignore.

It should be noted, however, that the verbal literacy required is not (only) the verbal literacy of an age dominated by print books. Instead this is a verbal literacy which not only understands the operation of the verbal text, but also appreciates the interrelation of verbal and visual text in the production of a page. And it is a verbal literacy which recalls and extends the awareness of the verbal as a graphic construction—just as the Concrete Poets or novelists such as Lawrence Sterne made use of the graphic features and layout of the verbal text. Effectively, then, the contemporary reader is reminded of the technology of verbal text (print) production, which is now so familiar that users often no longer perceive it as a technology. Walter Ong's classic text, *Orality and Literacy* is useful as a reminder of the development of print-based technologies. The contemporary reader/user needs also to be aware of the developing graphic conventions of the verbal text in a multimedia age: for example, the use of default colours in website construction or of particular contractions such as FAQ (Frequently Asked Questions). As in any kind of reading exercise, the value of knowing the conventions of a particular kind of text is that the reader is able not only to explore the possible significance of particular conventions, but also to trace deviations from the conventional and what that might mean for a particular text and its meanings.

As Stone's (1995) analysis suggests, therefore, website analysis requires a verbal literacy which is so highly developed that it is not even an issue; that literacy is invisible or transparent. It also, apparently contradictorily, requires a verbal literacy which is self-conscious about its own technology—understanding the meanings of specific genres of verbal text (e.g., genres such as exposition, essay, report, and narrative which frequently appear on websites), as well as the graphic features of verbal text which can also contribute significantly to the meaning of a text.

ii. visual text

As with verbal literacy we are dealing here with a semiotic system which has developed over a long period of time, so that a history of visual literacy exists, which includes the conventions by which we read and make meaning from visual texts. As the website analysis above suggests, this visual history is important in enabling us to read the images at a particular site—whether that means images which operate as the focus of a particular page or icons which interact with verbal text to construct the meanings of a page.

Images scanned into a website must be situated generically (e.g., photograph, illustration, artwork, film still, etc.) so that the reader/user can explore their meanings. For example, an image which began life as an illustration to a nineteenth century newspaper brings some of that meaning to the website, but it is also recontextualised by the website to generate quite different meanings—about its original context of production (the attitudes and values of nineteenth century Anglo-Australian society) and about its current context (the ideology of the institution which presents it in a particular manner to the user). In other words, the image also needs to be situated in relation to other material on the site—verbal text, sound, other graphic features— in order for its meanings *at this site* to be understood.

Visual icons feature widely on Internet sites, often as shorthand references to the institution or individual represented by the site. Again, the generic history of the icon needs to be explored in order for its significance at the particular site to be determined. If, for example, it appears in different forms as it did on the website discussed above, we might ask the significance or meanings of these different uses. That analysis included a study of the generic history of this kind of graphic—with the more realist version of the icon seen as more familiar to a contemporary user than the stylised version. Because of that familiarity (which arises, we might argue, from the popularity of realist art-forms) the realist form of the graphic signifies the more familiar, traditional form of the institution—bricks and mortar—whilst the stylised icon represents the new online version. The colours used in an icon might also be examined for what they convey socioculturally. So colour, size, style, positioning, and more recently movement, all contribute to the meanings of the icons used on websites.

As with the verbal text, we might also explore the use of visual texts in this new medium for new conventions, which will ultimately come to influence the ways we view visual image offline as well as online. For example, the use of a home page icon situated at top left might be seen as a way of inducting users into the literacy of the medium, familiarising them with the use of the visual as a mode of communication on a par with the verbal.

So, the visual texts used on a website also require a high visual literacy, which includes a generic and historical understanding of the development of visual imagery and our (sociocultural) readings of that development. In this way the user is able to explore the meanings of the images and icons used on the site, by reference to that semiotic history, and also to situate these meanings in relation to meanings generated by other elements of/on the site—verbal, visual, aural.

iii. composition and design

With the transparency of print technology, relatively little attention has been paid to the composition or design of a particular page (or more) of text. Of course, as noted above, writers have at times exploited this aspect of the technology in their own meaning production; however, there has been little systematic study of the sociocultural significance of composition. This might be considered a strange omission, given the prevalence within our society of multimodal texts—newspapers, magazines, posters, advertisements, labels, film, television. Of course, there are studies of each of these specific genres or media of text, which trace their development socioculturally and historically. These studies also address the meanings of particular texts, but tend to focus on the separate elements of the text rather than the way they are configured. That is left to the designer whose primary task is not seen to be critical.

The work of Gunther Kress and Theo van Leeuwen in *Reading Images* has brought together the study of design and composition with sociocultural analysis. They explore the history of the composition of western visual images, noting conventions which are used repeatedly both in visual text alone, and in texts which employ both visual and verbal material. These include the positioning of different elements of the text, the colours used in the composition and the construction of vectors within the composition which direct the attention of the reader in particular ways. Kress and van Leeuwen analyse the use of these conventions not just as a design feature, but for what meanings the conventions carry in particular contexts; that is, how they interrelate with the meanings produced by specific text elements to generate new or other meanings. Ultimately the concern is not only what meanings are conveyed to the reader by the composition of a text, but also what subject position(s) the text thereby offers the reader.

As noted earlier, the website analysis depended heavily on an understanding of the composition of the site, so that it seemed that, in a sense, the composition *is* the site. Of course, that formulation underestimates the verbal and visual literacy required for the composition to be intelligible; however, it does draw attention to the relative poverty of critical writing on composition and design.

iv. multimodal/multimedia text

All the above sections refer to issues which arise from the multimodal or multimedia nature of the IT text. And as noted, this is not a new issue, as the wealth of multimodal and multimedia texts in our society attests. However, the use of a new technology does highlight features of this multimodality which have been ignored or elided in studies of more familiar technologies and their production. The interrelation of meanings generated by verbal text, visual text, and (sometimes) aural text, as mediated by the composition or design of the site, produces a meaning or set of meanings which is/are the meaning(s) of the site—and of the individual or institution which the site represents/constructs. It is crucial, therefore, that contemporary verbal, visual and aural literacies be understood both intrinsically (in terms of the sociocultural history of their own semiotic) and intertextually (in terms of how they interact with other texts which carry different meanings and readings). For example, in the website analysis discussed earlier, it was not sufficient to read the page which focussed on a visual image as simply a frame for that image. Instead the image itself was explored in some detail, as was the verbal text which accompanied it and the links available on the page. The meaning of the page was seen as the interrelation of the meanings generated by each of these different elements—as well as by the material which was not there (the original context of publication, etc.).

Multimodal or multimedia literacy has, therefore, to be seen as a combination and interrelation of skills—verbal literacy, visual literacy, aural literacy, compositional literacy. We all have those skills to some extent, as they are the basis of most of the popular media of our time. However, we do not always have a critical understanding of those skills—a critical literacy. This consists in not only the ability to read each of these separate meaning-making systems, but also a sociocultural and historical understanding of their development and of the ways in which they position readers. Further, it means being able, therefore, to trace how information technology impacts on the conventions of these media/genres—constructing new conventions (and their meanings) and modifying the familiar (and their meanings).

v. links

The final meaning-making element of the site to be discussed is the link, which Nicholas Burbules regards as the characteristic feature of the technology. Burbules notes that: 'links do not only express semic relations but also, significantly, establish pathways of possible movement within the Web space; they suggest relations, but also *control access to information*' (Burbules, 1997, p. 105). In my website analysis the role of the link was explored specifically in relation to the page which focussed on the visual image. That exploration pointed to some fundamental issues which the institution needed to address: for example, the interrelation of verbal and visual text to generate meaning, which in this case implied a disturbing avoidance by the institution of the ethical complexities involved in storing and making available a particular archive. It also suggested that the institution had not clearly considered the relationship between data, information and knowledge and, therefore, how it positioned users as social subjects. This was clear not only from the information verbally given or not given, but also from the links which were not there; in particular, a link which would enable the user to more fully (socioculturally) situate the visual text and its meanings.

As Burbules notes, the link is characteristic of information technology and, because of the speed with which it (sometimes) happens, 'the link-event becomes invisible' (Burbules, 1997, p. 104). That is, if the reader of a book is referred to another book or article and then has to go to a library to find that book or article, in the time and effort required for the task the reader might well begin to question the reasons for this particular choice of reference; however, when the reference (that is, link) is (almost) instantaneous, there is no time (or motivation) to ponder the choice. For this reason the assumptions which create the link are also invisible. That is, the reader/user is not encouraged, or provoked, by the tedious process of finding a reference to question the philosophy and/or politics behind a choice of reference. The instantaneity of the link tends to make such questioning unnecessary: if the reader/user finds the reference useful, it can be immediately assimilated; if not, the return to the source is again virtually instantaneous. So the philosophy and/or politics which have motivated the generation of a link are left unremarked and unchallenged.

When a reader/user moves from data to contextual information of a particular kind, and then assimilates that relationship as part of her/his own perspective or set of values and attitudes, s/he generates knowledge uncritically. This reader/user does not question the reasons that a specific practice or event or individual is being situated in a particular way; rather s/he implicitly relies on the authority of the individual who produced the site. And just as readers are encouraged to be critical of the inferences and relationships theorised by authors of all kinds, so this critical attitude should extend to the website. Yet as Burbules notes, there are technological reasons that it does not, including not only speed of access, but also the effect of net surfing, of games-playing, and of the commodification of information (1997, pp. 108-110). The link, then, demands equally critical attention from the reader/user—particularly as it relates directly to the formulation of knowledge and so of the nature of the individual subject.

In summary, then, analysis of the text of a website requires a range of literacies, most of which are based on contemporary literacy practices—but which are also modified by both their interrelation and their use in this new medium. This website did not use sound, but many other websites do—and again the literacy required is drawn from the sociocultural analysis of the specific sound, as well as from an intertextual study of the role of the sound within a multimodal, multimedia context. The website is highly conventional in construction, though users/readers may not always comply with those conventions or the subject positions they offer. Which is not to say that conventionality means conservatism; after all, the self-reflexivity of a contemporary film such as Baz Luhrman's *William Shakespeare's Romeo + Juliet* demonstrates how a text which is highly conventional (that is, a major studio motion picture) can generate a reading practice which is critical—socially, culturally, textually—and does not simply situate the viewer as ideologically passive.

The following section focusses specifically on the theories and metaphors used to describe the working of the Internet, which includes the act of reading/viewing. This analysis assumes that the Internet only exists in what Chris Chesher (1997) calls the 'invocation'—the address by a supplicant for immediate aid; that is, the Internet is not always already there but is invoked by the individual user each time she/he logs on, in order to respond to her/his request for information. Chesher's conception of the Internet also points to the crucial role of information technology in the formation of the contemporary social subject—and so the need to develop ways of understanding this (inter)relationship. In particular, it addresses the issues of conventionality and of readership, suggesting that at least one of the metaphors which has become almost synonymous with the Internet itself might be more appropriate as a description of the role of the user.

CONNECT II: Readers and/as rhizomes

The Internet has been promoted as a major force for democracy: all of us, so the rhetoric claims, can take part in debate over local and global issues; all of us can vote on them—all of us who have computers, that is! Similarly, hypertext will explode the limits of the book, giving us works which are not limited by a certain number of pages and bound between covers. Instead we will have open-ended texts with multiple authorities, leading to an interrogation of social and cultural norms and the development of a truly multicultural society[1]. As the website analysis described in CONNECT I shows, however, cybertexts are not anarchic constructs but are highly conventional—even if those conventions are currently in the process of development. And since cybertexts now play a major role in the formation of the individual subject—either directly or via their influence on other familiar texts—it is important to explore this rhetoric about the Internet and its everyday reality.

1. In which some of the metaphors used to describe the Internet are considered

The theorists whose work is repeatedly cited in relation to information technology are Deleuze and Guattari, and their most-cited essay is 'Rhizome'. In this essay they distinguish 'the rhizome' from earlier models of text production, which they visualise as 'the root' which reflects 'the tree-world' above it. That is, the world has been conceptualised via a tree-like logic, which relates all events (branches) back to a central set of concepts or ideas (the trunk). This is an image for the modernist belief in a set of grand narratives or discourses (in Foucault's sense) which generate and can explain everything that happens in the world; discourses such as psychoanalysis and cultural materialism. And reflecting the tree-world is the root-book which is composed and analysed in a similar way, to reflect the world above. According to Deleuze and Guattari (1983, p. 11), disciplines such as linguistics, which study the language in which the book is composed, also use this 'tree' logic, though linguistics is represented here by the formal linguistics of Noam Chomsky:

> The linguistic tree according to Chomsky still begins at point S and proceeds by dichotomy. In a rhizome, on the contrary, each feature does not necessarily refer to a linguistic feature: semiotic chains of every kind are connected in it according to very diverse modes of encoding, chains that are biological, political, economic, etc., and that put into play not only regimes of different signs, but also different states of affairs.

The rhizome, then, is an image of the textual freedom predicted for the Internet and its texts, including hypertext. The rhizome differs from the tree or root in that it does not necessarily return to its origins; in fact, its operation questions the whole concept of origin. The rhizome is seen as connecting different semiotic chains, not maintaining modal purity, and relating them to social and cultural events and organisations. The rhizome places semiosis in the context of power and authority; as Deleuze and Guattari (1983, p. 13) say: 'There is no language in itself, no universality of language . . . There is no mother tongue but a seizure of power by a dominant language within a political multiplicity'. From a rhizomic perspective, language can only be analysed by 'de-centring it onto other dimensions and into other registers' (p. 13). For Deleuze and Guattari, language[2] studied as a system in and of itself is not too abstract, but not abstract enough; (formal) linguists fail to position language as a semiotic system in relation to the social and cultural practices in which it is embedded as a major player.

Deleuze and Guattari conceptualise the rhizome as based on a principle of multiplicities which spread out to form vast networks — like the web of the Internet, or the neural net of Data's brain in *Star Trek: The Next Generation.* Rhizomes do not trace multiples back to any generative One, again signalling their rejection of modernist grand narratives. The rhizome is also likely to rupture at any point into what they term 'lines of flight', generated by the rhizome and remaining part of it though directed out and away, referring to one another and so avoiding simple dichotomies. So the rhizome can not be contained within a simple abstract structure, like a tree or root, though its lines of flight often encounter such stratifying structures along the way. And they may be temporarily trapped by such structures, forming the 'nodes or points of structuration' on which many of our theories (such as psychoanalysis or formal linguistics) focus.

Deleuze and Guattari also use terms such as 'reterritorialisation' and 'deterritorialisation' to describe the processes whereby lines of flight, eruptions of the rhizome interact with institutions. Deterritorialisation is an image for the dissolution of the boundaries which constitute and contain institutionalised or disciplinary knowledge—the knowledge which is safe for society, cleansed of its multiplicities and its references to its sociocultural practice. So there is a sense in which Cultural Studies as an interdisciplinary practice operated to deterritorialise the disciplinary practices of Sociology, English and Communication Studies. Reterritorialisation occurs when that line of flight is recaptured, as when Cultural Studies itself becomes a discipline and starts erecting its own boundaries.

Related to this set of spatial metaphors is another set—the smooth and the striated, where the striated space is the space in which rules operate. It is the space of the State apparatus—or the space defined by the warp and woof of fabric, defined and regulated. Smooth space, on the other hand, is the space uncontained by regulations, which individual subjects traverse in a desire to avoid regulation; it is like felt, an entanglement of fibres rather than the orderly intertwining which constitutes woven fabric. For example, we might think of our everyday life as a mixture of regulated (striated) space—a home in the suburbs, a regular job, and the smooth space of our occasional voyaging out of domesticity—as political activists or as drop-outs, for example, though again with the sometimes uncomfortable realisation that the two are intertwined. And, as Deleuze and Guattari (1987, p. 474) note, 'the two spaces in fact exist only in mixture: smooth space is constantly being translated, traversed into a striated space; striated space is constantly being reversed, returned to a smooth space.'

2. In which these metaphors are used to explore hypertext reading practices

Referring this specifically to hypertext, it is necessary to distinguish between different types of hypertext—texts which are read-only and those which are read-and-write and to which the reader can add material (though it may be that this distinction is less clear than we might at first think). With the read-only texts, some operate as a simple list of links: logo at the top, then a set of verbal or visual cues to particular information sites. A lot of websites operate this way, and they constitute a very recognisable root function: a main stem which is the site itself, from which a series of branches takes you to other sites or to different parts of the same site—and back again to the main stem for more or different information. The website analysed in CONNECT I is essentially of this type. Verbal and visual literacies, principles of composition and design, and multimodal literacy practices can be deployed to deconstruct the significances of the site: what does it tell us about itself, consciously or unconsciously?

A number of educational hypertext documents follow a similar logic, with the links operating in a similar way to conventional footnotes. Perhaps even more explicitly than with a conventional footnote, the reader is directed back from the reference to the main body of the text. It is a root-text and typically encodes a particular version of reality, knowledge and truth which is guaranteed by a particular non-intrusive and undeclared authority. That is, such texts refer readers to specific information which explicates the text under scrutiny, but do not always explain the premise for selection of a particular piece of explanatory information. In other words, the authority of the author is not placed under challenge by the text itself. If we add to this the research which shows that students using these texts actually consult the links far more often than students consult reference texts with textbooks (Landow, 1994, p. 18), then the scope of that authority is considerably broader than that of the textbook writer.

The write-and-read text is often compared with this form of hypertext, as it seems to offer many more opportunities for multivocality and so to challenge the authority of a single controlling voice. With these texts it is wise not to underestimate the generic constraints which operate on the participants. For example, for those who contribute to ongoing stories, it is arguable that they all do so with the structure of narrative firmly embedded in their consciousness and, subsequently, in their contribution—even if it is primarily in the form of a reaction against narrative. Which is not to say that new insights cannot develop or new meanings cannot be made out of the kinds of experiences and issues introduced to a particular ongoing story-in-the-making, but it does challenge the notion of the Web as a space of total freedom from all rules. As Deleuze and Guattari (1987) say, smooth space and striated space exist in a mixture: where there is one, you will find the other. Furthermore, we might want to argue that new meanings are generated, and creativity takes place, in the interrelationship of the two.

Hypertext documents, whether primarily verbal or visual or a mixture of the two, and sometimes with an aural dimension as well, are all composed according to particular rules. Sometimes the rules are quite obvious, as with the root-type or linear-hierarchical sites; with others, the rules of composition require more analysis, but they are there. Sometimes the rules are there in the breaking, as with the multi-author stories which seem to break all the rules of a single controlling voice, until we realise Barthes' (1977) point that that voice has never simply been that of an individual speaker/writer, but is the voice of a society and/or of a culture—and that a text is a 'tissue of quotations from the innumerable centres of culture' (p. 146).

It has been noted often in the last twenty years that a transformation has taken place in our thinking—from the logic of the temporal, to that of the spatial. Postmodernism is rife with spatial metaphors— 'site', 'terrain', 'geography', 'topology', 'mapping', 'tracing', 'location', 'positioning'. We are preoccupied with the power of the visual, whether in the conduct of a war such as the Gulf War or the death of a princess. And spatial metaphors seem more appropriate to that logic—the logic of the snapshot or of the film still. Yet we do not experience the snaphot alone, but the snapshot as it fulfills our sense of a particular context and history, a particular social narrative; we experience the film still not devoid of context, but as it encapsulates some essence of the film narrative. Perhaps the metaphor which most clearly expresses this fusion of movements in space and time is the vector or the rhizome.

There is a semiotic history at work in our reading/viewing which dictates that the contemporary focus on spatiality and the visual takes place in the context of the verbal and the temporal. We look at visual images now and they are not ever simply isolated, stand-alone images, but are embedded in already-existing narratives and genres from which they derive at least part of their significance and power. So there is a sense that contemporary readings of the verbal and visual are somehow metatextual; that is, that they can never be naively representational, as it was perhaps once possible to be. It is this characteristic of contemporary verbal, visual and aural literacy which is signified by the unrelenting intertextuality or allusiveness of contemporary multimodal, multimedia texts.

3. In which the metaphors for cybertext are referred instead to cyber-readers

As noted in the discussion above and in the analysis in CONNECT I, cybertexts are rule-governed and invite particular kinds of reading. It is our reading of them which seems less so. It is in our reading as embodied social subjects that our experiences and perceptions enter into our understanding of textual practice. It is in our readings of these texts that we start to put together the semiotic with the social, cultural, biological, political, economic; we remake the text in the image of our everyday lives.

Our readings as embodied subjects generate lines of flight which take us from our starting point to areas not obviously predicted by that starting point. To use contemporary understandings of reading, we may generate tactical readings which incorporate that reading practice into everyday life (de Certau, 1984; Fiske, 1989), where it becomes part of a rhizomic practice by which we position ourselves in the world. A simple example of a rhizome might be traced in the 'Go' function of *Netscape*, which traces the sequence of sites we have traversed in a particular session on the Internet. This rhizome or vector is our trajectory through our contemporary time/space. It may at times be directed by a particular site, but we very often move beyond the links suggested at a specific site, to explore others which our own experience suggests might be useful.

The semiosis of contemporary multimodal texts must be read in the context of the already-existing narratives of life in a bourgeois state, though a state which is under interrogation. Some contemporary texts are root-books, whether they are multimodal or not, whether they are hypertext or not. They operate according to particular rules which give voice to a particular social order. We may not read them compliantly, of course, but embed them in our own rhizomic chains which challenge their authority. Other texts, including multimodal texts and some hypertext documents, may work metatextually with the root-structures which are familiar modes of text production. By means of recontextualising those structures/practices, deconstructing their aesthetic and political meanings, it is possible to produce texts which critically explore the nature of their/our contemporary society. Understanding those practices as sociocultural strategies in themselves (which means also understanding the semiotic history in which they are embedded) and positioning those practices within the complex semiotic, social and political context in which we operate requires, in Deleuze and Guattari's terms, more abstraction than most of our disciplines have traditionally been familiar with.

So the rhizome is less useful as a metaphor for the website, which is heavily rule-governed and intertextually and socioculturally specific, than for the reading practices by which users/readers access these sites. Of course, the reading practices themselves are rule-governed; we tend to read texts in ways which are familiar from our readings of other, similar texts. However, reading practices necessarily involve readers, who bring their own specific histories and identities to the process. Because of that history and identity, the individual reader enacts a particular individual reading practice, the path of which might be described by Deleuze and Guattari's rhizome. Like the rhizome it encounters nodes or points of structuration, which include hypertext documents and websites and their conventional reading practices. It is essential that the reader have the skills to deconstruct these sites—the data they present, the information they offer—in order that she/he is not positioned simply to accept the ideologies they encounter on their travels. Donna Haraway (1997, p. 36) wrote:

> Knowledge-making technologies, including crafting subject positions and ways of inhabiting such positions, must be made relentlessly visible and open to critical intervention.

Haraway's statement recognises that knowledge-making technologies such as information technology and its cybertexts generate not just meanings, but the positions which individual users/readers must occupy in order to understand those meanings. In the process they intervene in, and are part of, the formation of individual subjectivity. We made them; they make us.

The literary literacy of the late nineteenth and early to mid-twentieth century has been seen as actively producing a class system in which the educated middle-class were positioned to control the flow of information, and in so doing to dominate all major social institutions. The challenge for literacy education in the late twentieth and early twenty-first century is a literacy which is both multimodal and embodied. And this is not necessarily recognised by the rhetoric referred to at the beginning of Section II—which resulted in advertising campaigns such as Macintosh's 'Power to the People'. Which 'People'? It is an argument for a critical multimodal, multimedia literacy which goes beyond the liberatory rhetoric of a society which is, simultaneously, knee-deep in conspiracy theory; in which, as Stone (1995) noted, crucial demands on individuals such as high proficiency levels in both technical skills and English verbal literacy are ignored. This means a literacy which is responsive to (and so, critical of and creative with) the semiotic possibilities and practices of multimodal, multimedia texts, including cybertexts—their semiotic histories, generic practices, sociocultural significances. It also means a literacy which recognises that the embodied, literate, contemporary subject may operate within a number of different positionings, of class, gender, sexuality, ethnicity, 'race', age, ability—and that her/his reading practice will reflect the complexity and diversity of interests, values, attitudes, feelings which are generated by that embodiment. Accordingly, this contemporary individual subject will trace her/his own path through the information offered by information technology and develop ways of transforming that information into knowledges which enact her/his everyday life—dreams, aspirations, fears and desires. In the process this individual may form alliances which enable her/him/them to work socioculturally and politically for ideals which may not be recognised by major social institutions—textual, cultural, social, economic, political. So this is a literacy which operates from a recognition of difference, not an assumption of sameness; and which, rather than submitting to authority (textual, cultural, social, economic, political), actively interrogates it.

Endnotes

1. Chapter 11 further explores the notion that the language of the Internet not only has the potential to bring about a convergence of communities and cultures, but also to cause division as new subcul-

tures with unique languages are established.

2. Note that language here is read as synonymous with semiotic—a meaning-making system—and so may be verbal, but also visual, or aural, or tactile, etc. This is not to say that grammars developed for the verbal can be simply transferred to other semiotic systems, such as the visual or aural; those models apply quite distinctly to verbal language. However, it does seem that, just as verbal language can be understood as a rule-governed practice which articulates social and cultural values and has a distinct social and cultural (ideological) significance, so too may the other semiotic systems.

References

Barthes, R. (1977). *Image/Music/Text: Essays* (S. Heath, Selected & Trans.). London: Fontana.

Burbules, N. C. (1997). Rhetorics of the web: Hyperreading and critical literacy. In I. Snyder (Ed.), *Page to screen: Taking literacy into the electronic era* (pp. 102-122). St Leonards: Allen & Unwin.

Chesher, C. (1997). The ontology of digital domains. In D. Holmes (Ed.), *Virtual politics: Identity and community in cyberspace* (pp. 79-92). London: Sage.

De Certau, M. (1984). *The practice of everyday life.* (S. Rendall, Trans.). Berkeley, CA: University of California Press.

Deleuze, G., & Guattari, F. (1983). Rhizome. In *On the line* (J. Johnston Trans.), (pp. 1-65). New York: Semiotext(e).

Deleuze, G., & Guattari, F. (1987). *A thousand plateaus: Capitalism and schizophrenia.* (B. Massumi, Trans.). Minnesota, MN: University of Minnesota Press.

Eagleton, T. (1983). *Literary theory: An introduction.* Oxford: Basil Blackwell.

Fiske, J. (1989). *Understanding popular culture.* Boston: Hyman Unwin.

Haraway, D. (1997). *Modest_Witness@Second_Millennium.FemaleMan ©_Meets_OncoMouse™: Feminism and Technoscience.* New York: Routledge.

Holmes, D. (Ed.). (1997). *Virtual politics: Identity and community in cyberspace.* London: Sage.

Kress, G., & van Leeuwen, T. (1996). *Reading images: The grammar of visual design.* London: Routledge.

Landow, G. P. (1994). What's a critic to do?: Critical theory in the age of hypertext. In G. P. Landow (Ed.), *Hyper/Text/Theory* (pp. 1-48). Baltimore: The Johns Hopkins University Press.

Ong, W. (1982). *Orality and literacy: The technologizing of the word.* London: Methuen.

Stone, A. R. (1995). *The war of desire and technology at the close of the mechanical age.* Cambridge, MA: MIT Press.

Willinsky, J. (1991). *The triumph of literature/the fate of literacy: English in the secondary school curriculum.* New York: Teachers College Press.

Part 3

Cultures and Communities in Cyberspace

Chapter 8

Online on time: The language of Internet Relay Chat

Juliet Mar

Introduction

To the uninitiated, the popular press can give the impression that the Internet is a playground full of exciting people just waiting to strike up a conversation with them. As a result many people can be disappointed when they sit before an 'online' computer for the first time. They may feel cheated that email is merely a cheap, efficient and paper-free form of letter writing, and the World Wide Web just another way to receive information. It is only when synchronous forms of communication (such as Internet chat rooms) are discovered that the promises of the popular press become viable. In this chapter, I will discuss Internet Relay Chat (IRC)—the interactive side of the Net—explaining firstly what it is and then describing the contextual features which impact on the discourse which occurs 'in' it. The linguistic examples are taken from an actual IRC session which took place in March 1997, the log of which appears in Appendix 1 at the end of this chapter.

What IRC is

Internet Relay Chat is a type of computer-mediated communication (CMC) in which two or more users in different locations can interact in real time. Technologically, it is similar to email in that it requires the use of a modem, phone line and certain software programs. It is also similar in that the medium is text-based, rather than audiovisual. What distinguishes the two is that whereas time may lapse between the sending and reading of email messages, IRC is synchronous.

IRC is just one of a number of synchronous CMC, or 'chat', systems which allow users to type messages to each other in conversation—as opposed to letter—style. Others include what have been referred to as 'text-based virtual reality' such as MUDs (Multiple User Dungeons or Multiple User Domains)—creative games in which users take on the personae of fantasy characters with various powers and skills; MOOs (MUDs-Object-Oriented); and ICQ ('I seek you')—which is essentially IRC between people who have a pre-existing relationship.

IRC was first used in Finland in the late 1980s. It was designed by Jarkko Oikarinen who based it on the unix 'talk' utility which enabled synchronous CMC between two users. As public domain software[1], it is accessed by thousands of users in countries all over the world. In order to 'meet' other chatters, a user must first[2] choose which *channel* (the technical name for a chat room) s/he would like to visit. The available channels (those which at the time have at least one other user) can be listed, giving channel name (preceded by the hash symbol '#'), number of speakers present in the room, and current topic of chat. Examples of how these are listed on the screen are provided in Table 8.1 below.

Table 8.1 Typical computer screen display of open IRC channels

Channel name	Number of speakers	Current topic of chat
#ana	2	come on in for good food an fun chat
#cafe-moo	2	All wiyht. Rho sritched mg kegtops awound?
#classical music	7	happy birthday to singapore
#Cyberchat	49	I got the hookup! M00 if ya hear me!
#Funshack	5	Welcome to Funshack
#JoesPlace	3	We need People to get this Party going.....
#hottub	6	to bring up the change colours menu press alt and f4
#pagan	4	Pagan98 festival this weekend. Friday to Sunday ...
#paranoia	1	
#youwanna	2	THE END

Having chosen which channel s/he would like to chat in, the user types the command

```
/join #channelname
```

and will instantly be 'transported' there. However, users are not restricted to joining just one channel at a time; unlike real life, it is possible to be in two or more 'places' at once. Each channel appears in a different window which can be tiled on the computer screen so that the user can 'be part of' (read the 'scripts' from) every room simultaneously. In each channel window, the right hand column displays the names of the other chatters present, and upon entry into the chat room, the conversation starts to scroll up the main part of the screen as it occurs. A narrow bar at the bottom of the screen displays a blinking cursor for the user to type his/her own messages to the others. By pressing the ENTER key, these contributions will immediately[3] appear on all the screens of those present in the room, forming a type of script of the conversation.

There are also commands at the users' disposal which enable them to perform functions such as changing their nickname (*/nick*), finding out more information on other chatters in the room (*/whois*), sending a private message to one other chatter (*/msg*) and leaving the channel (*/leave* or */quit*). Anything that is preceded by the slash does not appear on others' screens as written.

For instance, if a chatter with the nickname *batman* typed:

```
/leave #funchat
```

others in the *#funchat* channel would see on their screens:

```
*** batman (...4) has left #funchat
```

or if he typed

```
/nick Robin
```

the others would read:

```
*** batman is now known as Robin
```

This command feature enables activity amongst the chatters which is not part of the verbal conversation, but still contributes to the interaction in the chat room.

The context of situation of IRC and its implications for language

According to Halliday (1978, 1994; Halliday & Hasan, 1985), the three most important elements of context of situation which impinge on language choice are Field, Tenor and Mode. Briefly,

Field deals with what sort of activity is occurring, Tenor with the social relationships amongst the interactants, and Mode with the specific way that language has been organised to transmit meanings in this situation. In the sections below, I shall describe each of these contextual features—Field, Tenor and Mode—in detail with respect to IRC, and I shall show what sort of an impact these features have on the language that is used in the chat rooms.

Field: What is going on

When one is asked to give information about a particular extralinguistic context, the elements that usually come to mind include what sort of people (e.g., bank tellers with customers), doing what sort of activity (e.g., processing cash deposits), under what sort of circumstances (e.g., in a bank on a week day). Such elements—i.e., 'what is going on' in a situation—make up what is known as Field. Specifying the activity and the topic(s) under discussion allows one to predict which linguistic choices are likely to be taken in this situation.

i. the activity

Although IRC usually involves individuals sitting alone typing at a computer terminal, it is more similar as an activity to having a casual conversation than to writing an essay or a document, even an email letter. This is due to features of the Mode of the context, such as the fact that there is immediate feedback from readers (see pp. 163-4 below). In IRC, any number of people who usually have not met each other face-to-face gather together in virtual rooms to exchange ideas about anything at all. It is perhaps most analogous to a conference call or partyline which links up three or more telephone lines for the one conversation. The activity begins when two interactants initiate contact in a channel by exchanging greetings, and terminates when the second last person leaves the channel[5]. To be a participant in IRC, however, one need not be present from the beginning until the end of the session. Rather, one may join and leave a channel and may contribute to the conversation for as long as one desires. It is the exchange of messages through the computer network, not the mere typing of words at individual terminals, which comprises the activity.

ii. topic

As is the case in casual conversation, IRC interactants negotiate amongst themselves what the topics of conversation will be. While sex is often assumed to be the most popular topic of discourse, especially in certain channels set up specifically for meeting and chatting with other singles, Gimon points out (1996) that a surprising amount of conversation simply revolves around relaxation and silliness. There are also several channels devoted to providing help to new IRC users and technical advice to more experienced ones.

IRC is a unique register in that the current topic of discourse must be identified and named by the chatters. This is so that it can be publicised on the channels list which allows others to choose whether or not they would like to join that conversation. This 'official topic' (which also appears on the top banner of the screen in that channel's window) is controlled by certain interactants known as *(channel) operators*. In general, chatters are not compelled to write exclusively on that designated topic, but if an individual insisted on trying to change the topic without consensus or if the 'rules' are particularly strict in a certain channel, s/he may be *kicked* from the channel by one of the operators.

iii. the effect of IRC Field on language choices

As was mentioned above, IRC is like casual conversation in that there is no restriction on choice of topic. However, it differs because there is no shared physical environment. This means that there are very few examples of exophoric reference (i.e., demonstratives such as *this* and *that*, referring to things in the physical context). Most demonstratives are anaphoric—they refer to items retrievable from preceding discourse. For instance, clause 17[6] of the IRC log example included in Appendix 1 has:

```
<wolvie>      ok who made it say that?
```

which refers to what the bot[7] says in clause 12:

```
<GonnaGetU>  [wolvie] I am a dickprick fucknut
```

Then again, IRC is different from other forms of writing because interactions occur in real time. This leads to discussions that one would not find on asynchronous CMC such as the following:

```
<bamboo>      What time is it over there?
```

<bamboo>	I told her to try and meet me!
<bamboo>	at 5pm....but it's around 6 now I hope!
<Chutzpah>	almost 8PM
<bamboo>	Can you give Ev a call and tell her to come on

(clauses 32-40)

Asking about the time or weather highlights the different locational but shared temporal contexts of the various chatters. These topics are similar to those found in long distance overseas telephone conversations. However, with IRC, chatters have a strong tendency towards speaking as if they do actually share a locational context, a virtual chat room where people can not only see each other but physically interact. There is an IRC command (i.e., typing */me* as the subject) which allows chatters to describe their actions in the third person. An example of this is in clause 60. <bamboo> has typed:

```
/me checks his pants
```

which has appeared on everyone's screen as:

```
* bamboo checks his pants
```

Other common actions include handing people things such as drinks (since chat rooms are often regarded as sites for virtual parties), hitting, hugging, kissing, sleeping, and laughing. Some of these are used so often that abbreviations have developed[8]. This pretence that there is a shared external context (i.e., virtual reality) means that, to chatters, the IRC activity is much more than merely typing words into a computer, or even sending messages to others; rather it is regarded as *attending* a social function. In depicting IRC as a sophisticated type of playing, Danet, Ruedenberg-Wright and Rosenbaum-Tamari (1997) use Goffman's (1974) concept of frames to show the different levels of interaction and make-believe in synchronous CMC.

Tenor: social relationships

Describing the activity and the topic of a situation goes a long way towards indicating the sort of language that will be used there. However, a much more accurate prediction about the verbal interaction will also require a more delicate description of the participants, specifying the relationship(s) between them. This register variable is referred to as Tenor.

Because CMC is a new and unique way of communicating, it has given rise to a new and unique culture to which the term *virtual community* has been applied, coined in the early nineties by Rheingold (1993). Various viewpoints about the nature of this community—in particular about the people who communicate by the Internet—exist, such as the cynical view presented by Fletcher and Greenhill (1996) that it is merely 'a place of seedy pornography markets populated by wayward teenage techno-freaks' or, on the other extreme, 'a place for do-good Silicon Valley hippies looking for a utopian existence or plotting to subvert all forms of now, apparently, archaic governmental and social organisations' (p. 184). Although most of the interactions occurring on IRC seem a little less colourful than these descriptions imply, it is still clear that an IRC environment is conducive to relationship building, rather than merely groups of individuals collaborating on a joint task, or playing a video arcade game together.

The sort(s) of communities that form through CMC depend(s) on the sorts of relationships that the particular computer program allows. So, in describing the Tenor dimension of IRC, we also need to take into account the Mode in terms of visual and aural contact (see p. 163 below).

It has been suggested (see Eggins, 1994; Eggins & Slade, 1997; Martin, 1992; and Poynton, 1985) that there are three important dimensions of Tenor: power (or status), contact and affective involvement (or affect). I shall briefly describe each separately with respect to IRC.

i. power

As was mentioned in the previous section, in any particular chat room or channel, there will be at least one operator. An operator has more control over what goes on in the chat room than other users. His/her powers include the rights to: change the topic of discussion, *kick* (i.e., expel) uncooperative users from that chat room and ban their future entry, refuse entry to potential users, give operator status to other users, and designate the room as private. One does not need more experience or expert knowledge in order to become an operator; it is a privilege conferred on those who first enter the channel[9], or who are made operators by other operators. A bot, which appears as a dummy chatter in a particular chat room, can be programmed to perform various functions such as confer operator status on its programmer whenever s/he enters that chat room, stay in a chat room to keep it open, and say certain lines upon cues from other (real) users. Operators are identified by an @ sign preceding their name in the list of users. For instance, on the right hand side of the #life channel window (see Appendix 1) would be a list of the #life chatters' names, with the operators, such as @wolvie listed first and then the other chatters in order of arrival.

Apart from the officialised type of power operators possess, some users have power arising from more conventional sources such as greater experience with CMC[10], greater expertise in the particular topic of discussion, and a more aggressive style of communicating. Newcomers (called *newbies* in IRC) are often found making reference to or apologising for their unfamiliarity with the system and politely asking those with experience for assistance.

Generally, however, there is a rather flat hierarchy amongst users in a chat room due to the fact that people are anonymous. Many researchers into CMC (e.g., Chesebro & Bonsall, 1989; Feenberg, 1989; Kiesler, Siegel, & McGuire, 1984; Murray, 1989; Tofts, 1996; and Werry, 1996) make reference to the fact that judgements as to age, race, gender, rank and class—ordinarily made from visual or aural clues—are impossible, which means that everyone starts off on equal footing. Interactants' cultural features remain unknown, as judgements cannot be made on the basis of clothing, physical features (e.g., physique, hair/skin colour, shape of eyes or mouth and so on), accent or pitch of voice. In IRC it is perhaps even more difficult than with other forms of CMC to be prejudiced against another user because people go by aliases and these nicknames are often ambiguous as to gender. Furthermore, with IRC, one's real email address[11] (in which information such as place of work can sometimes be revealed) need not be supplied.

ii. contact between interactants

In the 1980s, it was not uncommon to find CMC depicted as an impersonal way of interacting, with comments such as 'when unique and personal communication is desired, a computer connection is highly inappropriate' (Chesebro & Bonsall, 1989, p. 120) taken as self-evident. It seems that as the technology has become more sophisticated (for instance, enabling real time discussions between more than two people), accessible and popular, this view is no longer held.

With respect to IRC, the degree of intimacy and frequency of contact between the interactants varies from channel to channel. In general, chatters in IRC, unlike ICQ, tend not to have met each other face-to-face before. Although interactions occur amongst perfect strangers, self-introduction—as would be done in a face-to-face situation—is rare. One IRC convention used to ask about another user is to type 'A, S, L?' which stands for 'Age, Sex, Location (i.e., place of writing)'. One would never find someone asking another IRCer 'What's your name?' because: (i) the user's nickname appears on everyone's screen as soon as s/he arrives; and (ii) IRC prides itself on providing an 'anonymous forum'—it does not compel or even encourage self-disclosure of one's 'real life identity'.

Regular chatters tend to frequent the same channel(s) and thus form relationships with other regulars who keep the same nickname every time they use IRC. Some will visit the same channel every day and will spend hours chatting, so intimacy between users can be established and maintained. A *DCC*, or *Direct-Client-to-Client*, chat can be initiated by one chatter to another which enables them to have a private dialogue away from the others in the chat room. This also promotes intimacy between users, as they can exchange information about their 'real' selves which they may have been reluctant to do in the frivolous atmosphere of the chat room proper.

iii. affective involvement

As the name suggests, Internet Relay Chat tends to provide light-hearted casual interaction. Because the chatters do not have (and are unlikely ever to have) any real life contact, the affective involvement amongst them would presumably be low. They do not have a lot at stake if they are not accepted or appreciated, as they can simply leave the channel and join another without embarrassment, or even turn off the computer completely.

However, it seems to be the case that the general mood of IRC is positive and there is a lot of cheeky banter and teasing which is characteristic of friends who feel very comfortable and happy with one another. There are also cases, often reported in the popular press, of couples who have met on the Internet—presumably in an IRC-type environment—who eventually get married to one another.

It seems that the anonymity and freedom from prejudice which CMC affords, coupled with the guarantee of a captive audience and lack of visual/aural signs from others expressing lack of interest or boredom, lead to an abandonment of social inhibitions and a tendency towards self-disclosure. However, real life self-disclosure is not as common on IRC as it is in other types of CMC because it is more like a frivolous game (see Danet et al., 1997)[12]. People are more likely to express how they 'really' feel towards each other in less public electronic environments such as email, ICQ, and DCC-IRC.

While the mood of IRC is generally positive, CMC also provides means to express negative feelings such as anger or disapproval with other users through the practice of *flaming*. This may consist of overt abuse, name-calling, 'dumping' lines and lines of pre-copied text/nonsense symbols to fill the screens of other users, severe swearing and profanity, and other generally antisocial behaviour. Flaming not only tends to be disapproved of in many IRC channels, but can be a reason for the banning of a user from IRC completely.

iv. the effect of IRC Tenor on language choices

In IRC, status differences tend to be realised with the same linguistic choices as in casual conversation amongst friends. For instance, interactants who use more interrogatives to request information, use fewer direct imperatives, and seem not to have reciprocal rights in the use of vocatives to construct themselves as less powerful than the others. As an example, <bamboo> appears in this conversation to be of lower status than the others because he asks more questions:

```
Have you seen tori?
or ev?
Do you know if Ev is coming on today?
WHat's happened since I was last here?
```

(clauses 5-6, 29-30, 57-58)

Perhaps <bamboo> realises that he is asking a lot of questions because he provides the explanation on two occasions that he has not used IRC for three months. <Sheedo> appears to have higher status in this chat room. He seems to be regarded as more knowledgeable not only about computer programming:

<wolvie> sheedo do you know who changed my info message?

<Sheedo> no idea

...

<wolvie> i can't change it back either

...

<Sheedo> wolvie why can't you change it back?

...

<wolvie> it's locked

...

<Sheedo> fixed it wolvie

...

<wolvie> yeah? cool

(clauses 63-65, 70, 81, 88, 102, 106-107)

<bamboo> Chutz: do you know if I'm still on the userlist?

<Sheedo> I'll check bamboo

<bamboo> thanks sheed

...

<Sheedo> bamboo- you're dns has changed

<Sheedo> I can add you to the bot if you'd like

(clauses 109-112, 115-117)

but also about the activity and chatters in this particular chat room:

<bamboo> [to <Sheedo>] What's happened since I was last here?>

...

<bamboo> Sheedo....CAn you give ev a call and tell her I'm on please?

...

<Sheedo> well, I would

<Sheedo> but, two things stopping me

<bamboo> two things?

<Sheedo> 1, she lives on the other side of

```
              the country
<bamboo>      what are they?
<Sheedo>      and 2, I don't have her number
<Sheedo>      :(
<bamboo>      ok sheeds....thanks anyway!
```

(clauses 57-58, 67-69, 72-80)

Intimacy and/or frequency of contact can also be seen in the way chatters address each other. In order to use IRC, one must use a nickname. Knowing a fellow chatter's real name implies intimacy. For example, as soon as <bamboo> discovers that <Sheedo> has joined the channel, he says 'Richard!'. Once <Sheedo> has recognised <bamboo>, he initiates an old joke they have shared in the past:

```
<Sheedo>      bamboo?????
<Sheedo>      what's up!!?!?!?!?!
...
* bamboo checks his pants..nothing's up!
```

(clauses 54-5, 60-61)

Shortening someone's nickname not only saves time, but also implies intimacy and contributes to the friendly atmosphere of the room. For instance, <bamboo> calls <Sheedo> 'Sheeds' and <Chutzpah> 'Chutz'.

Another way of expressing emotional responses in CMC is by using *emoticons* ('emotion icons'), the most popular being the sideways smiley :-)[13]. There are many variations on this theme, enabling a range of other facial expressions; or writing out non-verbal noises such as laughter (e.g., *hehe*— clause 7, and *argh*— clause 42). The use of eccentric orthography, capitalisation and/or punctuation (referred to by some in CMC as *ranting*) also has interpersonal meaning. These can be used to amplify an emotional response, emphasise a particular word/phrase, represent a pause, imitate an accent or express playfulness. They also confirm a user's membership in the exclusive IRC group.

Mode

Mode covers broadly 'the role that language is playing in realising social action' in the particular situation (Martin, 1992, p. 508) or how language is being used by the interactants. It can be described more specifically in terms of the way that messages are transmitted from the sender to the receiver including such features as the presence or absence of visual and/or aural contact, and the availability and immediacy of feedback. These features will be described below with respect to IRC.

i. visual and aural contact

IRC is similar to written discourse in that there is no visual contact and no aural contact between the interactants, that is, chatters can neither see nor hear one another. They are therefore prevented from retrieving meanings in the conversations from many of the semiotic systems at work in face-to-face conversation such as facial expressions, gestures, proxemics, posture, tone of voice and so on. Much research (e.g., Baron, 1984; Chesebro & Bonsall, 1989; and Kiesler et al., 1984) has been undertaken into the effects of the absence of these contextual cues on communication, with conclusions that, with these 'cues filtered out', on the one hand there is more equal participation by all interactants (presumably because the anonymity reduces inhibitions), but on the other hand decisions and consensus take longer to reach.

Much of this research has investigated the use of CMC in task-oriented settings, and concludes that anonymity and the lack of 'socioemotional information' of CMC (such as subtle, sometimes involuntary cues including smiles, directed glances, winces, raising of eyebrows) make it ill-suited for the forming of social communities. However, Baym (1994) challenges this view, claiming that in certain other CMC settings 'hundreds of participants have voluntarily created communities rich in social information, prominent personalities, valued relationships, and behavioural norms' (p. 141), as was evidenced in her study of a particular newsgroup on Usenet, an asynchronous type of CMC. The real-time environment of IRC is even more conducive to this sort of community formation, as is discussed below.

ii. availability and immediacy of feedback

Whereas the lack of visual contact and aural contact features of IRC liken it to typical written discourse, the availability and immediacy of feedback make it much more similar to speech. What distinguishes chat systems from the majority of other types of CMC is that interactants must be present at their computers at the same time in order to read the messages being sent and to contribute to the interaction. Even though there is a *log* function in IRC[14], there is no record of the interactions to which users may refer if they want to read what has happened while they were absent.

Messages are delivered and read by (online) receivers within seconds of the sender pressing the ENTER key on their keyboard. Feedback is very nearly immediate; the amount of time between sending a message and receiving a reply is dependent on the time taken for:

- the original message (or 'initiating move' (Berry, 1981; Martin, 1992)) to be transmitted through the network to the other users;
- the message to be read;
- a reply (or 'responding move' (Berry, 1981; Martin, 1992)) to be typed; and
- the reply to be transmitted.

Since all messages are transmitted to all of the other users in the chat room, any of the users may provide a response. The order in which these responses appear depends on the time taken for the four factors listed above. These factors will differ with different users: some users' systems will have quicker transmission times, while other users may be more efficient at typing or will type very short responses so as to claim the floor before anyone else. In general, IRC turns tend to be short. Werry (1996, p. 54) found that they averaged six words each, so that the interaction flows more like face-to-face conversation.

iii. the effects of IRC Mode on language choices

The most obvious difference between a transcript of a spoken conversation and a log of an IRC session would be the difference in the organisation of the conversational sequences. Whereas turns in spoken discourse are organised into adjacency pairs (see Sacks et al., 1974) which in turn form exchanges[15], synchronous CMC seems to operate on a completely different pattern of organisation[16]. IRC turns appear on the screen as they are received, which can be some time (in seconds) after the sender started typing. This means that overlaps, interruptions, and backchannelling are impossible. It also means that a sender may make a second move before receiving a response to the first. As Murray (1989) notes, second pair parts are not obligatory in CMC. In multiparty conversations, different topics are often interwoven as interactants subdivide into smaller groups. A good example of this unique organisation of conversation sequences can be seen below:

Clause	Log	
81	<Sheedo>	wolvie why can't you change it back?
82-86	<bamboo>	So how are you? I haven't seen you for about 3 months now! Ev says everyone misses me!!! :P
87	<LeniAnne>	bamboo: I haven't seen you
88	<wolvie>	it's locked
89	<Sheedo>	only 3 months? it must have been longer than that
90-91	<Sheedo>	I'm doing pretty good :) my work is about to run out
92	<Sheedo>	since basketball season is ending
93	<Sheedo>	but still, it's kewl
94-96	<wolvie>	i don't remember you. weird how many peole you miss even though you get on almost every day
97-98	<bamboo>	Well, could be a bit longer...can't remember the last time I talked to you!
99	<bamboo>	Everything's changed...
100	<wolvie>	must be all the vacations
101	<Chutzpah>	oh, yeah
102	<Sheedo>	fixed it wolvie
103	<Sheedo>	has it?

There are a few exchanges intertwined here. Many 'adjacency pairs' do not have adjacent pair parts. For instance, the question in clause 81 is answered in clause 88 and then followed up in clause 102, and <bamboo>'s 'So how are you' in clause 82 is answered in clause 90 'I'm doing pretty good'. Similarly with the exchange initiated by <bamboo>'s estimate of three months in clause 83. <Sheedo> questions it in clause 89, and <bamboo> responds in clause 97. There is also an example in clause 94 of more than one person responding to a turn, when <wolvie> seems to be commenting on <bamboo>'s turn which presumably was intended for <Sheedo>. Because of the confusion which could arise from this apparent discourse chaos, and because there are no visual cues, the use of vocatives is much higher than in other registers.

Another main effect that the Mode of IRC has on language is the length of turns. As was mentioned earlier, in order to make the discourse as synchronistic as possible, turns tend to be short. It is also not uncommon to find a turn has been sent in multiple parts in order to reduce waiting time for receivers. For instance,

<bamboo>	What time is it over there?
<bamboo>	I told her to try and meet me!
<bamboo>	at 5pm....but it's around 6 now I hope!

(clauses 32-36)

and

<Sheedo>	I'm doing pretty good :) my work is about to run out
<Sheedo>	since basketball season is ending
<Sheedo>	but, still, it's kewl

(clauses 90-93)

This can lead to strange effects when messages from others squeeze in between, such as in the following example:

<bamboo>	Sheedo....CAn you give ev a call, and tell her I'm on please?
...	
<Sheedo>	well, I would
<Sheedo>	but, two things stopping me
<bamboo>	two things?
<Sheedo>	1, she lives on the other side of the country
<bamboo>	what are they?
<Sheedo>	and 2, I don't have her number
<Sheedo>	:(
<bamboo>	ok sheeds...thanks anyway!

(clauses 67, 72-80)

<bamboo> splits what would have been spoken in one turn ('two things? what are they?') into two parts, but <Sheedo> begins to answer before the second part is received, leading to a very unusual looking sequence which appears to contravene the basic turn-taking conventions taken for granted by conversation analysts.

Finally, as with other forms of CMC, abbreviation is a default feature of IRC. Its main motivation is to save time, but it also has the interpersonal effect of increasing solidarity amongst those familiar with the conventions and excluding those who are not. Forms of abbreviation include: the truncation of words by omitting vowels (e.g., *ppl* for people, *msg* for message); the exclusive use of lower case (even for the first person singular nominative pronoun 'I'); syntactic ellipsis (e.g., omission of Subject and Finite as in 'fixed it wolvie' for 'I have fixed it, Wolvie'); and the use of acronyms for common phrases (e.g., *brb* for '[I'll] be right back', *wb* for 'Welcome back' and *btw* for 'by the way').

Conclusion

The language that is used in chat rooms carries the hallmarks of the particular Field, Tenor and Mode features of IRC. The computer medium and real-time aspects encourage interactants to use a style of language that lies somewhere in the middle of spoken and written discourse. Furthermore, rather than restricting or de-personalising communication, the lack of visual and aural cues tends to lead to less prejudice, the discarding of inhibitions, and a creativity with the keyboard which can draw interactants into closer relationships.

Internet Relay Chat provides an interesting and still relatively novel way of interacting, even within computer-mediated forms of communication. As the Internet becomes more widely used by people from different walks of life and for a greater variety of social purposes, it is likely that the boundary between speech and writing will become increasingly blurred and our assumptions about socialising, physicality and identity will be further challenged.

Endnotes

1. There are many different chat software programs (called 'clients') available such as WSIRC, mIRC, InteRfaCe and ChatMan. They are available by anonymous ftp (file transfer protocol) or can be downloaded from the World Wide Web. The *IRC Intro File for Newbies Using Windows* (http://www.mirc.co.uk/ircintro.html) provides their

URLs.

2. This is assuming that the user has already set up an IRC client which connects the computer to a server on one of the IRC networks, such as EFNet, Undernet and Dalnet.
3. Sometimes a message may take a few seconds, or occasionally minutes, to be transmitted, depending on individual users' modem speeds and other network time lags.
4. What appears here is a computer IP (Internet Protocol) number or alias email address.
5. The channel, however, will remain 'open' (i.e., will still appear on the list of available channels for newcomers to join) until the last person leaves.
6. Clause numbers refer to the IRC log example provided in Appendix 1.
7. A 'bot' (short for robot) is a computer program which appears as a chatter in an IRC channel to keep the channel open when no-one else is there. Bots can be programmed to perform other functions too (see below p. 158).
8. Some of the ways in which abbreviations and typographic symbols are used to express ideas and feelings in online communication are taken up by Donna Gibbs in chapter 1 above, and by Annette Wong in chapter 9 below.
9. Being the first to enter a channel creates that channel: empty channels do not exist.
10. Concerning status in the Internet community in general, Fletcher and Greenhill (1996, p. 192) make the interesting observation that electronic prestige seems to correlate with online longevity: those who can claim to have held an email account before the Internet was popular are highly respected, as are programmers who have designed significant software for the Internet and those who control World Wide Web computers, especially important websites.
11. To register as an IRC user, an email address must be supplied. However, this is merely a formality as alias email addresses are accepted. The most information that a user would be able to glean (using the */whois* function) about another user would be the country from which that other is logging in, and their server.
12. This is true even/especially in the case of the channels set up specifically for the purpose of allowing chatters to show affection to each other openly. These channels tend to have names such as *#hottub* or *#Lovezone*, which indicate the nature of their discourse.
13. For a discussion of Japanese emoticons, see below chapter 9.
14. *logging* means the computer saves (and prints, if the user desires)

the conversations occurring in any or all of the channels which the user has joined. This function is available only when the user is online.

15. For a Systemic Functional linguistic approach to exchange structure, see Berry (1981), Ventola (1987) and Martin (1992).
16. Murray (1989) suggests that CMC has a 'commitment to action' organisation which enables it to succeed despite the flouting of conventional turn-taking rules. However, her study focussed on a type of CMC helpdesk which was more task-oriented (problem solving) rather than chatty. IRC discourse 'succeeds' not so much because tasks are achieved, but because the users become used to constructing what Werry (1996, p. 51) refers to as 'multidimensional text' in which 'disparate strands of conversation are juxtaposed'.

References

Baron, N. S. (1984). Computer mediated communication as a force in language change. *Visible Language, 18* (2), 118-141.

Baym, N. (1994). The emergence of community in computer-mediated communication. In J. Jones (Ed.), *Cybersociety: Computer-mediated communication and community* (pp. 138-163). London: Sage.

Berry, M. (1981). Systemic linguistics and discourse analysis: A multi-layered approach to exchange structure. In M. C. Coulthard & M. Montgomery (Eds.), *Studies in discourse analysis* (pp. 120-145). London: Routledge & Kegan Paul.

Chesebro, J. W., & Bonsall, D. G. (1989). *Computer-mediated communication: Human relationships in a computerized world.* Tuscaloosa, AL: University of Alabama Press.

Collot, M., & Belmore, N. (1996). Electronic language: A new variety of English. In S. C. Herring (Ed.), *Computer-mediated communication: Linguistic, social and cross-cultural perspectives* (pp. 13-28). Amsterdam: Benjamins.

Danet, B., Ruedenberg-Wright, L., & Rosenbaum-Tamari, Y. (1997). HMMM... WHERE'S THAT SMOKE COMING FROM? Writing, play and performance on Internet Relay Chat. *Journal of Computer-Mediated Communication, 2* (4). Available: http://207.201.161.120/jcmc/vol2/issue4/danet.html [1998, December 12]

Eggins, S. (1994). *An introduction to systemic functional linguistics.* London: Pinter.

Eggins, S., & Slade, D. (1997). *Analysing casual conversation.* London: Cassell.

Feenberg, A. (1989). The written world: On the theory and practice of computer conferencing. In R. Mason & A. Kaye (Eds.), *Mindweave: Communication, computers and distance education* (pp. 22-39). Oxford:

Pergamon Press.

Fletcher, G., & Greenhill, A. (1996). The social construction of electronic space. *Social Semiotics, 6* (2), 179-197.

Gimon, C. (1996). The Net in real time: Parts 1 and 2. *InfoNation Magazine* No.169.

Goffman, E. (1974). *Frame analysis: An essay on the organization of experience*. New York: Harper and Row.

Halliday, M. A. K. (1978). *Language as social semiotic: The social interpretation of language and meaning*. London: Edward Arnold.

Halliday, M. A. K. (1994). *An introduction to functional grammar* (2nd ed.). London: Edward Arnold.

Halliday, M. A. K., & Hasan, R. (1985). *Language, context and text: Aspects of language in a social-semiotic perspective*. Geelong: Deakin University Press.

IRC Intro File for Newbies using Windows. Available: http://www.mirc.co.uk/ircintro.html [1998, December 10].

Kiesler, S., Siegel, J., & McGuire, T. W. (1984). Social psychological aspects of computer mediated communication. *American Psychologist, 39* (10), 123-134.

Martin, J. R. (1992). *English text: System and structure*. Amsterdam: Benjamins.

Murray, D. E. (1989). When the medium determines turns: Turn-taking in computer conversation. In H. Coleman (Ed.), *Working with language: A multidisciplinary consideration of language use in work contexts* (pp. 319-335). Berlin: Mouton de Gruyter.

Poynton, C. (1985). *Language and gender: Making the difference*. Geelong: Deakin University Press.

Rheingold, H. (1993). *The virtual community: Homesteading on the electronic frontier*. Reading, MA: Addison-Wesley.

Sacks, H. E., Schegloff, & Jefferson G. (1974). A simplest systematics for the organization of the turn-taking for conversation. *Language, 50* (4), 696-735.

Tofts, D. (1996). Cyberbabble: The grammatology of on-line communications. *Social Semiotics, 6* (2), 263-272.

Ventola, E. (1987). *The structure of social interaction: A systemic approach to the semiotics of service encounters*. London: Pinter.

Werry, C. (1996). Linguistic and interactional features of Internet Relay Chat. In S. C. Herring (Ed.), *Computer-mediated communication: Linguistic, social and cross-cultural perspectives* (pp. 47-64). Amsterdam: Benjamins.

Appendix 1

Transcript of Log of IRC session
Channel name: #life
March 1997

Clause	Log	
	...	
1	<bamboo>	Hi GUys!!!
2	<bamboo>	Long time see!
	***Giddeon has quit IRC (Ping timeout)	
	*** badinflue has quit IRC (Ping timeout)	
3	<Chutzpah>	hi banboo
4,5	<bamboo>	Hi Chutz! Have you seen tori?
	*** AcIdFrEEk is now known as AcIdFrEaK	
6	<bamboo>	or ev?
7	<AcIdFrEaK>	hehe
8	<LeniAnne>	bamboo : I haven't seen tori
9	<Chutzpah>	bamboo
10	<AcIdFrEaK>	i got my name back
11	<bamboo>	Have you seen Marbles
	*** wolvie (...) has joined #life	
	<GonnaGetU>	*chat
12	<GonnaGetU>	[wolvie] I am a dickprick fucknut
13	<Chutzpah>	um, last night, i think
14	<wolvie> hello	
	*** GonnaGetU sets mode: +o AcIdFrEaK	
15	<Chutzpah>	hi wolvie
16	<wolvie>	nope
	*** GonnaGetU sets mode: +o wolvie	
17	<wolvie>	ok who made it say that?
18-21	<bamboo>	yeah...I haven't used IRC for 3 months...and I haven't seen al the regulars anymore....I can see it's changed a lot!
	-> [Dev-]PING	
	-> [Dev-] FINGER	
22	*Chutzpah has been a reg here on and off for over a year and a half	
23-4	<bamboo>	Yeah, I know Chutz....I've met you before!
25-7	<bamboo>	...however I haven't spoken to you for a while...so I've forgotten your name! Sorry!
28	<Chutzpah>	:)
29-30	<bamboo>	Do you know if Ev is coming on today?

Clause	Log
	-> [Dev-] FINGER
	-> [Dev-] VERSION
	-> [Dev-] TIME
	-> [Dev-] USERINFO
	-> [Dev-] CLIENTINFO
	-Dev –No CTCP Friend Access. You had your fun, now GO AWAY
31	<Chutzpah> ev hasent come on in quite awhile
32	<bamboo> What time is it over there?
33-4	<bamboo> I told her to try and meet me!
35-6	<bamboo> at 5pm....but it's around 6 now I hope!
37	<Chutzpah> almost 8 PM
38-40	<bamboo> Can you give Ev a call and tell her to come on?
41	<Chutzpah> i don't know ev
42-3	<bamboo> argh....that's ok...
44	<bamboo> doesn't matter
45-6	<Chutzpah> i know dylanger, tamerax, sd, insectkin, retoss and exodus, but not ev
47-8	<bamboo> I've met dylang er and tamerax, and sd...but that's it
49	<Chutzpah> the others are fairly recent
	*** Sheedo (...) has joined #life
50	<bamboo> Richard!
51	<GonnaGetU> [Sheedo] The King, has returned.
52	<bamboo> Hi!
53	* wolvie is an old-timer
54	<Sheedo> bamboo?????
55	<Sheedo> what's up!!?!?!?!?!
56-8	<bamboo> The king has returned??? WHat's happened since I was last here?
59	<Sheedo> how's school??
60-1	* bamboo checks his pants..nothing's up!
62	<Chutzpah> sheedo!!
63-4	<wolvie> sheedo do you know who changed my info message?
65	<Sheedo> no idea
66	<Sheedo> ;/
67-9	<bamboo> Sheedo....CAn you give ev a call, and tell her I'm on please?
70	<wolvie> i can't change it back either
71	<wolvie> fucking annoying

Clause	**Log**	
72	<Sheedo>	well, I would
73	<Sheedo>	but, two things stopping me
74	<bamboo>	two things?
75	<Sheedo>	1, she lives on the other side of the country
76	<bamboo>	what are they?
77	<Sheedo>	and 2, I don't have her number
78	<Sheedo>	:(
79-80	<bamboo>	ok sheeds...thanks anyway!
81	<Sheedo>	wolvie why can't you change it back?
82-6	<bamboo>	So how are you? I haven't seen you for about 3 months now! Ev says everyone misses me!!! :P
87	<LeniAnne>	bamboo: I haven't seen you
88	<wolvie>	it's locked
89	<Sheedo>	only 3 months? it must have been longer than that
90-1	<Sheedo>	I'm doing pretty good :) my work is about to run out
92	<Sheedo>	since basketball season is ending
93	<Sheedo>	but still, it's kewl
94-6	<wolvie>	i don't remember you. weird how many peole you miss even though you get on almost every day
97-98	<bamboo>	Well, could be a bit longer ... can't remember the last time I talked to you!
99	<bamboo>	Everything's changed...
100	<wolvie>	must be all the vacations
101	<Chutzpah>	oh, yeah
102	<Sheedo>	fixed it wolvie
103	<Sheedo>	has it?
104	<Sheedo>	how's school?
105	<Chutzpah>	marbles closed up the userlists on the bots
106-7	<wolvie>	yeah? cool
108	<Chutzpah>	u can't do ANYTHING
109-110	<bamboo>	Chutz: do you know if I'm still on the userlist?
111	<Sheedo>	I'll check bamboo
112	<bamboo>	thanks sheed!
113	<Sheedo>	chutz, he was never ongonnagetu
114	<Chutzpah>	doesn't look like it

Clause	Log	
115	<Sheedo>	bamboo- you're dns has changed
116-7	<Sheedo>	I can add you to the bot if you'd like
	...	

Chapter 9

Cyberself: Identity, language and stylisation on the Internet

Annette Wong

'The bodiless exultation of cyberspace'?—images and realities

> In modern everyday life, it is difficult (and becoming impossible) to definitively classify experience as "real" or "not real" . . . The frames we once used . . . to set the real apart from the unreal . . . they betray us. (Chayko, 1993 as cited in Jones, 1995, p. 7)

New technology changes not only our material reality but also the way we think about reality. Chayko believes that 'The frames we once used . . . betray us' but maybe we were doing things back-to-front anyway, trying to fit reality into the 'frames' and throwing away, or ignoring what did not fit. In an age of information proliferation more and more does not 'fit', consequently drawing attention to the inadequacies of our current 'frames' and presenting us with enormous challenges about the way we process data/information/knowledge.

Yet somehow we keep using the same 'frames', falling back on those easy dichotomous distinctions: 'Man' - 'Woman', 'Human' - 'Machine', 'Image' - 'Reality'. We use these terms as if they were foundational when they are only labels stuck onto the surface while the concepts shift and change below the surface. The labels are tethered but not stationary—shifting, colliding and sometimes overlapping. And there are gaps between the labels, unnamed but still part of the overall process. Perhaps it is like the restless on-and-off binary flux of digital processing where the two components [I and O] are easily labelled but what is accumulated in the flickering spaces in-between the components keeps escaping definition. An elusive energy which shimmers in and around the familiar until even the familiar becomes transformed whether we notice it or not. For instance, how have concepts of 'Human' and 'Machine', 'Life' and 'Death' changed in an age of artificial intelligence, virtual reality, life support systems, cloning, bionics and genetic engineering? What role does new technology play in changing the way we view even the most basic concepts let alone more complex formations of identity?

In all of this, the 'frames' are still useful, not as heavy antique structures that fix something upon a wall but as a camera frame in motion, defining that moment's boundaries of perception—changing, moving, flickering through numerous accumulated moments which are juxtaposed in differing relations to one another. This chapter begins by exploring some key concepts in relation to cyberspace and the Internet and raises questions about the relationships 'in-between'. It also considers the ways in which interpretations of these concepts affect attitudes towards the Internet, the style of interaction and the perceived possibilities of identity formation.

Cyberspace is a dream of transcendence

> Cyberspace . . . A world in which the global traffic of knowledge, secrets, measurements, indicators, entertainments, and alter-human agency takes on form: sights, sounds, presences never seen on the surface of the earth blossoming in a vast electronic night . . . The realm of pure information . . . siphoning the jangle of messages transfiguring the physical world . . . letting it fly free in the soft hail of electrons that is cyberspace. (Benedikt, 1992, pp. 1-3)

In *Neuromancer,* as with many other cyberpunk novels, the physical world is described as a 'meatworld' where the body is 'a prison of flesh' (Gibson, 1993, p. 12). Cyberspace, however, promises the possibility of escaping this 'meatworld' and transcending the body into a 'realm of pure information'. A human-created world of technical perfection.

Human technology has probably always been about transcendence of the limitations of the 'natural' body. The relentless 'improvement' of Nature. But cyberspace is about more than just the excitement of a new technology. It is not just a new technology but the promise of a new kind of place. Cyberspace is about an utopian ideal which has many similarities to the imagery surrounding various religions, drug cultures, sex, gambling, surfing and racing. Many of these things promise transcendence to some higher state of being—Heaven, Nirvana, Utopia, Paradise. But, even more importantly, all of these things emphasise the addictive excitement of the transcendence itself—that 'one great ride' —the climax, the awakening, the enlightenment, the liberation, the transcendental moment.

Consequently, the imagery of cyberspace[1] is often drawn from these other transcendental influences. For example, in William Gibson's *Neuromancer* (1993) the experience of cyberspace is described as being 'on an almost permanent adrenaline high . . . jacked into a cyberspace deck that projected his disembodied consciousness into the consensual hallucination that was the matrix . . . Case . . . lived for the bodiless exultation of cyberspace' (pp. 11-12). Analogies of surfing, sex, car racing, space travel, and drug addiction abound in cyberspace.

Even though some form of cyberspace does technically exist, cyberspace is also an imaginary place heavily reliant on the proliferation of mass media images (cyberpunk novels, comics, movies, etc.). Cyberspace may be thought of as a revolutionary 'new' place but we do still carry many older influences along with us. Importantly, there are many people who do not have access to cyberspace technologies but know about cyberspace from other media forms. Cyberculture tags, terminology and labels attest to this intertextuality: *cyberpunks, technopagans, mondoids, infomaniacs, zippies* and *cyberdelics; technocrats, technoprats, technobrats* and *cyberkids, computer geeks* and *cyberphreaks; hackers, slackers,* and *cyberspace backpackers; cyborgs* and *bots, alters* and *cyberspace 'mirror creatures'* and *avatars; cyberjocks* and *cyberrockers, technoravers* and *Deadheads;* and *MUDders* and *players* and *users* and *InterNETters, technicians* and *operators* and *Wizards, cyberspace cowboys, channel-surfers, site-hoppers* and *skim-readers*—'all watched over by machines of loving grace' (Dery, 1996, p. 30)[2].

Many of these cybercultures have been hybridised from existing subcultures by adding the prefix 'cyber-' or 'techno-'. These prefixes do, admittedly, suffer from overkill, though many of these compound terms have a certain irony to them. 'Cyberdelics', for instance, is a pun on psychedelics. Also many of the subcultures are related to music styles. Cyberpunk, as the name suggests, was heavily influenced by punk rock music. William Gibson played music by *The Velvet Underground* and *Joy Division* to 'set the mood' while he was writing *Neuromancer*, and one of the characters, Molly, was based on an album cover photo. Rap and techno music also influence the rhythm and style of cyberspace language[3].

Cyberspace is over-rated

> To a man with a hammer everything looks like a nail. (Postman, 1993, p. 14)

Is *cyberspace* the answer to everything? As with a lot of new technology, blind enthusiasm is a problem, with many descriptions of cyberspace technologies tending to conflate possibility with reality. This is a condition which we might call 'Acceleration Blindness' where the novelty of 'newness' causes an inability to distinguish the imagined future from the present. Addicted to speed, and racing into the future, all we tend to see is what is further ahead—the desired destination. The peripheral becomes a blur. Sometimes the futuristic imagery is so seductive it distracts us from reality. As Dery (1996, p. 49) comments

> cyberdelic rhetoric represents what Walter Kirn has called "an eruption of high-tech millenarianism—a *fin de siècle* schizoid break induced by sitting too long at the screen . . . ultimate detachment is not the same as freedom, escape is no substitute for liberation and rapture isn't happiness".

Working in conjunction with these idealistic visions of cyberspace is the welter world of advertising images. Advertisers tend to exploit the fascination that people have for new technology in an effort to pump up consumerism. For instance, in selling the Internet, they happily conflate Internet technology with the seductive (and fictional) imagery of cyberspace. Consequently, a lot of cyberspace imagery is hyped-up, overblown and often misleading.

For some people, though, cyberspace is no great mystery. It is just an abstract place of communication in the same way that a telephone, or a short-wave radio, or a letter creates an abstract place beyond the material world of the human body. For these people, cyberspace may raise some interesting issues about social relations but it is hardly an utopia. If anything, ambivalence is the style of cyberspace with attitudes to cyberspace relentlessly flickering between idealism, cynicism and indifference. Exhilaration alternating with mundanity. As Jon Casimir (1996, p. 9) points out: 'For millions and millions of us, most cyberdays are remarkably uneventful. It's been, oh, weeks since I used the Net to save somebody's life or make myself another million bucks'.

What is the Internet, anyway?

While cyberspace is the dream, the Internet is the main technology for manifesting the dream[4]. But this has its limitations. For instance, it is not actually a 'bodiless exultation'. The Internet is a mask of sorts, it hides the colour of our skin, the shape and size of our body, its beauty and its blemishes, our age, our accents, our incomes and our fashion sense. Identity is reduced to the love affair of the words typed across the screen. Behind the mask, however, we still remain in our bodies and our language reflects this.

The Internet *is* 'bodiless' in the sense that it is a text-based (and in many cases, text-only) communication, therefore bodily signifiers are mediated (as well as masked) by text. Language becomes the primary marker of identity. And this is more than just electronic pen-pals. Typewritten letters, for instance, also provide a similar technical capability for 'disembodied' communication yet this technology cannot compare to the immediacy and 'real-time' conversational capacity of the Internet. Typewritten letters also cannot compare to the immense image power of cyberspace (and by association, the Internet). The Internet has become one of the major symbols of 'the Future' (whatever that may be) and its possibilities have been exaggerated out of proportion with the actual practicalities, and mundanities, of its present usage.

The Internet has also heralded a new invigoration of writing as a conversational art at a time when media forms have tended to become dominated by the audiovisual. Many people seemingly lost to the literate arts, particularly adolescents, are now devoting enormous energy to relationships built on written communication. Probably one of the main attractions of Internet communication is that it allows both an easy immediate intimacy and anonymity.

Furthermore, while most people do not confine themselves to one particular form of communication technology, and may use various forms of communication in a relationship with another person, the Internet subcultures do tend to facilitate the formation of a particular persona for Internet communication. For instance, many people create a pseudonym or 'nickname' for Internet communication. This particularly occurs in IRCs[5] and MUDs[6], though it is also quite prevalent in email postings and websites. While many people merely use the Internet as a supplement to other forms of communication, for those immersed in Internet subcultures, the Internet can become a kind of identity in itself. This is perhaps because the Internet has the image of being another place defined from 'real world' communication where 'bodiless' transcendentalist imagery encourages people to believe that they have somehow transcended their bodies into an ultimate state of connectedness. In all of this, the body has not really disappeared. Even though the body is masked from others by the mediation of technology, the personal experience itself is still embodied. And the Internet users themselves still have assumptions about the types of bodies they are communicating with.

Various other mass media forms are also busily promoting cyberspace imagery, consequently amplifying the Internet's influence far beyond just those who use it. There is a lot of conflicting description of the Internet. Perhaps the confusion lies in the contradiction between the technically correct definitions and the more colloquial, generic usages. This has a lot to do with the overload of marketing campaigns surrounding the World Wide Web in particular, and cyberspace in general, where the population is bombarded with the terminology and the images, the catchphrases and buzz words, without any substantial information. Therefore, a lot of people are aware of these technologies in a peripheral way, just as people are aware of various other parts of popular culture without being directly interested in it as such. Many people have enough stylistic knowledge to talk about the Internet without having any technical/utilitarian knowledge of how to use the Internet. In this way, the Internet is a style not just an utility, with various subcultures proliferating in and around it.

Style over Utility

> If you do not understand a particular word in a piece of technical writing, ignore it, the piece will make perfect sense without it—Mr Cooper's Law. (Barry, 1992, p. 89)

In *Technobabble*, John Barry talks about the term *technobabble* as being inspired by a book called *Psychobabble* by Richard Rosen which defined psychobabble as 'writing or talk using jargon from psychiatry or psychotherapy without particular accuracy or relevance' (Barry, 1992, p. 3). As Barry notes, 'The definition of technobabble is similar' (pp. 3-4). A lot of technoculture in general is also like this, where style outweighs utility.

In analysing language and identity in relation to technology, one of the most important concepts to understand is the relationship between style and utility. An utility is more about function than appearance. It is something that is almost 'anaesthetic' (where aesthetic quality is not so much absent as irrelevant). To be reduced to mere utility is to become machine-like, dehumanised. The modernist nightmare of a world dominated by machinery.

Technology is, of course, about utilities—tools and machines. And there are certainly technologies where utility is favoured over style, particularly in industrial mass production and the massive information systems used for raw data processing (for instance, faceless behind-the-scenes bureaucratic systems). In a cold machine world, personality is reclaimed by 'human' stylisation. And stylisation is important in the age of mass production where items are churned out with numbing regularity.

However, style and utility are not simply oppositional. It is also possible to have an 'utilitarian' style, where something or someone may appear to be utilitarian. For instance, the way an actor might play 'an efficient rational scientist', or an architectural style may be designed to look purely functional even if it isn't. Furthermore, style is not merely decoration or labelling or image. It is about a way of interacting and identifying with others (people, objects, concepts, images).

Humans have often used stylisation to indicate aspects of their identity which are not physically apparent in the 'natural' body. For instance, while gender identity is indicated by genitalia, or racial identity is indicated by skin colour or facial features, identities such as class or sexuality are often only indicated by styles of clothing, speech or body movement. Stylisation is also often used by 'borderline' identities, emphasising (or de-emphasising) certain features so that a hybrid, 'in-between' identity will be more ambiguous, or more firmly placed within one category rather than another.

More than mere identification, stylisation is particularly important as a strategy for situations where people are disenfranchised from the means of production. Even if they do not have power over what is produced they do have a certain power to stylise the reception of products and practices—a marginal re-appropriation. In *Subculture: The Meaning of Style,* Hebdige (1979) notes how youth cultures use the strategy of stylisation in consumer practices. Consumer goods are 'mobilized for a "semiotic guerilla war" ':

> Available cultural resources — consumer goods, leisure activities, popular culture in the form of music and dress—are appropriated and reassembled through a process of *bricolage* into meaningful patterns — styles—which can be understood in terms of the meanings, responses and strategies through which youth copes with its contradictory situation. (as cited in Slater, 1997, p. 165)

This is also often the case in colonial cultures. People with little or no 'official' power, and forced to adopt certain practices or products, syncretise it for their own use; not passive reception but negotiated resistance. For instance, the way that a number of Afro-Caribbean cultures have syncretised Christianity with Voodoo. Similarly with language—for those who do not have the power to define their own language they create styles, creoles, dialects, accents, jargons.

In some cases, however, stylisation is also exploited by consumerist forces to promote desire for consumer items and accelerate the sense of obsolescence. As Smith (1993, p. 86) points out:

> In his discussion of the striking emphasis on styling in the consumer practice that filled the American landscape after the Second World War, for example, Thomas Hine (*Populuxe*, 1987) elaborates the simple notion that this was merely a means to ensure premature obsolescence and boost consumption. He observes that through styling, which primarily evoked the past or the future, objects that had become ordinary necessities retained the appearance of extravagant luxuries.

Or as Stacy Warren (1993, p. 180) phrases it in her article 'This Heaven Gives Me Migraines—the problems and promise of landscapes of leisure', consumerism is 'stealing our dreams and selling them back to us'.

Consequently, stylisation is a chaotic process of appropriation and re-appropriation, often being turned around on its creators. For instance, many feel that cyberspace has been invaded by mercenary marketeers who appropriate cyberspace jargon, turning it into corny sales pitches and slogans. The SPAM[7] home invasion is a constant source of irritation for many Internet users who do not wish to be bombarded with advertising. However, relentless image promotions, profiteering and the proliferation of junk mail are all so much a part of the Internet experience. The general impressions of new technologies that we receive from the popular media, even if they are not accurate, factual or relevant, have an enormous influence on our cultural attitudes, perhaps even more than the actual technology itself. For instance, compare the actual usage of the Internet (and the relatively small percentage of the population that are actual users), with the mass media hype about cyberspace and the enormous reach that the highly stylised images about the Internet and associated cybertechnologies have through films, books, newspapers, comics and magazines, advertisements, video arcade games, music, TV and video, and word-of-mouth.

Even while acknowledging that people are often bombarded with cyberspace imagery it is important to analyse the way these images are received, and the way people interact with these images and stylise them into personal identity. Literal translation of technobabble will not get you very far if you do not understand something about the styles involved, the attitudes, personalities and codes of conduct. Consequently, when we talk about technobabble and Internet jargon we are not talking about a separate language for the Internet but how language is stylised by the influences of the Internet as it becomes interwoven throughout society.

Cartoon cultures — New technologies and 'adolescent' identity

Cyberspace is an 'adolescent' space. A place of transient experimental 'adolescent' identities where hormones are running high, where emotions and experiences seem more emphatic. Like adolescence, cyberspace is often a place of apathy and melodrama, carelessly fluctuating between the extremities of emotional experience. And since adolescents form one of the major population groups on the Internet, it is not surprising to find that cartoon culture is one of the most prominent stylistic influences on the Internet. Emoticons [smileys * < : O) and ass-cons (_!_)] and other visual stylisations of punctuation symbols, for instance, have a strong cartoon influence[8]. The choice of pseudonyms is also heavily influenced by cartoon intertextual references, as are the conversation topics and jargon in general. Cartoon culture is likely to become an even more significant influence in cyberspace as MUDs become more visual and more like animated comic strips rather than text-only playscripts. The cartoon-style MUD is also likely to facilitate more cross-cultural interaction.

Cartoon culture has long been popular with adolescents. Cartoons, like adolescents, tend to span that hybrid place between childhood and adulthood. There is something both clearly defined and experimental about cartoon culture. For instance, the style of cartoon illustration—its heavily defined outlines around each scene, around each dialogue bubble—is somehow always aware of its constructedness. There is something comforting and childlike about the clearly defined edges and the exact divisions of colour and form. The story, on the other hand, is usually fantastical and escapist. It is often extreme and experimental, crossing the boundaries of the conventional. It is not reality but fantasy—away from the ordinary world ruled by adults. Cartoons are more than just a style of illustration or a medium of storytelling. They also involve certain attitudes and styles of interaction.

Importantly, the 'virtual' space of the Internet is often one of the few places that adolescents can feel they own. MUDs, for instance, allow players to create not only their own identities but their own spaces and belongings which can be 'locked' for privacy. Players often spend hours creating textual architecture, creating their own spaces while in 'Real Life' they live in other people's houses. More than just an alternative place, MUDs facilitate an easily accessible alternative community. An interactive place where a person's fantasy life can be shared without ridicule.

This is not to say that only adolescents are attracted to cartoon culture. It does have a wide appeal for many age groups but it is widely acknowledged as having a strong identification with adolescents. While other age groups may participate, cartoon cultures do have a certain 'adolescent' style. (And this is often the reason why other age groups are attracted in the first place.)

Furthermore, there are many interesting parallels between adolescents who are initially becoming aware of their disempowered status in society, and marginalised subcultures who are often forced into a similarly low social status to the adolescent. Both groups have little or no voting power, little consumer power and no authority to speak on matters of political importance. Of particular interest is the way that these 'adolescent' identities, often disenfranchised from the means of cultural production, use stylisation as a strategy for entering and leaving the 'mainstream' cultures.

'Adolescents' learn the language to negotiate their way through 'the mainstream' but they also stylise it to define themselves from 'the mainstream'. Stylisation is a form of negotiated resistance. For smaller marginalised groups, subcultures and youth cultures which cannot afford to be totally rejectionist/separatist, stylisation becomes an important way of expressing non-conformity. Many marginalised or counter-cultures do not flatly reject all of 'the main-stream'. They disagree with particular aspects of it but often do not have the knowledge or the requisite power to change society. Rather than flatly submit to what they cannot overtly change, they use negotiated, discrete tactics. For instance, the Op Shop clothing style of wearing mismatched, worn, torn and grungy second-hand clothes represents a refusal to buy into the throwaway consumerist society. Stacy Warren (1993, p. 177) notes how Hebdige, in *Subculture: The meaning of style* (1979), 'has applied this argument to style and appearance, demonstrating that even a non-commital object such as a safety pin can be transformed into a symbol of resistance when worn on the human body'.

On the Internet, language is, of course, one of the most prominent features of the 'adolescent' style with language experimentation including neologisms, creolisation, word games, patterns and styles. As with many other parts of 'adolescent' subculture, music is an important influence and there is often an implicit 'soundtrack' which influences the rhythm of communication. Meaning is often contextual, accumulated and intertextual, not encapsulated in each word. Keeping the rhythm and flow of the words going is often more important than the meaning of each word. 'Rapping' and 'chatting', rather than talking, speaking or writing. As John Barry notes in *Technobabble* (1992, p. 61):

> Keeping up with all the changes requires an ever-increasing vocabulary . . . Perhaps the most notable characteristic of these techniques is expediency . . . Many of its frantic denizens are "high energy" types. They have to think fast — although not necessarily coherently — to keep up . . . nearly anything goes. Coin a word to fit a singular occasion, and then discard it.

Playing in the MUD — Identity creation in cyberspace

'This is more real than my real life.' (as cited in Turkle, 1995, p. 10)

'Falling in love with words' @}-'-,-'-

While identity creation and experimentation occurs throughout the Internet, the MUD raises some particularly interesting identity issues because of its emphasis on 'adolescent' community role-playing in a simulated environment, and its emphasis on the personal creation of place, belongings and identity. MUDs usually have an intricate 'textual architecture' on database—the archival files of players' rooms, prop descriptions and characters (what Rheingold (1995, p. 178) calls 'the community memory'). The MUD reads like an interactive playscript with stage directions, dialogue, character, costume, prop and scene descriptions. Numerous simulated 'body actions' are possible, so the MUD is certainly not 'bodiless'. The excitement of this kind of playscript is that the work is widely collective and open-ended, carried along by the energies of hundreds of contributors. The 'play' is literally being composed by numerous participants even as it is being performed, so that the writing of the 'play' is, itself, a kind of performance art[9].

The interesting thing about this kind of activity is that it is unique to Internet technology. A real life collective production such as this could not be sustained for any significant length of time. And this kind of event has only become possible through computer technology which speedily handles the more mundane and laborious aspects of the production in progress such as collation, transmission and coordination of contributions.

Default identities

Have we transcended the body through cyberspace or have we merely transcended the 'difficult' marginalised identities, making it easier for people to 'pass' as the more dominant 'acceptable' identities? Perhaps, the Internet both foregrounds identity and makes it easier to ignore.

On entering the Internet you are not provided with a neutral identity so much as a default identity. And people tend to assume that you are the default unless otherwise specified. While many of the prejudices of a person's initial appearance are transcended, so are many of the subtleties of visual communication. In some ways it becomes more difficult to identify as other than the default without it becoming an issue. In face-to-face communication you can indicate things about your identity through your appearance without it becoming an awkward confrontational issue. On the Internet, some of this is overcome by the choice of pseudonym. However, this is often not a very reliable signifier because so many of the pseudonyms are fantastical (or assumed to be fantastical). The burden of proving identity is shifted onto those who do not have the default identity while the default identity is rarely challenged, if at all.

Privilege is about not having to explain yourself. About being able to take your rights for granted. On the other hand, being forced to explain your identity is an act of debasement, a lowering of status. The identities in cyberspace are not equally privileged in this way, with some coming under more scrutiny than others.

Challenges to identity are quite common on the Internet. For instance, this situation occurred in an Internet debate (recounted in Dery, 1996, pp. 202-203) where one 'female' player accused another 'female' player of not really being a woman. This was closely followed by a challenge to the accuser's gender identity and exchanges of image scans and phone calls to outprove each other's identity with various interjections from other participants. Ultimately, debates such as this are unresolvable and only seem to peter out because of stalemate situations. As Ross (1990, p. 24) comments in his article 'Hacking away at the counter-culture', 'there exists a crucial operative gap between authentication and identification'.

Further to this uncertainty is the presence of *'bots'* and *'alters'* (automated programs which can engage in limited conversation) on the Internet. As DiGiovanna (1996, p. 456) puts it: 'there is the possibility that whoever you are talking to is no one at all. Or perhaps a new kind of someone'. While most bots and alters are fairly crude and easy to identify because of their limited responses, some are very sophisticated, such as the speech synthesizer bot, which learns dialogue and vocabulary from everyone it engages with: 'The speech synthesizer bot would essentially be . . . the creation, in fact, of everyone it talked to' (p. 456). The perfect cyberspace 'mirror creature'.

What the Internet has actually facilitated is mobility of identity. This is hardly the same thing as freedom of identity. While this mobility of identity contains the possibility of transcending bodily prejudices, the most prominent actual effect that the Internet has had is an expansion of the parameters of identity leading to more as well as less prejudice. This is because, even though the Internet may facilitate more mobility of identity, and more acceptance of experimentation and ambiguity, in some ways it also creates more anxiety. In a world of shifting, uncertain identities, suspicions are often aroused. For instance, scanning through various 'newsgroup' postings there are many irate discussions about 'violations' of identity. The Internet is, supposedly, a place to experiment with identity but there are a lot of irate users highly offended by the 'violation' of certain identities by 'imposters'. Consequently, there is a lot of conflict about which kinds of identity are acceptable for role-playing.

MorFs and the DragNET

> Users who pose as members of the opposite gender are commonly known as "MorFs". The term, short for "male or female", is also a pun on "morphing", the computer animation technique used to seamlessly dissolve one image into another. (Dery, 1996, p. 202)

What is the purpose of identity experimentation on the Internet? Frivolous entertainment? Soul-searching? Sometimes, it is curiously both. Gender-swapping, for instance, ranges from a pubescent game to serious questions about gender politics. After having interviewed a number of people about gender-swapping on the Internet, Dinty Moore (1995, p. 57) reported this response from a college student:

> ... he explains to me that CEE is a friend, a fellow Greensburg student, now home in New Jersey. "He's a guy, but he's had cybersex with I think about five guys and about seven girls."
>
> > "Is he bisexual?" I ask naively.
> >
> > "Oh no, he has a girlfriend."
> >
> > "Why does he do it?" I ask, meaning, why would a heterosexual young man want to get on his computer and pretend to be female and have "sex" with other young men.
> >
> > "He does it because it is so funny."

This kind of pubescent trivialising of gender-swapping is also evident in the related cybertechnology of computer video games, where players can choose to play overly-endowed skimpily-dressed female characters. This kind of gender-swapping seems more motivated by the chance to 'watch the boobs bounce' rather than any genuine experimentation with gender identity.

This criticism is not meant to trivialise many of the more genuine explorations of gender identity[10]. However, there is a significant gender inequality in MorFing experiences. While many males have more 'freedom to' experiment with gender identity and are often guilty of MorFing for gratuitous reasons, many females tend to MorF for reasons of camouflage (as a 'freedom from' harassment)[11]. This, again, highlights one of the main concerns of Internet role-playing—that the 'difficult' identities will tend to be abandoned except in cases of controversy or novelty.

Flame Wars — provocation and entertainment

Unfortunately, freedom of expression also tends to give people more freedom to be obnoxious, and the reason why many Internet users assume other identities is not as a genuine exploration of identity but as a form of provocative (and often offensive) entertainment. Some sites are particularly set up for 'flaming'. The more controversial and provocative the better. To borrow DiGiovanna's phrase: 'It's like booking yourself on Oprah' (1996, p. 446). Within context, these sites can be entertaining and even, perhaps, cathartic. However, it becomes a serious problem when 'flamers' invade other sites with the express purpose of provoking a scene—the textual version of a home invasion. As Jon Casimir (1996, p. 17) notes:

> Since the people in cyberspace are the same people as those in the real world, it isn't surprising to find all the usual extremists: neo-Nazis, skinheads, Holocaust deniers, anti-Semites, Asian bashers, the Ku Klux Klan, the Nation of Islam . . . the entire hate parade.

There are also times when it is hard to tell whether a site is meant to be serious or not, particularly with more extreme sites. An important issue that has not, as yet, been fully explored in cyberspace critique is the issue of authenticity and sabotage. There are, for example, the problems of imposters who misrepresent other identities with the intention of defamation and sabotage, or the setting up of 'shadow sites' with almost identical addresses, or the bombarding of sites with hate-mail[12].

'It's only a game'

This is a common disclaimer on the Internet. All that is obnoxious, offensive, unacceptable can be easily trivialised under the magic command 'It's only a game', which is another way of saying 'I'm not sorry'. Things tend to be excused under the guise of experimentation or frivolity. Some people think that the 'bodiless' anonymity of the Internet gives them the license to let free all the more obnoxious, annoying parts of themselves that they would not dare normally reveal. While Internet communication allows some people to be more sensitive, others feel less inhibited about hurting other people's feelings. For some people, letting go of their inhibitions means giving expression to all their baser desires. Rheingold (1995, pp. 184-185) reports on the research of Kiesler and others into this phenomenon:

> Sara Kiesler and others have studied the social effects of CMC in business groups and have noted that the lack of social context cues encourages both positive and negative disinhibition. Normally shy people react by speaking up, and people who would never shout at others or hurl insults in a physical gathering sometimes behave that way online . . . Antisocial behaviour is not rare in IRC. Racist and homophobic outbreaks are regular events. Hostile individuals can program their bots to flood a channel by sending out a stream of characters to IRC.

'It's only a game' also sums up the attitude that many people have about the ephemerality of Internet identity. Pavel Curtis (1996, p. 353), the creator of LambdaMOO, estimates that 90% of the MUD players are affiliated with colleges and universities. MUD participation is encouraged by colleges and universities because most of the facilities are provided free, and experimentation with new computer technology is so often part of the educational experience. However, after students graduate, the responsibility for Internet connection shifts solely onto their shoulders unless they happen to have easy access through the workplace. And even then, work commitments often deprive them of the leisure time they had as students. The drop-off in the participation rate after graduation tends to be enormous, though quickly balanced by the influx of new students. Despite the intensity of many MUDders' experiences of identity during their student years, a large number of these identities are transient.

And even for other longer-term Internet participants, the escape key is always in front of them. While the Internet has facilitated the formation of more numerous relationships than we could ever achieve face-to-face, it also allows an easier exit from these relationships. 'Disembodied' communications compress distance but they can also rapidly decompress that distance. This is not peculiar to the Internet—telephones can be hung up, letters can be returned unopened. But again we have that uneasy question—what does a 'bodiless' identity built out of words mean in terms of commitment? Has our 'freedom' of 'bodiless' identity also made it easier to run away from the more 'difficult' or marginalised identities? Masking the differences does not necessarily solve our problems of prejudice. Sometimes, all it really does is help us to ignore the problem more easily.

Colonising cyberspace? — Cyberspace cowboys and the pretensions of the World Wide Web

> *Cyberspace is perceived as a new human-created alternative place to the 'Real World'. A place which is seemingly a* tabula rasa, *a* terra nullius. *A place without history, without prior inhabitants. Is this a place that can be colonised without guilt?*

In 'Nintendo and new world travel writing' (1995, p. 59), Mary Fuller and Henry Jenkins discuss the association between the Renaissance 'discovery' of America and computer software, noting how the appealing imagery of discovery tends to reinvigorate the spectre of colonial imperialism:

> One has to wonder why these heroic metaphors of discovery have been adopted by popularizers of the new technologies just as these metaphors are undergoing sustained critique in other areas of the culture . . . part of the drive behind the rhetoric of virtual reality as a New World or new frontier is the desire to recreate the Renaissance encounter with America without guilt.

Discovery, exploration, technological progress, the collection and dissemination of knowledge, global connection—these are all seductive and seemingly positive but it is important to examine what underlies the rhetoric. Are these globalisation processes consensual, harmonising, equitable? Or are they processes of cultural domination, acquisitiveness, exploitation?

Frontier mentality and the obsession with 'going where no one has gone before'

The Internet is like a new kind of world tourism which allows some people to travel the world more easily. The world seems a more accessible place. However, other people who do not have access to the technology have not become more mobile. They have become more objectified, more available for scrutiny by the tourists with their technology. For instance, if you scan through newsgroups or the World Wide Web there are numerous sites devoted to different countries and their 'ethnic' cultures. But, most of these sites offer a 'tourist' perspective *about* a culture, though not necessarily authored by people *of* that culture. And if they are authored by people of that culture they are often constructed for the Western voyeur.

Is cyberspace just another Western frontier? — ASCII world domination

Despite all the rhetoric about worldwide, global connection through the Internet, language remains a barrier. English is *the* language of technology (American English, that is). But this is more than just a linguistic translation problem. The technology itself creates cultural barriers. There is hardly global equality of access to Internet technology (or technology in general for that matter. What is a computer when you cannot even afford a lightbulb, let alone a reliable electricity supply to plug it into?). Of the countries that have access to the Internet, many only have Usenet-type access and sometimes only email. The World Wide Web is a relatively new phenomenon which is a lot more expensive to implement and access. The tag 'World Wide' is, as yet, a pretension. Furthermore, the World Wide Web is more of a passive broadcast medium which tends to subdue interactivity. And it still relies on email and newsgroups as a supplementary feedback system in much the same way that television relies on telephones and letters for feedback.

As with the default identity problem, the Internet also has default languages. Within each country or 'marketing frame' there is a default language which influences the standard issue of keyboards and software. For those wishing to use other than the default, things become more difficult (and more expensive). Multilingual/cross-cultural communication tends to be obstructed. This is particularly the case if your system is defaulted to English ASCII. ASCII is the 'American Standard Code for Information Interchange character set' (Barry, 1992, p. 47). It refers to the technobabble term for the English-based character set that cyberspace is dominated by[13]. While non-English languages based on the Roman alphabet are technically available in the full ASCII set, access to accented characters depends on keyboard layout and software compatibility. Most other character sets incorporate ASCII, in addition to others.

Many Internet systems cannot even transmit another language if it is in an incompatible character set unless the system software has been specifically set up to do so or the appropriate conversion software has been installed. Instead, it will 'corrupt' the text by replacing it with a lot of nonsense symbols [¥£Ü¢çÑ-ô£Ä¥¢é¥*], or it will 'block' the text (that is, replace it with blocks or boxes) [□□□□□]. This is more obstructive than the telephone system or postal service which at least allows equitable delivery of a message in another language character set. Furthermore, many language character sets are not even accommodated at all by the technology. Because ASCII so dominates cyberspace it becomes incumbent on those with character sets other than ASCII to anglicise their communication. In the textual realities of the Internet, global communication is a war of words where some languages are more readily silenced than others.

While the Internet may have compressed time and space, making the world a conceptually smaller place, the language barriers have been built higher. The Internet is segregated into different language character sets — not one cyberspace, but a variety of unequal cyberspaces. And yet, the curious thing is that the image of global communication is so prevalent in perceptions of the Internet, even though it is not matched by the reality. This has a significant influence on the way that people interact with the Internet, and the way they perceive the role of the Internet in their lives. People tend to be heavily influenced by the global rhetoric of the Internet and talk about the division between the Real world and the Virtual world as if there were only *one* Real world and *one* Virtual world. The danger of some Internet global rhetoric is that it subdues difference even while enjoying the novelty of all the differences it can seemingly access. There is, undeniably, diversity in the subcultures of the Internet, but it is important to question what kinds of diversity are actually appearing . . . or appear to be appearing—as Moore (1995, pp. 59-60) does so tellingly in the following account:

> "Around Greensburg, people are basically all the same, they're all here, everyone goes to the same mall, everyone does the same thing. On the Internet, you've got people from all over the world. Like, there are people on here from the Philippines."
>
> It sounds good, and Rob is sincere, but I haven't seen him have any sort of substantive conversation with anyone all afternoon, and most everyone he has met on the Net has been a college student somewhere in the United States. I ask him what he talks to people about, people from the Philippines, or wherever.

Techno-cultural-colonialism remains a problem, not only on the Internet but throughout technological 'development' in general. The relationship between technology and culture is convoluted. As Stephen Hill (1988, p. 6) argues: 'Technology is a cultural product, and cannot be reified above the ground of social and cultural forces that create it, or use it, or which fit particular technologies into a meaningful relationship to daily life'. Technologies are not mere utilities which can be traded between cultures unencumbered. The trade of technologies carries all kinds of complicated expectations of cultural indebtedness which extend far beyond the material price tag. The technological imperative of 'advancement' and 'progress', with its emphasis on new and exciting discoveries, also carries heavy penalties for inefficiency, incompatibility or obsolescence. And these judgements, though they have the image of objectivity, are hardly free of cultural bias. We have to be careful about the ideologies that pervade our technologies and lead us to coldly rationalise the obsolescence of other cultures. It is also important to note that these cultures have not passively accepted this domination. For instance, there are numerous projects working at resisting ASCII domination, not through sheer opposition but rather through incorporation, integration and adaptation. Some of these projects are discussed below.

i. Populopolis, JIS and the Japanese Internet

> JIS is the Japanese Industrial Standard character set. As with ASCII, there are a number of variations though the most popularly used set "includes 6879 characters, among which are the hirigana and katakana syllabaries, 6355 kanji, the Roman, Greek and Cyrillic alphabets, the numerals, and a number of typographic symbols." (*Japanese text encoding*, n. d.)

The Japanese character set is more culturally inclusive than ASCII and reflects something about the Japanese approach to technology research. While American technology research is quite egocentric, aware that it culturally dominates the technology market, Japanese technology has tended to be more culturally adaptive, with an awareness of export markets. For instance, notice the hybrid aesthetics of Japanese video arcade games where the cultural diversity of characters is not just segregated into the usual racial stereotypes (as are most American and Australian multicultural images), but also offers more cross-cultural possibilities, both realistic and fantastical. The American cultural influence in these aesthetics is prominent and yet it has been hybridised in such a way that it is also unmistakably, almost quintessentially, Japanese.

Furthermore, with a different character set, visual textual elements such as emoticons tend to vary across cultures. Some languages and their associated cultures are also more visual than others. Compared to the starkness of the 26 character Modern Roman alphabet that ASCII is based on, many languages use extensive character sets where accents and ideographs transform mere writing into the art of calligraphy. The visual becomes an important part of the communication. Not just the words themselves but also their presentations have meaning. In the puritan efficiency of ASCII-dominated CMC how might culturally-specific visual inflections be communicated? While emoticons are hardly a substitute for the subtlety and beauty of many ideographic characters they may go part of the way towards re-inserting some of the richness of visual inflections of meaning. Perhaps as (or if) CMC becomes more globalised, the use of emoticons will become more abstract and culturally-specific in the same way that standardised character sets seem to have developed out of pictograms. Though hopefully CMC will come to facilitate easy and equitable access to a wider range of character sets.

Japanese emoticons, for instance, while still using ASCII punctuation symbols, are quite distinctively different from American emoticons. For instance, there is a 'girl smiley' (^.^) because, as Keeley (1997, message 5, n.p.) explains: 'it is considered impolite for a woman to bare her teeth in a grin', as is apparent in the regular smiley (^_^). Moreover, Keeley explains that 'when someone is confused, apologetic or embarrassed in Japan, s/he often scratches the back of his or her head. So the > represents a bent elbow' (n.p.) in the following emoticons expressing the phrase 'excuse me' (Sumimasen): (^^;>) or (^o^;>). Other examples of Japanese emoticons are reproduced in Table 9.1 below.

Table 9.1 Japanese emoticons and associated meanings

Emoticon	Meaning
(^_^;)	cold sweat, nervous, stressed
--	time to bow
(^o^)	Ureshii - Happy!
*^_^*	Big Joke
\(^_^)/	Banzai!
*^_^;	this may be a joke
(-_-)	secretive smiley
(;_;)	crying, sadness
(_o_)	Gomen nasai - I'm Sorry

Within Japan, research is also being concentrated on visual Internet technologies more tailored towards Japanese cultural needs. The virtual community of Populopolis provides a good example of this process of cultural adaptation. Populopolis was developed by Fujitsu, which bought over Lucasfilm's *Habitat* virtual community and redesigned it for use in Japan. Populopolis is similar to a MUD but with sophisticated graphics. Instead of using text only, players in Populopolis use animated characters called avatars which have a certain number of facial expressions and action commands. Like a comic strip the characters use dialogue bubbles to indicate speech[14].

In an interview with Howard Rheingold, Joichi Ito, one of the co-founders of TWICS (a virtual community in Tokyo), argues that: 'it is difficult for the Japanese to participate in the Net culture as it exists today . . . It wasn't designed for the Japanese' (1995 as cited in Rheingold, 1995, p. 219). Speculating about Japan's role in the future of the Internet, Ito comments:

> I think the Japanese will make their own version of online communication media and the Net will grow to include it . . . the product of such a fusion may be the greatest transmission of Japanese culture to the West yet . . . Imagine what might happen when the West begins to use communication tools based on Japanese/Eastern ways of communicating. (Ito, 1995 as cited in Rheingold, 1995, p. 219)

ii. Minitel and the FROGNET crusade

While most people tend to think of the US when they think about the origins of the Internet, it was actually France that first popularised Internet-style communication through their Minitel system implemented in 1981. The Minitel terminal, a small keyboard and screen which plugs into the phone system, was distributed free by the French government as a nationwide project to both replace the printed phone book and compete with British experiments in videotext. However, with a little help from the hackers, the Minitel system quickly expanded its capacities from a mere database service to a real-time chat service. This became known as the *messageries*. And because everyone who had a phone in France was also entitled to a Minitel terminal, the system easily became widely popular (Rheingold, 1995).

While national projects such as this have encouraged a very high French participation rate in the use of new technologies, language remains a barrier for more international participation. The jargon of technology presents a constant challenge to the French in their battle against being overwhelmed by Americanisms[15]. Technical incompatibility of character sets is another ongoing problem which is being addressed by projects such as FROGNET (French Research Organisation Net) created by M. Bruno Oudet. This project involved improving the standards for email and other communications protocols to facilitate the use of the French language between researchers around the world and institutions in France. Cerf (1994, p. xxvi) comments that Oudet's efforts

> . . . also encouraged schools with Internet access around the world to join in, so that children taking French can correspond in that language with others. I take that as an encouraging sign that while the *lingua anglica* prevails in the net, other tongues will thrive there as well.

iii. From the Margins

Internet technologies have an enormous potential for facilitating community activism at the 'grassroots' level as a many-to-many communication medium. The Internet has been valuable as a relatively inexpensive medium for those marginalised community groups who are not well represented in the mass media and do not have access to the mainstream broadcast networks. For instance, there is the Native American Share-Art gallery whose goal is to:

> . . . use telecommunications to help Native Americans learn the skills and knowledge they will need, by getting them first to be the teachers of the rest of us about their culture, and in their preferred modes (graphic art, storytelling, native language expression) rather than just feed the white man's view of the world into them by satellite educational feeds, or impose upon them only white man's ascii text. (as cited in Rheingold, 1995, p. 250)

Setting up a website is often a lot more economical than running a TV or radio station. It also easily reaches many overseas audiences. Ironically, rather than just submitting to the ASCII-dominated global rhetoric of the Internet, a number of cultural communities have utilised the capabilities of the Internet as a way of preserving and publishing material related to their diverse cultural heritages[16].

The Style of Internet usage and identity — peripheral realities and multi-tasking

For many people, the Internet is not a total immersion in cyberspace. It is a supplement to other forms of communication. It is also about multi-tasking. For instance, MUDs and IRCs allow peripheral participation where people are logged in for several hours or even days, aware of the proceedings but only actively participating for short periods of time (Curtis, 1996). As Turkle (1995, p. 13) notes, 'your identity on the computer is the sum of your distributed presence'. Or as one user informs Turkle: '[I] turn pieces of my mind on and off—I split my mind' (as cited in Turkle, 1995, p. 13). The way we function becomes influenced by the immense power of the metaphorical imagery of the machinery that surrounds us. Ironically, while computers may be modelled on the human brain we also model ourselves on computers.

Fragmentation and multi-tasking also influence the way we use email. While it can be used for writing conventional letters, the main advantage of email is that it combines writing with CB radio communication. As with the open airwaves of a CB, a person can be online without requiring the devoted attention that a telephone call requires. Consequently, it is quite possible to keep up an ongoing conversation (or even a conference with various people) for several hours without disrupting other activities. The style of conversation is also similar to the CB—short transmissions such as one line comments, punchlines or interjections which can be sent in a volley of messages and replies every few minutes. However, unlike CB radio, email is silent, and incoming messages can easily be ignored until a more convenient time. It is also a lot more private than CB and allows the easy production and transmission of excessively long conglomerated documents.

IRCs occupy a similar peripherality, or peripheral reality, where a person can be aware of an ongoing conversation and just participate in idle times between other activities[17]. As Rheingold (1995, p. 177) notes:

> many people who work for long hours in front of computer workstations—college students, computer programmers—leave a small "window" on their computer screens tuned in to IRC while they go about their day's work.

In this way, Internet technologies allow us to maximise our social relationships by interspersing them in our more mundane and methodical activities. While it is true that this peripherality can be distracting and time-wasting for some, for others it increases their productive time by allowing them to utilise what would otherwise be idle time spent waiting for something to process, or download, or arrive. This multi-tasking, fragmentation feature also allows people to act out multiple identities and explore alternatives. It allows people to maintain a sense of a working community even if they are physically isolated in separate work cubicles.

Then there are those who just watch—the peripheral reality of the voyeur. On the Internet, they are called *lurkers*, though there are also a lot of people who watch the development of the Internet from afar. The Internet is surrounded by a virtual audience of numerous voyeurs who watch cyberspace via other media. (And, some of the best images of cyberspace and the Internet still come from other media. Cyberpunk for instance, was popularised by books.) Voyeurism is an important part of the broadcast experience. As with other broadcast mediums such as TV or radio, even the most private viewing or listening is imbued with the sense of a larger audience which we cannot see or hear or touch. People we will never meet have shared the same imaginary space we have—'the imagined community'. The Internet magnifies this sense of community because it offers the possibility of interactivity where the broadcast show is transformed into a forum, loosening the distinction between audience and performer; and added to this is the pervasive rhetoric of global connection. In a curious way, the implied presence of numerous lurkers influences the way people interact on the Internet. Silence is not the same as absence. The possibility of lurkers encourages a sense of 'being on stage'.

'Writing as a performing art'

Internet communication in general tends to encourage what Rheingold (1995, p. 38) calls 'writing as a performing art'. Because of this, there is often a performative aspect to Internet writing which combines the need for speed with the need for entertainment. This encourages one-liners, catchphrases and incisiveness, as well as quotability. It also often encourages more directness, if not brazenness. As with speech performance, sentences and phrasing are usually shorter and clearer. Vocabulary tends to be more colloquial. As Dery (1996, p. 203) comments: 'being able to type fast and write well is equivalent to having great legs or a tight butt in the real world'.

The Internet has brought a new vitality to the art of writing. If text-based identity continues to hold a significant place in Internet communication perhaps creoles, accents and dialects may evolve as they have evolved in speech performance, as a subtle (or sometimes not so subtle) signifier of identity. The last half of the century has witnessed the rising significance of multicultural nations where people have an 'official' national language with a diversity of cultural accents, creoles, and dialects. This diversity of language forms has been present for many centuries but this period is particularly interesting because it has facilitated a proliferation of diverse populations and their language forms while also globally unifying languages in a way that has not been previously possible.

Perhaps a more phonetic way of writing will develop. This is already evident in some Internet communication. Literatures written in English have experimented with representing accents for a long time. However, the Internet presents a particular situation because it is a type of communication that can be simultaneously person-to-person and broadcast, combining speech performance, publishing and intimate personal interaction in the same moment. As Reid (1995, p. 171) observes: 'The language of MUD players is a hybrid one and contains elements of both written and spoken forms . . . MUD interaction is not enacted to be read but to be experienced'.

Furthermore, in his discussion of the form of cyberspace, Marcus Novak describes cyberspace as liquid architecture and poetry as liquid language (Novak, 1992, p. 229). Perhaps this is the way to imagine language on the Internet—as the liquified hybrid of speech (air) and writing (solid).

Conclusions — back to the body — Extropians, Posthumanism and Nerdvana[18]

In sci-fi visions of aliens we imagined anaemic, large-headed, skinny-limbed glowing green beings. Perhaps we dreamed up our own children—anaemic, large-headed video kids hypnotised by the green phosphorus glow of the magical light box and its flickering images transporting their minds to distant places while their bodies remain seated and sun-starved, or hopping to the rhythm of Nintendo, Sega, Atari, their fingers always on the button, the pulse of life, 'Point and Press, Point and Press'. Electron-zapping and frying those aliens they are becoming . . .

While we may revel in the images of physical transcendence and bodiless exultation, cyberspace technologies also continue to influence our bodies and our future visions of our bodies. For instance, cyberspace has spawned subcultures of 'Extropians' and 'Posthumanists' who envision either 'bodiless' existence or atrophied visions of the future body. The body is perceived as a burden. Or a kind of machine which can be detached from the person inside. As Dery (1996, p. 234) comments: 'I am in my body the way most people drive their cars'. Dery speculates that in a world where boundaries become more amorphous, the body would also become more 'liquified': 'Redesigned for zero gravity, the human form might resemble an octopus' (p. 298).

Despite the creativity of this imagery, it does tend to oversimplify the relationship between our bodies and our minds, as if all our flaws can be projected onto the body and 'it' can be calmly, coolly jettisoned into the vacuum of cyberspace. The pure, detached mind is a delusion. In Pat Cadigan's *Synners* this kind of transcendental desire is given an ironic twist when a character called Gabe achieves the ultimate transcendence into cyberspace. After a while he loses his exhilaration: '*I can't remember what it feels like to have a body,* . . . He wanted to scream in frustration, but he had nothing to scream with' (Dery, 1996, p. 317).

And 'bodiless' communications such as those facilitated by the Internet have not made the body disappear. In some ways, the body has become a more prominent concern. For instance, anxieties about the body's seeming obsolescence have created a new emphasis on the body and body-building. While people once built up their bodies primarily through their everyday labour, in contemporary times exercise now occupies a separate activity. For some it becomes an ironic obsession where people rage against the 'superiority' of the machine by 'making themselves over in the image of the machine' (Dery, 1996, p. 261).

And how might we imagine the future? While cyberspace may be limitless our imaginations remain tethered by the narrowness of our current image resources. The Internet may encourage experimentation but all the other media that it refers to remain dominated by certain role models and stereotypes. As the name suggests, the Internet is *inter* as in interactive and interwoven with the other technologies that surround it. We cannot really expect to expand our horizons when our Real world remains so narrowed by prejudice. Perhaps our Virtual worlds will help us create the impetus, the imagery and imagination we need to expand the boundaries of our

Real world. Perhaps that is what our Virtual world is for—as the test case, the scaffolding, the sketch or the aspiration for the new expanded boundaries of the Real world. If we cannot continue to expand our Real world then our Virtual world is only a useless delusion, no matter how beautiful and utopian. But more than that, a dangerous delusion that distracts us from all the Real work we still have to do: 'Once we can surmount time and space and "be" anywhere, we must choose a "where" at which to be' (Jones, 1995, p. 32).

But not only 'where'. Not only a place at which to be.
Who will be the people in our cyberspace Utopia?

Endnotes

1. For discussion of the ways in which this imagery has changed over time, see chapter 2 above.
2. For discussion of various cybercultures see Mark Dery's *Escape Velocity* (1996).
3. For discussion of the music origins of cyberpunk see Dery (1996, pp. 90-96).
4. See Introduction, Endnote 1 (p. 6).
5. IRCs are like the cyberspace version of a telephone partyline or CB radio, where 'real time' discussion is literally typed across the screen as you watch. These chat 'channels' started out as an experiment by a programmer in Finland. For more discussion of IRCs see Rheingold (1995, pp. 176-188) and Juliet Mar's chapter 8 above.
6. MUDs were developed at the University of Essex. As Howard Rheingold (1995, p. 155) describes it: 'The first MUD was a Multi-User Dungeon, modeled on a Tolkienesque domain of dwarves and treasure, warriors and wizards, swordplay and magic, known as "The Land" . . . Narrative is the stuff of which MUDworlds are made'.

   Though not all MUDs (and its later variants, MUSE, MOO, MUSH, MUCK) are fantasy/roleplaying narratives, the association between MUDs and roleplaying subcultures is still very strong. There are also visual versions of MUDs (Lucasfilm's *Habitat* is an early version of this) which look something like an animated comic strip. Players use what are called 'avatars' which have a limited set of facial expressions and body actions. Compared to the text-only version, the visual version is not yet widely available. (The exception to this is the Japanese Internet, further discussed below on pp. 195-196. It is not likely to supersede other forms of the Internet though it is likely to grow a lot more popular with MUD players, particularly with those Internet subcultures which are attracted to Cartoon culture.) For more discussion see below p. 183. Also see Curtis (1996), Turkle (1995), and Rheingold (1995, pp. 145-175).

7. SPAM is the Internet term for 'junk mail', probably named after that tasteless over-processed product in a can. SPAM has been notorious for choking some 'newsgroup' sites to death. There are a number of these dead 'newsgroup' files on the Internet, so choked with 'junk mail' that they have been abandoned.
8. For a discussion of Japanese emoticons see below p. 195.
9. For a discussion of Internet Relay Chat (IRC) which has some similarities to the MUD playscript, see Juliet Mar's chapter 8.
10. For additional discussion of gender identity and the Internet see Moore (1995, pp. 93-95) and Reid (1995, pp. 180-181).
11. For some comments on this see Reid (1995, pp. 180-181), Curtis (1996, p. 355) and Robin Keeley (*Culturally Adapted Emoticons,* Message 12, April 14, 1997).
12. See Rheingold (1995, p. 135) for the account of a BBS called CommuniTree which was destroyed by 'flaming'. For a personal account of the well-known LambdaMOO MUDrape case see Julian Dibbell, 'A Rape in Cyberspace; or How an Evil Clown, a Haitian Trickster Spirit, Two Wizards, and a Cast of Dozens Turned a Database into a Society' (*Village Voice* Dec 21, 1993) reprinted in Ludlow's *High Noon on the Electronic Frontier* (1996).
13. For basic and extended ASCII charts see http://www.jimprice.com/jim-asc.html; Webdesk - ASCII table can be accessed at http://members.tripod.com/~plangford/ondex.html; and http://www.bbsinc.com/symbol.html.
14. For a detailed description of the older version of this, called *Habitat*, see Morningstar and Farmer's 'The Lessons of Lucasfilm's *Habitat*' in Benedikt (1992, pp. 273-302).
15. See Barry (1992, pp. 189-191) for a discussion of this problem and a glossary of French equivalents to American technobabble. For other projects similar to FROGNET see *L'association FDN: French Data Network* and *HAPAX: French Resources on the Web*.
16. See, for example, how various Australian Aboriginal cultures have set up websites. See *The Kamilaroi/Gamilaraay Dictionary* or *Bunyip's Australian Aboriginal Links Page.*
17. For more discussion of IRCs see chapter 8 above.
18. Like most cyberspace jargon, these terms are a play on words. 'Nerdvana' is the computer nerd's Nirvana. 'Extropian' plays on the idea of utopian existence outside of or beyond the body (i.e., 'extro-' or 'extra-' terrestrial or corporeal). 'Posthumanism' looks beyond the 'natural' human body towards a cyborgian (human-machine) consciousness. The term also alludes to poststructuralism and postmodernism. For more discussion of this topic, see Dery's (1996) *Escape velocity* (pp. 227-319).

References

A Guide to Japanese Email. Available: http://davinci.sla.purdue.edu/academic/fll/JapanProj/Je-mail/key.html [1998, November 12].

Barry, J. (1992). *Technobabble* (2nd print). Massachusetts, MA: The MIT Press.

Basic and extended ASCII charts. Available: http://www.jimprice.com/jim-asc.html [1998, November 12].

Benedikt, M. (1992). Introduction. In M. Benedikt (Ed.), *Cyberspace: First steps* (pp. 1-26). Massachusetts. MA: The MIT Press.

Bunyip's Australian Aboriginal Links Page. Available: http://www.midcoast.com.au/~bunyip/indig/aborig.html [1998, November 12].

Casimir, J. (1996). *Postcards from the Net-An Australian's guide to the wired world*. Sydney: Allen & Unwin.

Cerf, V. C. (1994). Foreword. In P. Gilster (Ed.), *The Internet navigator: The essential guide to network exploration for the individual dial-up user* (2nd ed.), (pp. xxv-xxvi). New York: John Wiley & Sons.

Culturally adapted emoticons. Available: http://reach.ucf.edu/~reach/wwwboard/data/enc4932-3/messages [1998, November 12].

Curtis, P. (1996). MUDding: Social phenomenon in text-based virtual realities. In P. Ludlow (Ed.), *High noon on the electronic frontier: Conceptual issues in cyberspace*. Massachusetts, MA: The MIT Press.

Dery, M. (1996). *Escape velocity: Cyberculture at the end of the century*. London: Hodder & Stoughton.

DiGiovanna, J. (1996). Losing your voice on the internet. In P. Ludlow (Ed.), *High noon on the electronic frontier: Conceptual issues in cyberspace*. Massachusetts, MA: The MIT Press.

Fuller, M., & Jenkins, H. (1995). Nintendo and new world travel writing: A dialogue. In S. G. Jones (Ed.), *CyberSociety: Computer-mediated communication and community* (pp. 57-72). Los Angeles: Sage Publications.

Gibson, W. (1993). *Neuromancer*. London: HarperCollins.

HAPAX: French Resources on the Web. Available: http://hapax.be.sbc.edu/home.html [1998, November 12].

Hill, S. (1988). The tragedy of technology: Human liberation versus domination in the late twentieth century. London: Pluto.

Japanese text encoding. Available: http://www.lfw.org/text/jp.html [1998, November 12].

Japanese with English Windows in *Algorithmica Japonica*. Available: http://www.tpc.ml.org/tpe/9703/japanese.html [1998, November 12].

Jones, S. G. (1995). Understanding community in the information age. In S.

G. Jones (Ed.), *CyberSociety-Computer-mediated communication and community* (pp. 10-35). Los Angeles: Sage Publications.

Keeley, R. (1997). Message 5-Culturally adapted emoticons. Available: http://reach.ucf.edu/~reach/wwwboard/data/enc4932-3/messages [1997, March 14]

L'association FDN: French Data Network. Available: http://www.fdn.fr [1998, November 12].

Ludlow, P. (1996). *High noon on the electronic frontier: Conceptual issues in Cyberspace*. Cambridge, MA: MIT Press

McFadden, T. (1992). Notes on the structure of cyberspace and the ballistic actors model. In M. Benedikt (Ed.), *Cyberspace: First steps* (pp. 335-362). Massachusetts, MA: The MIT Press.

Moore, D. S. (1995). *The emperor's virtual clothes: The naked truth about internet culture*. Algonquin Books of Chapel Hill.

Morningstar, C., & Farmer, F. R. (1992). The lessons of Lucasfilm's *Habitat*. In M. Benedikt (Ed.), *Cyberspace: First steps* (pp. 273-302). Massachusetts, MA: The MIT Press.

Novak, M. (1992). Liquid architectures in cyberspace. In M. Benedikt (Ed.), *Cyberspace: First steps* (pp. 225-54). Massachusetts, MA: The MIT Press.

Postman, N. (1993). *Technopoly: The surrender of culture to technology*. New York: Vintage Books.

Reid, E. (1996). Communication and community on Internet Relay Chat: Constructing communities. In P. Ludlow (Ed.), *High noon on the electronic frontier: Conceptual issues in cyberspace*. Massachusetts, MA: The MIT Press.

Reid, E. (1995). Virtual worlds: Culture and imagination. In S. G. Jones (Ed.), *CyberSociety: Computer-mediated communication and community* (pp. 164-83). Los Angeles: Sage Publications.

Rheingold, H. (1995). *The virtual community: Finding connection in a computerized world*. London: Minerva.

Ross, D. (1990). Hacking away at the counter-culture. In *Postmodern Culture, 1,* 1-43.

Slater, D. (1997). *Consumer culture and modernity*. Cambridge: Polity Press.

Smith, J. (1993). The lie that blinds: Destabilizing the text of landscape. In J. Duncan & D. Ley (Eds.), *Place/Culture/Representation* (pp. 78-92). London: Routledge.

The Kamilaroi/Gamilaraay Dictionary. Available: http://coombs.anu.edu.au/WWWVLPages/AborigPages/LANG/GAMDICT/GAMDICT.HTML; www.webnet.com.au/clients/koori/index.html [1998, November 12].

The Unofficial Smiley Dictionary. Available: http://www.queensu.ca/eegtti/eeg_286.html [1998, November 12].

Turkle, S. (1995). *Life on the screen: Identity in the age of the internet*. New York: Simon & Schuster.

Using Japanese language on your computer. Available: http://www.kanzaki.com/jinfo/japanese.html [1998, November 12].

Warren, S. (1993). This heaven gives me migraines-The problems and promise of landscapes of leisure. In J. Duncan & D. Ley (Eds.), *Place / Culture / Representation* (pp. 173-86). London: Routledge.

Webdesk - ASCII table. Available: http://members.tripod.com/~plangford/ondex.html; and http://www.bbsinc.com/symbol.html [1998, November 12].

Chapter 10

Critiquing <the> Internet 2000: Knowledge, language and freedom

Ray Archee

Introduction

The aim of this chapter is to critically examine the usefulness of the Internet as a potential vehicle for communication and education. Given the extraordinary popularity and widespread coverage of the Internet today, it ostensibly should be the perfect tool for the dissemination of knowledge to potential clients and students as we enter a new century. The Internet's history as a research collaboration facility also makes it a prime candidate for the creation of new ways of working. But as it will be shown, there is a range of problems which need to be overcome before professionals can fully embrace the Internet.

THE Internet not 'Internet'

We need to get our definitions correct. *The* Internet is a unique presence in this world like the Taj Mahal and Mount Everest, and as such is labelled a proper noun. The term stands for the particular agglomeration of hardware, software, and 'bioware' which connects hundreds of countries, and millions of users around the world on a daily basis. Depending on an individual's usage, however, the Internet can be defined as:

- a network of networks based on the TCP/IP computer network standards;
- a vast collection of resources which can be obtained (usually for free) from those networks;
- the world's largest library;
- a term to collectively describe facilities such as electronic mail, the Usenet, the World Wide Web and chat sites; and
- the community of people who develop and use those networks.

The media are responsible for headings such as 'Internet pulling in regular investors' (*Age*, September, 1998), and 'Cheating on

Internet puts HSC at risk' (*Illawarra Mercury*, October, 1998). These are the standard reductions of 'headlinese'. But it is misinformed people who talk of 'getting on to Internet'. Such populist usage of 'Internet' (no article) reminds one of generic labels used by old-style nurses such as 'doctor' ('Doctor will see you now') and 'baby' ('How is baby doing today?') which appear innocuous but translate into an abuse of language. In this vein there is also the British citizen's use of the word 'Concorde' ('The Prime Minister flew back to London on Concorde') which elevates the jet airplane to superplane status. The use of 'doctor' or 'baby' in this way prioritises the roles played within an institutional setting, but it is more than that. By unilaterally emphasising the person's role at the expense of their individuality, the nurse exerts his/her own form of control over the relationship and the people involved. It establishes that 'doctor' refers to all doctors as being the same, as having the same skills and abilities, and in some ways, as being god-like and omnipotent; somewhat similar to 'Concorde'. 'Baby' refers to the cuteness and helplessness of the infant. By using such terms the user not only stands in judgement of the referent but also of the people being addressed in this style. The user's need to exercise control by means of language over all the participants ultimately devalues the term.

If the populist usage of 'Internet' (no article) goes beyond mere genericism then what is its significance? I believe that users of the article-less concept are in fact, non-computer users unaware of the history and development of computer networks in general. These people often spuriously attribute somewhat magical power to the Internet. Such people also seem to make no distinction between Internet applications such as electronic mail, the World Wide Web, the Usenet, gopher, chat and listservs. Every online activity is amalgamated into an amorphous term absolving the (non-)user of responsibility for their behaviour and ignorance of the real Internet.

The seductive appeal of hypertext

The World Wide Web began in March, 1989 when Tim Berners-Lee wrote the original Web proposal whilst working for CERN, the European Laboratory for Particle Physics. Berners-Lee had been enamoured with the idea of hypertext, which was previously conceptualised as a way of interacting with a document on a local computer, not a network. He wanted to develop a system which would allow researchers to collaborate with each other, and which would support data scattered across the globe.

Almost ten years later we have a system that has grown beyond Berners-Lee's wildest dreams. In 1997 the figures showed the Internet hosts to be over 16 million; web server hosts over 1.1 million; with 80% of all web traffic originating in the USA (*survey.net*). The World Wide Web has the ability to link almost all the academic disciplines, as well as education, government, military and corporate sectors. But it is now a system in which researchers play a minor role, and in which collaboration is minimal compared with the huge volume of web advertising content and graphics.

Whilst the Web is appealing in its use of graphics and multimedia, it is most seductive in its utilisation of hypertext, often regarded as a metaphor for human cognition (Carmel, 1992; Rouet, Levonen, Dillon & Spiro, 1996). Contrary to popular belief I contend that much of the current Web interpretation of hypertext is not a metaphor for anything except a web designer's ability to insert hyperlinks into otherwise ordinary electronic documents.

The term *hypertext* was coined in 1965 by Theodore H. Nelson to concretise a form of electronic text, which was a radical departure from the printed word, and which involved the use of information technology. Before the advent of the Web, hypertext used to denote non-sequential writing, which embodied branches that allowed textual choices for the reader (Landow, 1993). Readers could become decision makers choosing various pathways to enter, backtrack and choose again. In one sense hypertext, as originally conceived, was a new form of writing, a new creative genre in which the reader never quite finished the text, since there was always the possibility of unchosen paths opening up. Whilst the World Wide Web certainly makes use of hypertext, the original meaning of the word has been changed. The Web's utilisation of hypertext is basically as a support mechanism for a primary, but somewhat abbreviated text. The incidental links (not the menus) within most webpages are not really the point of the homepage content, but simply technological add-ons.

A good example is the Vannevar Bush website (see Figure 10.1 below). Bush in 1945 is credited with being the first scientist to discuss the merits of hypertext-like technology. Notwithstanding the article's rhetoric, it is instructional to analyse how this milestone article, 'As We May Think', is presented in the medium it purports to champion. The paper on the Web is split into its original nine sections. The division of a longish paper into digestible units for some reason is theoretically supposed to enhance the comprehension of online information. What this also enables is a menu system which can be arranged by the web editor, allowing serendipitous discoverers of this article to then 'browse' different sections without necessarily downloading the entire article.

Figure 10.1 Excerpt from Vannevar Bush website: 'As we may think'

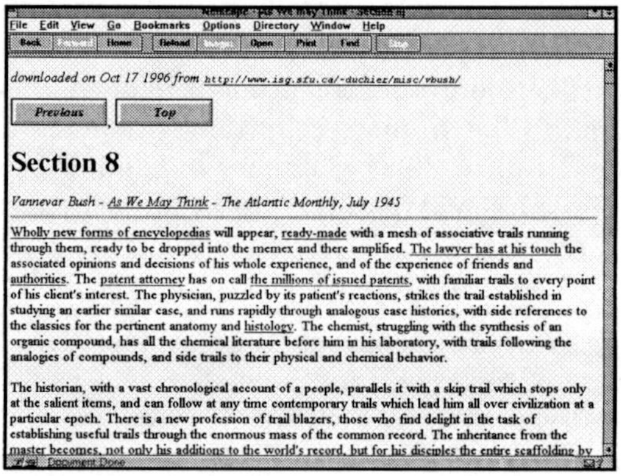

Source: http://www.isg.sfu.ca/~duchier/misc/vbush/

Unfortunately web editors are not technical communication specialists, so the Web's rendition of this momentous text mitigates against easy saving or printing of this paper since it is in nine separate sections. What is more problematic is the fact that throughout the article, the web editor has thought it prudent to hyperlink the most unusual concepts, so that we might visit other sites to clarify our curiosity. For example there are links to dictionary definitions of 'platen' and 'adze', a link to the Encyclopedia Brittanica's commercial website, and several links to law schools and patent explanations. Whilst the hypertext used in this article could be judged to be patronising to the reader, or distracting at best, it also changes Bush's original language by providing points of emphasis never intended in the original *Atlantic Monthly* version. What the hypertext reveals is not what the author intended but what appeals to the web editor in terms of difficult concepts needing explanation, and the availability of other sites to which to link.

Hypertext might be an appropriate metaphor for the human mind's associative ministrations, but the real-life application of hypertext as seen on much of the Web today is trivial, boring and totally at the behest of the computer geek wishing to showcase his or her minor talents.

The notion of (discourse) community

The Internet has quite often been described as a community. Although some real life communities, such as schools, clubs and organisations actually use the Internet to communicate, the focus for many advocates has been on the unique sense of community engendered by electronic communication and computer networks. People who interact (usually via writing) on a regular basis, report that they feel a sense of identity with their fellow members leading to the suggestion that the Internet has permitted new kinds of communities to emerge, where there were previously none. *America Online* is now the largest Internet Service Provider (ISP) in the USA, if not the world, and originally became popular because of its unique interactive discourse facilities. Email listservs and Usenet newsgroups have been cited as innovative examples, with many afficionados also citing web users, especially those of educational sites, as forming another sort of 'virtual' community (Chaplin, 1996).

If you perform a search on the Web itself for the keywords 'Web community' the *Hotbot* search engine returns over a million hits. One of the first is *www.geocities.com* which bills itself as the 'largest community on the Web' (see Figure 10. 2 below). Upon inspection, straight after the geocities logo you find a huge banner for a Surplus Auction Sale. This is like finding a billboard for IBM in the middle of your local primary school. More advertisements follow from Amazon.com, Surplus Direct computer hardware, CDNOW music/ video wholesalers, and credit cards from Platinum. There is a large number of interesting topics from Art and Literature to Travel and Women which can be accessed, but the problem is that there is no evidence of a community on the geocities homepage.

My definition of community importantly includes the component of interacting with people, and it is here that the Web has major limitations. Apart from web chat and hypertext versions of newsgroups, the vast majority of websites are not set up for interaction. Their sole purpose is the one-way dissemination of information—personal, advertising, educational or otherwise. Users of these websites

Figure 10.2 Excerpt from the GeoCities homepage

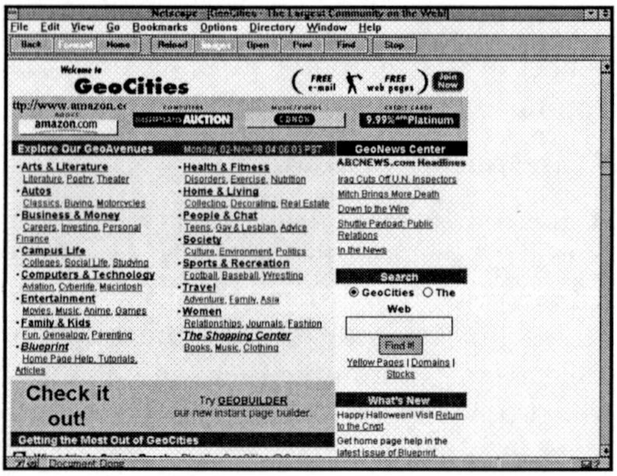

Source: http://www.geocities.com

are not expected to talk to other users. They are expected to browse, to assimilate information, not to ask questions. Thus most business websites are not much more than glitzy shopfronts constituting more than 80% of the total number of sites on the Web (*NetNames*, 1998).

Sclove and Scheur (1994) in examining the freeway metaphor for the Information Superhighway warn us that the metaphor may in fact be too close to the real thing. They blame the construction of the asphalt highway system of the US for both the destruction of poor neighbourhoods, and their marginalisation into ghettoes. Sclove and Scheur argue that highway noise and pollution forced children from the street pavements, and families off the front porch. With employment in small towns becoming scarce, communities lost their breadwinners who were forced to find work in the big cities. Alienating shopping malls were only made possible by the freeway system. The community spaces of the general store, the soda fountain, the Main Street sidewalk and the Town Square vanished with the advent of the freeway. Undoubtedly the Internet has enabled the creation of new communities, but what about the loss of the old communities? Does anyone worry that when we are creating a community with our associates across the other side of the world, we are ignoring our neighbours, our familes and our friends? What are the side effects of Internet commerce if we no longer venture outside our homes and meet people?

The language of the Internet

The Internet has in many ways permeated our real lives. These days, we cannot view an advertisement in the media without some mention of a website, or email address. A few years ago the catch phrase was 'Virtual Reality', then the media seized upon 'The Information Superhighway'; these days it is 'cyberspace' and the 'Internet' which have become vogue expressions. Unfortunately these terms and the accompanying jargon which is needed to support these concepts read like secret codes for all but the most technical people. Try reading the manuals (if they exist) of your local Internet Service Provider. Or attempt to make sense of the salesperson's explanations when you ask for details about setting up a webpage for commercial purposes. The jargon of the Internet both perplexes and confuses novice computer users since there are often no other terms available to translate highly technical words. The Internet has also developed its own specialised language or slang which has led to hundreds of Internet glossary pages being written. Since most communication is achieved through keyboard typing, a number of shortcuts have evolved to speed up the process[1]. If you use the interactive parts of the Internet such as the Usenet or Internet Relay Chat, newcomers may in fact be overwhelmed by the acronyms and jargon they encounter.

Several commentators have noted the oral nature of much of the Internet (Langham, 1994; Ong, 1985; Vitanza, 1997). The fast turnaround of Internet interaction contributes to the informality characteristic of spoken language. Many users of Internet email, Usenet newsgroups and real-time chat systems tend to rely on short sentences, keyboard emphasis, 'emoticons' and abbreviated grammatical constructions because of the difficulty in reading complex arguments on a screen.

Figure 10. 3 below provides an example of a Usenet article which illustrates these linguistic features. The Usenet is an interactive sub-system of the Internet, consisting of thousands of computer conferences called newsgroups and categorised by the prefix to the newsgroup name. It is common to find abbreviations such as 'Alt' which stands for 'alternate', 'comp' for 'computer', 'rec' for 'recreation', 'soc' for 'social' and so on. The language of the Usenet is very closely tied to text-based written communication and the range of possible keyboard non-verbal communication. In Figure 10.3 we have a short advertisement from alt.business.career-opportunities. Note the frequent repetition, use of capitals for emphasis, colloquialisms (such as 'whole bunch' and 'galore'), slang/trendy expressions (such as 'mondo'), overuse of exclamation marks, and absence of verbs in sentences.

Figure 10.3 A Usenet article

> Date: Oct, 1998
> Forums: alt.business.career-opportunities
>
> There are currently 1,168 TCP/IP INTERNET AND WEB jobs at the WESTECH Virtual Job Fair.
>
> Search over 25,000 high tech jobs, cut and paste your resume confidentially, then apply for multiple positions simultaneously at:
>
> http://www.VJF.com
>
> Again, a whole bunch of TCP/IP INTERNET AND WEB jobs, more TCP/IP INTERNET AND WEB jobs than any other site that has TCP/IP INTERNET AND WEB jobs. TCP/IP INTERNET AND WEB coders--check us out! TCP/IP INTERNET AND WEB jobs galore! Mondo TCP/IP INTERNET AND WEB jobs!

Chat users also abbreviate their prose so much that it resembles typed speech (see Figure 10. 4 below). The immediacy of computer chatting creates the need for even greater brevity and succinctness which in turn leads to very short sentences, acronyms and often a distorted perception of tone and feeling in heated discussions. On IRC, users may join one of thousands of channels, or a user may choose to simply chat one-on-one without being in a channel[2]. Channels range from professional discussions to the most banal topics imaginable. Figure 10.4 displays a social channel discussion. Note the short declarative sentences, successive brief statements by Jay^ and DJ_Scott, abbreviations, and lack of punctuation. Typically, users are involved in more than one conversation in the channel, and often in more than one channel, so that successive statements from the same person will not be coherent to the casual observer. IRC is probably the only medium which is both public and private simultaneously.

Figure 10.4 Excerpt from an IRC channel

<DJ_Scott> heH I work for the Talk Station up here in Maine
<Jay^> but on the weekends I do Mobile DJ stuff spinning top40/dance remixes/rap, etc
<Rai99> hahaha... no idea about plastic surgery?
<Jay^> at this one bar I DJ the Saints Tailgate party
<DJ_Scott> WVOM 103.9 —-> http://wvom.midmaine.com/
<Jay^> and also do high school dances and stuff
<DJ_Scott> eyah I wanna do that stuff
<Jay^> doing high school dances is kinda fun
<DJ_Scott> yeah
<Jay^> club work is really cool...thats what I want to do since I like that type of music
<AzWildCat> i have no idea about sandra.....
<DJ_Scott> yeah I wanna club big time
<Jay^> i actually might get into a club if my DJ boss gets this club
<Jay^> i'll end up having Saturday and Sunday nights to spin
<DJ_Scott> yaeh
<Jay^> do you own any mobile equip?
<DJ_Scott> nope I have my Numark CD-7030 thats it
* Jess1 has returned!
<Jay^> the Pioneer CDJ 700s and the Pionneer mixer is NICE
<Jay^> whoa baby let me tell ya
<DJ_Scott> yeah they are
<DJ_Scott> I want the Numark CDN-34's
<Jay^> haven't even heard of those to be honest with ya
<Jay^> they any good

Democracy or anti-democracy

For most of its life, the Internet has been seen as the last remaining bastion of freedom and democracy in our society. Given the large student population on the Internet, its reputation as being an open, hospitable and democratic environment has been a natural extension of its users' ideology and politics. The main criticism of the early Internet was that it was difficult to learn the arcane Unix commands, and that access was for the privileged few, namely engineering and computer science students. The question for the Internet of the future is perhaps not whether or not this unique medium can maintain its vainglorious reputation, but whether it was ever a free and democratic environment in the first instance.

The experienced Internet user is typically young (under 30 years old, according to *survey.net*) (1998) and highly intolerant towards newer users, who are often called 'newbies'. My knowledge of adept users is that they are usually highly opinionated about technical issues, impatient towards others less skilled than themselves, and extreme in their attitudes about technology. Characteristically, experienced Internet users do not typify cooperation and affability. On the other hand, novice users, in needing information and help, usually epitomise openness and friendship.

Whilst the Clinton administration's so-called Communications Decency Act of February, 1996 created an anti-censorship movement leading to an eventual legislative reversal, the Internet itself is not the open and liberated place it proclaims itself to be. The Usenet, email, and chat systems all have their policies, norms and value systems. To transgress a tacit rule of the Internet will bring disfavour, and contempt. And if one continually flaunts the rules of cyberspace one will be censored.

A good example is the now infamous mass Usenet post of the Greencard lawyers, Canter and Siegel. The lawyers had a programmer quite legally 'spam' their ordinary advertisement to thousands of newsgroups. Millions of people received the same message, resulting in anger and retaliation on the part of the Net community. The extent of their activities was recognised so that within minutes 'flames' began pouring into the lawyers' mailbox—so many that their host system crashed repeatedly. In *Time* magazine (July 25, 1994) the lawyers reported that they made an extra $100,000 in new business. And despite the ill feelings, Canter and Siegel were unmoved and unrepentant over their actions. A later interview in the *New York Times* signalled that they would repeat the whole exercise, so the harassment swelled anew. The lawyers' fax machine became tied up with dozens of blank pages; hundreds of bogus customers signed onto their books; and a Norwegian programmer created a piece of software which looked specifically at Canter and Siegel posts, and deleted them before they spread.

Unsolicited electronic mail is the equivalent of ordinary junk mail, but there is one main difference; each piece of junk email costs the recipient a few fractions of a cent. However, apart from the cost burden, the Internet community detests unsolicited email so much that even public service announcements can result in extreme anger and retaliation from supposedly wounded recipients. Service providers, frightened of being black-banned by a sympathetic fraternity of users, also tend to respond badly to individuals who break this rule.

In 1997, an Australian company announced that it was offering a free copy of a historically significant document to any visitor to its website. The company spammed 50,000 Australian email addresses in order to inform the public of the significance of the gift. The response from the recipients varied from irritation and anger to praise and thanks. But it was the company's ISP that provides a salutory lesson in Internet democracy. Because the Service Provider also received a few angry email messages, they immediately blanked out the supposedly offensive website, spuriously claiming that the company had broken their policies. The company website was only reinstated when legal action was threatened against the ISP for breach of contract.

In the United States and in Australia the Internet is increasingly becoming a place for the marketing of political platforms. Websites espousing the policies of the Republican, Democrat, Labour, and Liberal parties stand side by side. On the Web, renegade politicians and alternative parties such as Neo-Nazis and the Ku Klux Klan also vie for the attention of the bypassing cybernaut who happens to accidently drop in. In the late 1990s, politicians have become commodity items with mass advertising in the media and on the Internet playing a key role (Rheingold, 1994).

President Bill Clinton's presidential campaign of 1992 particularly stressed 'electronic democracy' including digital town hall meetings and online voting. The Clinton administration was also responsible for the National Information Infrastructure Agenda for Action which can really only be found on the American Government's website. But a more recent and more sinister use of the Web can be seen to be occurring. The Office of the Independent Council for the American government, in using the Internet to publish the 'Starr report' which placed Bill Clinton under the watchful eye of the world, has brought impeachment proceedings one step closer. In the late 1990s, the Internet became more than just a marketing space for avante-garde *digerati* and their parties, it also became a battlefield for politicians peddling public humiliation. Ironically the network championed by the Clinton government as a model for leading the country forward may also become the medium of Bill Clinton's eventual undoing.

Epistemological considerations

The development of the computer is regarded as one of the major technological achievements of the twentieth century. Our shiny monitors and computers promise us perfection in the way in which words can now be processed, in the way that numbers can now be manipulated, and significantly in the way that information can now be stored and retrieved. Sherry Turkle (1995) in her book, *Life on the Screen* talks about the computer's 'holding power', its mystique as a machine that is right, and anything found on a computer as being true. The Web extends this mythology (and it is a myth) to all the computer's hosts on the Web. A belief now exists that useful information about any topic can be easily found, and once found this information's reliability is unlikely to be questioned.

We tend to regard information found on the Web through one of the search engines as a godsend— as a way of saving time and energy in dark musty libraries. As such, there is a tendency to regard this knowledge as free and therefore able to be copied and used without the usual restrictions of intellectual property and copyright protection. But this is not the case. Moreover the information we find is usually neatly and tidily packaged into small easily assimilated units called homepages. There are few books on the Web, few long academic treatises, but lots of short, self-opinionated magazine-style snippets which are fast becoming the norm for our students. Are we guilty of fostering a generation of young researchers who are accustomed to Sesame Street-style information grabs by erroneously placing our confidence in the Web?

Paradoxically, belief in the power of the Web also leads scholars to devalue the information acquired therein since this knowledge is intrinsically public knowledge. Jones (1994), in his essay entitled 'The Ethics of Research in Cyberspace', suggests that all the knowledge found on the Internet is in fact public knowledge. Academics pride themselves on their research skills. Scholars specialise in a particular field of knowledge in which they do research and compile precious bibliographies. Scholars are seen as experts in a particular field and are hired as professionals to teach, consult and do further research in these highly specialist areas. But what if an expert's knowledge was available to anyone and everyone? What if someone could do a search on the Web and find out the same things which have taken specialists years to acquire? Would they still be hired? Would a specialist's knowledge be worth anything at all? What is valuable about our experience and about our best students' work is the fact that the knowledge acquired is rare—it is painstakingly difficult to find.

The Web changes our perceptions of the value of information by placing online the fruits of many experts' collective labours. It is said to supposedly level the playing field in terms of access to this specialist knowledge, since we can locate all manner of esoterica. The Clinton administration has stated that electronic access to information enhances the country's democratic processes since all Americans can search for and find all the pertinent information relevant to an issue or problem. This claim not only totally ignores those citizens who cannot afford a PC, a modem and an Internet account, or who do not have the skills to use such technical tools, but it also presupposes that the information found on any government's websites is fair, unbiased and includes a range of policy opinions. This is simply not true. As stated earlier, websites provide a particular point of view which may be rhetorical at best, but also polemical in extreme cases[3].

Conclusion - technology redux

Some commentators have complained that the educational Web is growing too fast (Duin & Archee, 1997) or in the wrong direction of adult-oriented material (Archee, 1997). Whilst webpages change on a daily basis, they can also disappear overnight without warning. How can we have faith in a reference if it no longer exists? Books, once printed, may be referenced and checked time and time again. But webpages by their very nature are ephemeral and changeable. There are very few Internet documents and programs which still exist in their original form.

The Web's utilisation of hypertext means that a single mouse click can bring up completely different sets of information. Similarly the content of the Web may be digested by scanning and browsing as opposed to close reading and reflection—printing tends to be eschewed in favour of online assimilation. As it has been earlier stated, the very nature of hypertext mitigates against perusal in any other form except online format. Given present costs of Internet usage and printing, the normal process of reading and questioning may be reduced to mere minutes. If educators persist in placing all their course material online, then the vast majority of students will digest the same material *in situ*. The result is an imperfect reading, or at best a superficial perusal of significant documents by our students.

Ciolek (1996) asks if the Web, in fact, has much to interest academics or educators. He provocatively suggests that the future may hold in store a 'multimedia mediocrity' since the ratio of useful information is diminishing in favour of advertising. Ciolek also implies that the Web is too easy to access and thus also too difficult to control access to. Anyone from the youngest schoolchild to the most senior citizen can access the Web today. And whilst there are numerous benefits for all users by allowing ordinary people access to the largest database in the world, there are also dangers of which we, as responsible parents and educators need to be aware. The spectre of pornography raises its ugly head, not only as a danger, but also as a distraction. Unless you use a special web server or search engine, you cannot do any search on the Web without coming across a hyperlink to an 'adult site'. The most innocuous keywords will yield pornographic hits. You do not have to follow up these hyperlinks, but they still exist alongside your research results. The distraction of these hits can lead to frustration and dissatisfaction with the whole system.

In his book, *Travels in Hyperreality* (which predates the Web) Umberto Eco (1986) suggests that Americans (and Australians) adore creating hyperreal simulacra of real things that seem more vibrant than the originals. Whilst the Web is not American, the major web browsers, *Netscape* and the *Microsoft Internet Explorer* are examples of this tendency. Schoolchildren, the unemployed and students are able to publish online, and compete with multinational companies for user attention. Depending on their level of expertise there can be little difference between such personal homepages and those of huge corporations. The same computer screen displays both. The people as represented on the Web are hyperreal and so are the companies. There seems to be little distinction between the personal/private and the corporate/public. Rheingold (1994, p. 281) states succinctly:

> We live in a hyper-reality that was carefully constructed to mimic the real world and extract money from the pockets of consumers: the

forests around the Matterhorn might be dying, but the Disneyland version continues to rake in the dollars.

This is also true for the websites of other cultures, which are all beginning to look rather similar to the *Microsoft* or the *Netscape* homepage. Will the typical Internet user in 2000 and beyond be any more sophisticated in their choice and use of information sources? I would like to think that we shall impart caution alongside our enthusiasm for the digital. As educators and scholars we need to be aware of the problems inherent in the latest technology. And before we embrace the Web too wholeheartedly we need to determine why we are using it in the first place. What real benefits does it offer, and what are the costs involved for our students? Strange as it may seem some experienced web users are already complaining of boredom with much that they see on the Web. Are we turning our students into archetypal couch potatoes clicking mindlessly on 40 million web channels only to find that there is nothing worth viewing? <click>

Endnotes

1. Examples of some of the most commonly used abbreviations and acronyms are provided in chapters 1, 8 and 9 above.
2. A fuller discussion of IRC is provided in chapter 8 above.
3. For a critical interpretation of a government website, see chapter 7 above.

References

Archee, R. (1997, November). *The Australian Internet 1997—Behaviour and Attitudes*. Paper presented at the European Information Technology Conference 1997, Brussels, Belgium. Available: http://stc.nepean.uws.edu.au/~rarchee/oznet97.html [1998, December 21].

Bush, V. (1945). As We May Think, *Atlantic Monthly*, 1945. Available: http://www.isg.sfu.ca/~duchier/misc/vbush/ [1998, December 22].

Carmel, E. (1992). Browsing in hypertext: A cognitive study. *IEEE. Transactions on Systems, Man, & Cybernetics, 22* (5), 865-884.

Chaplin, D. A. (1996, May 1). Creating web communities. *Computer Mediated Communication Magazine*. Available: http://www.december.com/cmc/mag/1996/may/chaplin.html [1998, December 22].

Ciolek, M. (1996). Today's WWW-tomorrow's MMM? The specter of multimedia mediocrity. Available at: http://myweb.worldnet.fr/~bferris/medio.html [1998, December 22].

Duin, A. H., & Archee, R. (1997). Distance education via the World Wide Web: Information, engagement and community. In Stuart Selber (Ed.), *Computers and technical communication: Pedagogical and programmatic perspectives*. Greenwich: Ablex.

Eco, U. (1986). *Travels in hyperreality*. London: Pan.

GeoCities Neighborhoods. (1998). Available: http://www.geocities.com [1998, October 4].

Jones, R. A., (1994). The ethics of research in cyberspace. *Internet Research, 4* (3), 30-35. Available: http://www.mcb.co.uk/services/articles/liblink/intr/ethics.html [1998, December 22].

Landow, G. P., (1993). *Hypertext in hypertext - An expanded electronic edition of hypertext: The convergence of contemporary critical theory and technology*. Baltimore: Johns Hopkins University Press.

Langham, D., (1994). The common place MOO: Orality and literacy in virtual reality. *Computer-Mediated Communication Magazine, 1* (3). Available: http://www.december.com/cmc/mag/1994/jul/moo.html [1998, December 22].

Nelson, T. H., (1992). *Literary machines*. Sausalito: Mindful Press.

NetNames Ltd. (1998). Available: http://www.domainstats.com/internic.cfm [1998, December 22].

Ong, W., (1985). *Orality and literacy: The tehnologizing of the word*. New York: Routledge.

Rheingold, H., (1994). *The virtual community: Surfing the Internet*, Minerva: London. Available: http://www.rheingold.com/vc/book/10.html [1998, December 22].

Rouet, J., Levonen, J. L., Dillon, A., & Spiro, R. J., (Eds.), (1996). *Hypertext and cognition.* New York: Lawrence Erlbaum.

Sclove, R. E., & Scheuer, J. (1994, May 29). The ghost in the modem: For architects of the info-highway, some lessons from the concrete interstate. Sunday Outlook Section, *The Washington Post*, (p. C3). Reprinted (1995), *The Fifth Conference on Computers, Freedom and Privacy: CFP '95 Program* (pp. 51-58). Stanford, CA: Stanford Law and Technology Policy Center).

survey.net. Available: http://www.survey.net/hon1r.html [1998, December 20].

Turkle, S. (1995). *Life on the screen.* New York: Simon and Schuster.

Vitanza, V. (1997). *Writing for the World Wide Web*. New York: Allyn and Bacon.

Wild, M., & Henderson, L. (1997). Contextualizing learning in the World Wide Web: Accounting for the impact of culture. *Education and Information Technologies*, *2* (3), 179.

Chapter 11

Cyberlines

Kerri-Lee Krause

Introduction

The Australian Aboriginal people's way of perceiving their country and its origins provides a unique yet widely applicable means of interpreting the ways in which language creates, and is created in and by, the realm of cyberspace and those who journey through it. This chapter juxtaposes two seemingly disparate worlds—that of the ancient Australian Aboriginal Dreaming, with its focus on the significance of tracks in the dirt and a valuing of the lessons of the past; and that of the futuristic, high-tech world of computers and technology, with its focal point the speed and might of machines. Strangely, however, these two worlds are not so dissimilar. There are many points of comparison, one of the most significant of which is the potency of human language and the lines of communication which operate through the times and spaces of both worlds.

After briefly considering the parallels between these two worlds —the world of Aboriginal Songlines and that of cyberspace—this chapter will examine the subject of linguistic change, particularly in the cyber context. Discussion then turns to two specific aspects of cyberlanguage: its capacity to create communities by facilitating the sharing of values and cultures, and its power to precipitate division by establishing excluding boundaries between those who have the money, power and resources to muster and deploy the necessary linguistic tools, and those who do not.

Songlines in cyberspace

The native inhabitants of Australia depict their country in terms of ageless Songlines stretching in all directions across the continent and forming a 'labyrinth of invisible pathways' which act as constant reminders of the 'Footprints of the Ancestors' (Chatwin, 1987, p. 2). The totemic ancestors of indigenous Australians were thought to have scattered trails of words and musical notes which formed lines of communication between separate groups of people across the landscape of a massive continent. This image of the inherent connectedness between past, present and future, between individuals and groups, and between far-flung parts of the physical and spiritual terrain—facilitated through tracks of words and song—provides a window through which to view and investigate the energy and influence of cyberlanguage.

For those investigating the ways in which cyberspatial communication occurs and develops, there is much to be learned from examining the Songline analogies more closely. Some of these have already been noticed. For example, McLellan (1997) draws parallels between Aboriginal Songline imagery and the forging and maintaining of links between learning communities, emphasising the power of the Internet to connect and build cybercommunities. She likens this interconnectedness to a set of necklace beads on interconnecting strands, all dependent on the links between those strands for their patterned existence (c.f., the Buddhist imagery of the network of pearls, see p. 39). The Internet has brought into being an entirely new way of creating and sustaining community-like forms of social conversation. The ethereal transmission of such conversation, and its function as a promoter of forms of social bonding between distinct peoples, provide striking parallels with the mysterious linkages created by the Songlines.

While the Aboriginal origin story is a useful metaphor for examining the nature of Internet communities, there is even more to be gained from exploring the application of this 'way of talking, of seeing, of knowing'— as the Songlines have been described (Benterrak, Muecke & Roe, 1984, p. 19)—to the role and function of cyberlanguage. A nexus exists between our study of the language of the Internet and the normative role of Songlines, both of which operate as 'vessels for the values on which a culture can agree' (Brown, 1997, p. 149). There are lessons to be drawn from the Aboriginal understanding of the capacity of dreaming tracks to not only connect, but also to divide; and of the inherent power attributed to those who know the song and can therefore read the map and find their way in cybercountry. First, however, these lessons must be contextualised by briefly recalling the issue of language change and its social nature.

Cyberlines of change

A fundamental characteristic of language is its tendency to change. There is, however, an innate tension between this natural divergent tendency and the tacit agreement shared by language users, or communities, regarding the importance of maintaining the language as a means of safeguarding social identity and 'language loyalty'[1]. A predilection for convergence is constantly present as a contributing factor in the maintenance of social networks; yet as these networks, moulded by external forces themselves, change in character, so demands are imposed upon language to adapt accordingly. Social and technological developments create a continuing tension between the principles of language change and the maintenance of language conventions.

Language divergence is brought about by a range of external pressures exerted by social, political, cultural and technological forces—all imposing their demands on language users and requiring them to adapt and adjust their language. Cyberlanguage provides a striking illustration of this process. As Kitchin argues, cyberspace brings about a 'deep restructuring of society, challenging traditional notions of . . . community' (1998, p. 74). The concomitant demands on language are the focus of this discussion.

Cyberlanguage connects and creates communities and subcultures on and around the Internet in a range of ways. Those who inhabit the noncorporeal world of cyberspace have come to be known as virtual citizens and cyber citizens[2], connoting a sense of belonging, ownership and commitment to a 'country' or locale. The need to create communities and to feel as if you belong is explored by Rheingold (1994, p. 6) who refers to 'the hunger for community that grows in the breasts of people around the world as more and more informal public spaces disappear from our real lives'[3]. Cybercommunity members have their own language. They portray themselves via this language and, like other subcultures, they define their territory through their language. Wodak (1989) comments that members of particular subcultures 'act upon their surroundings by means of the power and dynamics of their language' (p. 138). While Wodak's concern lies with the power of political jargon, the principles of her theory apply equally to those who communicate through cyberlanguage.

The intricate nature of the interrelationships of language, culture and, in this case, the technology of the Internet, is impossible to quantify— each is interdependent and in turn develops and changes as a result of the other[4]. The intensity of these interconnections is vividly portrayed in communities such as those of the cyberpunks and hackers, which develop and often splinter into subcommunities as a result of the dynamic interplay of computer technology and the language which has grown up around it. It is not the intention of this chapter to present an exhaustive description of these complex subcultures, nor to engage in the debate as to whether hackers are a subgroup of the cyberpunk social movement or a community in their own right[5]. Rather, discussion of these communities will be used as a basis for elucidating some key principles which may be applied as the reader further explores the nature of Internet cultures and the languages that draw them together[6]. The following discussion mainly focusses on cyberpunk and hacker communities as cultural sites for the examination of those principles.

The cyberpunk community

Cyberpunk originated as a genre of Science Fiction some time prior to the Internet era and is associated with such well-known authors as William Gibson and Bruce Sterling (Wood, 1994). Over time, however, cyberpunk has become a social movement associated not only with literature, but also with such diverse activities as music (or 'industrial music' with groups such as *Machines of Loving Grace* and *Restless Machines*), computer-generated psychedelic ('cyberdelic') art, and designer drugs.

The cyberpunk culture—or counterculture (Elmer-Dewitt, 1993)[7]—borrows heavily from the rebellious attitude characteristic of the punk rock music of the 1970s, sharing with such groups as the *Sex Pistols* a defiance of the perceived oppression of mainstream Western culture (Wood, 1994). It is a community associated with a 'diverse set of cultural forms based around futuristic ideas of computing and communication' (Kitchin, 1998, p. 91). The complexity and diversity of these cultural forms[8] is reflected in the language of community members and examples of the vocabulary typifying the cyberpunk community and its related subcommunities may be found in numerous online specialist dictionaries[9]. Wood (1994, p. 132) suggests the need to learn some 'serious jargon' if you wish to find your way through the maze of subcultures that is cyberpunk. Rather than attempt to provide exhaustive lists of this idiosyncratic vocabulary, the purposes of this discussion are better served by posing some key questions about the role and function of language in such communities.

One question pertains to the categorisation of the language typical of the cyberpunk community, and others like it. With its 'unholy alliance of pop culture and street level anarchy' (Sterling n.d., as cited in Elmer-Dewitt, 1993, n.p.), this subculture which encourages a distrust of authority and urges members to 'Surf the Edges' and 'Fight the Power' (Branwyn, n.d., n.p.) demands a language or dialect consistent with its purposes. The term 'anti-language' (Montgomery, 1986) goes some way toward depicting such a language. Anti-languages come in a variety of forms and are defined as 'extreme versions of social dialects' (p. 93). They tend to arise among subcultures and groups that occupy a marginal or precarious position in society— particularly where their activities place them outside the law. Often the subculture has a rather antagonistic relationship with mainstream society. Notable examples of anti-language include the language of Polish prison life and that of the Calcutta underworld.

Anti-languages are based on a process of relexicalisation—that is, the substitution of new words for old. The grammar of the parent language is usually preserved, but a distinctive vocabulary develops to facilitate the functioning of activities that are central to that subculture. This vocabulary serves to set the group apart from established society. Taken to the extreme, anti-language is virtually impenetrable to outsiders, thus establishing a strong sense of solidarity between members of the group. In the case of cyberpunks, many of whom are engaged in active, self-confessed self-marginalisation from the mainstream and social resistance, the communicative possibilities offered by anti-language may be consistent with the values represented by some strands of their community. However, as Wark (1992) notes, there has been a shift from a 'negative subcultural style', typical of the 1970s and 80s, towards a 'positive celebration . . . of media technologies' (n.p.) among a large proportion of cyberpunks and those who hold similar beliefs. This renders any generalisations about the nature and categorisation of their language dangerous, to say the least. The principle nonetheless remains that the form of language known as anti-language is an integral component of the language of cyberspace and is apparent in some facets of the cyberpunk subculture.

The hacker community

Hackers, too, comprise a collection of subcultures (Raymond, 1996) with shared experiences, origins and values based around their interest in all things computer-oriented. There is, however, ambiguity as to the meaning of the term 'hacker': for some, it refers to a talented computer programmer able to solve difficult computing problems in creative ways, to others it contains more subversive undertones, suggestive of the activities of computer system crackers (Wood, 1994). This ambiguity is an illustration of the complex and sometimes ambivalent nature of cyberlanguage and the way in which its development is so closely connected to the rapidly evolving communities it serves.

One of the most comprehensive descriptions of hackers and their language is found in Raymond's *The jargon file* (1996). Here Raymond explains that the special vocabulary of hackers helps hold their culture together, while those who do not know how to use the language or use it inappropriately, are defined as 'outsiders'[10]. As a rule, hackers love wordplay and many see the evolution of the language as a game. These linguistic inventions and the ability to understand and use them have great power in any community.

Not only does the language of the hacker community unite its users, it may also serve to actively exclude outsiders[11]. This illustrates the dual role of language—both as a vehicle of communication and as a vehicle for concealment and secrecy (Edwards, 1985). Electronically mediated forms of communication provide numerous linguistic mechanisms by which individuals and language communities can keep their identity secret. This is evident in the language used to interact in Internet chat rooms[12], for example. Some hackers, too, have developed a unique coded language to preserve their rights to free communication (Cooke & Lehrer, 1993)[13]. Through the use of elaborately coded information, veiled in secrecy, they are able to communicate via a language virtually impenetrable to even the most advanced computer systems. In this way, uniquely coded languages form tight-knit bonds between members of an elite cyber-community who know how to use the resources of language to serve their purposes. The pragmatic use of language as a tool for maintaining privacy and secrecy and as a symbol rejecting what many hackers perceive to be the domination of cyberspace and data flow by a privileged few, illustrates once more the power of language to bind communities by, in this case, a united rejection of mainstream culture and normal values. Thus the operation of cyberlanguage as a form of anti-language to convey messages about hacker beliefs and values may be likened to the cyberpunk 'dialect'.

Classifying the language typical of cybercommunities, such as that of hackers, is not a simple task. In the case of hacker usage, three language forms have been identified: 'jargon', 'hackers' jargon' and 'techspeak' (Raymond, 1996). Jargon is a 'group language' (Wodak, 1989, p. 141)—it establishes group identity and consolidates the group and distinguishes it from the external world or outsiders. While serving pragmatic functions, it may also be said that speakers employ jargon in order to acquire prestige and to denote group membership. Hackers are said to use a specialised form of jargon—'hackers' jargon'—which tends to comprise vocabulary learned from textbooks, technical papers, and computer or software manuals. A related, but even more technical form of hacker language is known as 'techspeak' which is specifically related to the vocabulary of computer programming, computer science and electronics.

These three categorisations of the language used by the hacker community illustrate the complexity inherent in attempts to describe the language of the hacker community and its functions. This task is complicated by the fluidity of the language as, in the case of the hacker language, much techspeak originated as jargon, and a lot of jargon arises from techspeak. Thus as mentioned earlier, the interconnectedness and interdependence of the technology, the language and the community cannot be underestimated. The three can never be depicted as mutually exclusive or discrete entities. Rather they function, as Rheingold (1994) contends, within a complex ecosystem with all elements drawing from, and in turn giving life to, others.

The cyberpunk and hacker subcultures—with their associated offshoots and subcommunities—are but two of the huge range of cybercommunities residing in the virtual space of the Internet. While the hackers and the cyberpunks share a mutual interest in matters technological, there are also online communities for those more comfortable with familiar 'homely' spaces and the language that goes with them. For example, you may visit *SSI Online*[14] —a 'Cyber home' and a 'little world' where you can 'test-drive', 'build a home (page)', visit the Town Hall and even have an 'SSI Online Picnic'. Through the vehicle of language, a space between the real and virtual worlds is starting to be colonised. The potentially frightening enormity of cyberspace is somehow reined in and community members are made to feel that they belong by being involved in 'real' world activities, such as building a home, going on a picnic and test-driving a car. Turkle (1998, p. 310) comments on this process of between-world colonisation, noting that 'we are not being sucked into the virtual and we are not going to live completely in the physical. We are going to learn to live between the two worlds'. Language is a key to facilitating this process.

Internet communities offer a 'cozy little world' (Rheingold, 1994, p. 1) quite literally at the fingertips of some, yet there are many for whom the cyberworld and the sense of community it may offer, is hidden from view behind a 'secret door' (p. 2) that may only be accessed, it seems, if you know the password. This implied secrecy —perhaps even subterfuge—so effectively facilitated by language, highlights the fact that access to Internet communities, like that to the Songlines, is not necessarily open to all. Resources of language play a critical role in facilitating access to those 'secret doors'—doors which are barriers to those unable to 'talk the talk'. The power of language to divide and separate individuals and groups of people cannot be ignored.

Cyberlines of divide: How cyberlanguage separates

Boundary lines—like Songlines—contain connected individuals, engendering a sense of community and belonging on the other side of 'secret' doors; but they also operate as barriers to keep others out. Thus the cyberlines of communication which facilitate interaction across electronic spaces so effectively and efficiently also hold communities apart. There are, of course, many factors which contribute to this process—language being one.

In Aboriginal beliefs, Songlines were maintained as a result of cooperation between tribal groups. This process depended on goodwill and a willingness to subscribe to the norms and behaviours—including languages—of those whose particular Songline was connected to your own. Each group was, and remains, responsible for caring for the track, keeping the path open. As noted earlier, an individual or group travelled the Songline track by singing a song which functioned as a map, a direction-finder (Chatwin, 1987, p. 13). Provided you knew the words of the song, you could always find your way across the country, from one community to the next. Similarly in the vast cyberspatial terrain, if you know the language and how to use it, you can cross the boundaries. But what happens if you do not know the song, cannot remember the words, or never learned them in the first place? It is then that cyberlines become barriers to those who are excluded or marginalised.

While some might see cyberlanguage with all its variations as the new lingua franca with the potential to unite the global community, others perceive it in a very different light. For example, Aoki (1994, as cited in Kitchin, 1998) comments on the scepticism and suspicion with which the Japanese view the US-dominated CMC[15]. Aoki challenges the rhetoric which automatically assumes that CMC and the communities they form as a result will necessarily have a positive outcome. Kitchin also notes Davis' (1993) misgivings about cybercommunities and the dangers they may pose to our real-world society by rendering it even more 'polarised and segmented than at present' (as cited in Kitchin, 1998, p. 90). Like Davis, Cooke and Lehrer (1993, p. 4) observe that 'global networking is fragmenting and resorting society'. And Branwyn (n.d., point D) expresses similar sentiments in a rather hyperbolic but nevertheless enlightening summary of the cyberpunk worldview: 'The world is splintering into a trillion subcultures and designer cults with their own language, codes and lifestyles'. And language plays a key role in this 'splintering', 'fragmenting' process.

In exploring the ways in which language divides and sets communities and subcultures apart, the issue of power over language use and resources cannot be left out of account. Language communities operate as a result of the shared consent of members who enter into a social contract to abide by the various 'rules' of their language community. However, one must consider whose language is being used, who decides on the linguistic rules, and what happens if those with less power do not share consent. These and similar questions form the basis for a growing body of research critically examining broader questions of power and the hegemonic nature of the Net, and the significant implications of such issues for communities both on- and offline (see for example Bromberg, 1996; Brown, 1997; Kelly, 1994; Rheingold, 1991; and Robins, 1995). While this issue can only be examined briefly here, it should be considered central to any discussion of the relationship between technology, language, culture and community.

In a sense, language can be said to colonise cyberspace just as it colonises reality (Brown, 1997, p. 149). Consideration of the implications of such colonisation for those who do not use the language or have access to the power it conveys is just as important as a discussion of those communities who can appropriate these resources. Language both constrains and empowers (Poster, 1995), playing a crucial role in configuring human beings and conveying cultural beliefs and values. Online discourse is predominantly Western discourse which many believe reinforces and reproduces hegemonic structures within cyberspace (Kitchin, 1998, p. 70). This is achieved through control of access to economic, political and cultural resources, including the capital so potently embodied in language. As long as such control and ownership exists—dominated by a privileged few—we will need to ask questions about who is in control and who is determining the nature of our communication. Because language *is* power: it provides every user acquainted with its particular rules and mores 'with society's most powerful weapons of attack and silence' (Manguel, 1998, p. 21), while simultaneously marginalising unwelcome individuals and groups. Such factors as gender, race, sexuality and ethnicity may preclude citizenship of these spaces, but language, too, plays a determining role.

Conclusion

With its multiplicity of languages and its potential for creating global communities, the Internet is a compelling source of information for those interested in investigating ways in which language changes and evolves, conveys cultural values, and forms and reforms our society and its communities, whether virtual or real. As language communities develop on and around the Internet, bound by the cohesive forces of cyberlanguage, the need to critically examine the role and nature of this language is increasingly apparent. The implications of the Internet, its languages and the cultures it creates are critical to both the intellectual and spiritual progress of human society—particularly now, as we collectively endeavour to navigate our way through the interconnecting spaces of the virtual and the real.

The global linkages facilitated by cyberlines are embodied in the Aboriginal Songline tradition which inspired the title of this book:

> the Songlines were . . . universal: . . . they were the means by which man marked out his territory, and so organised his social life . . . I have a vision of the Songlines stretching across the continents and ages . . . these trails must reach back, in time and space, to an isolated pocket in the African savannah, where the First Man opening his mouth in defiance of the terrors that surrounded him, shouted the opening stanza of the World Song, "I AM!". (Chatwin, 1987, p. 280)

As individuals in the isolated pockets of homes or offices around the world open metaphorical mouths to communicate in the fast-paced, high-tech, sometimes daunting virtual world, it might be argued that Internet users are composing a World Song using cyber-language to declare their existence, to colonise their territory, and to find their place in virtual communities. But who is conducting the composition and who are the composers? And what of those deprived of the voice to speak, those excluded from the composition process? Such critical questions must be posed, as we continue the journey along communication cyberlines with the potential to unite and divide, to connect and exclude.

Endnotes

1. See Milroy (1992) for a more extensive discussion of the value of adopting a sociolinguistic approach when examining the ways in which language operates to hold communities together. Milroy also argues for the need to examine language in its sociocultural and sociopolitical context.
2. Rheingold defines virtual communities comprising cyber citizens as 'social aggregations that emerge from the Net when enough people carry on those public discussions long enough, with sufficient human feeling, to form webs of personal relationships in cyberspace' (1994, p. 5).
3. Gates (1995, p. 263), too, contends that 'people want a sense of belonging to . . . communities' and that such a need is met by the online communities of the Internet.
4. For further discussion of the nature of the interdependence of language, technology and culture, and the poststructuralist conceptualisation from which it is drawn, some useful references are Kitchin (1998) and Poster (1995).
5. The cyberpunk community is often said to comprise: hackers, cypherpunks and ravers (for example, see Wood, 1994). However, some commentators make clearer distinctions between these subcultures, identifying cyberpunks and hackers as separate communities in their own right.
6. In chapter 9 above, for example, Wong discusses the relationships between the Internet 'cartoon culture', language and identity.
7. For an informative discussion as to whether or not cyberpunk has moved beyond the status of subculture to that of mainstream culture, see Wark (1992).
8. Dery (1996) identifies cyberpunk subcommunities such as the Deadhead hackers, technopagans, New Age technophiles and ravers; and Wood (1994) provides an extensive list of cyberpunk-related websites and discusses some of the communities associated with them.

9. Scott Fitzgerald identifies a number of useful online dictionaries in chapter 3 above.
10. *The jargon file* (Raymond, 1996) also comprises a series of appendices devoted to discussion of the nature of the hacker subculture and suggestions for helping it to grow. For example, see the sections entitled 'Hacker Writing Style' and 'Hacker Speech Style'.
11. The power of language to unite and exclude is not, of course, limited to the hacker community. These principles apply to language communities in general, but the hacker subculture serves to illustrate the point effectively.
12. The language of Internet chat rooms and the provision for individuals to interact on a one-to-one basis in a language of their own, is discussed further in chapter 8 above.
13. It should be noted here that cypherpunks, too, are sometimes defined in terms of their strongly held belief in the 'privacy of personal communications and [they] use a variety of methods for securing it against any unintended receiver' (Wood, 1994, p. 131). Many cypherpunks are dedicated cryptographers who enjoy the challenge of computerised message encryption.
14. Similar sites include *One Cyber Square* and *WorldVillage* which contain an interesting mix of the language of the real and the virtual. *One Cyber Square* describes itself as 'the biggest little community on the internet . . . A safe way for the whole family to tour the internet'. Similarly, *WorldVillage* (1997) promotes itself as a website which has 'served the Internet . . . providing a great family-oriented community'. These and similar sites illustrate Kitchin's (1998) argument that while 'Cyberspaces do offer new forms of communication and are new spaces of interaction', forming new communities and subcultures, 'they are embodied spaces that are essentially extensions of real-world spaces, governed by the same cultural ideologies' (p. 170).
15. In chapter 9 Annette Wong enlarges upon the Japanese scepticism of Western-dominated cyberlanguage, noting their initiative to develop their own culturally inclusive Japanese character sets in place of those making up the English-based ASCII system.

References

Benterrak, K., Muecke, S., & Roe, P. (1984). *Reading the country*. South Fremantle: Fremantle Arts Centre Press.

Branwyn, G. (n.d.). Description of the cyberpunk worldview. Available: http://www.cyberspace.org/~cyborg/cp/worldview.html [1998, December 10].

Bromberg, H. (1996). Are MUDS communities? Identity, belonging and consciousness in virtual worlds. In R. Shields (Ed*.), Cultures of the internet: Virtual spaces, real histories and living bodies* (pp. 143-152). London: Sage.

Brown, D. (1997). *Cybertrends: Chaos, power and accountability in the information age*. London: Penguin.

Chatwin, B. (1987). *The songlines*. London: Jonathan Cape.

Cooke, K., & Lehrer, D. (1993). Available: http://eserver.org/cyber/talking.txt [1998, December 10].

Dery, M. (1996). *Escape velocity: Cyberculture at the end of the century*. London: Hodder & Stoughton.

Edwards, J. (1985). *Language, society and identity*. Oxford: Blackwell.

Elmer-Dewitt, P. (1993). Available: http://eserver.org/cyber/hyprtime.txt [1998, December 10].

Gates, B. (1995). *The road ahead*. New York: Penguin.

Kelly, K. (1994). *Out of control*. Reading, MA: Addison-Wesley.

Kitchin, R. (1998). *Cyberspace: The world in the wires*. Chichester: John Wiley & Sons.

Manguel, A. (1998). Tongue-tied. *The Australian's Review of Books*, [Special feature of *The Australian*] pp. 20-21.

McLellan, H. (1997). Cyberspace songlines: Building trails to learning communities [Excerpt of an article published in *Journal of Public Service and Outreach*, *2* (2)]. In Tech Head Stories. Available: http://tech-head.com/ [1998, November 21].

Milroy, J. (1992). *Linguistic variation and change: On the historical sociolinguistics of English*. Oxford: Blackwell.

Montgomery, M. (1986). *An introduction to language and society*. London: Methuen.

One Cyber Square. Available: http://www.cddoctor.com/mall.htm [1998, December 10].

Poster, M. (1995). *The second media age*. Oxford: Polity Press.

Raymond, E. S. (1996). *The jargon file.* Available: http://www.logophilia.com/jargon.html [1998, December 21].

Rheingold, H. (1991). *Virtual reality*. New York: Touchstone.

Rheingold, H. (1994). *The virtual community: Homesteading on the electronic frontier.* New York: Harper Perennial.

Robins, K. (1995). Cyberspace and the world we live in. In M. Featherstone & R. Burrows (Eds.), *Cyberspace, cyberbodies and cyberpunk: Cultures of technological embodiment* (pp. 135-156). London: Sage.

SSI Online – Cyber home to the playfully curious. Available: http://ism.ferris.edu/students/s/scherzer/index.htm [1998, December 10].

Turkle, S. (1998). The cyberanalyst. In J. Brockman, *Digerati: Encounters with the cyberelite* (pp. 303-314). London: Orion.

Wark, M. (1992). Cyberpunk: From subculture to mainstream. Available: http://eserver.org/cyber/cyberpnk.txt [1998, December 20].

Wodak, R. (1989). 1968: The power of political jargon – a "Club 22" discussion. In R. Wodak (Ed.), *Language, power and ideology: Studies in political discourse* (pp. 137-159). Amsterdam: John Benjamins Publishing Company.

Wood, L. (1994). *The Net after dark*. New York: John Wiley & Sons, Inc.

World Village. Available: wysiwig://127/http://206.50.232.100/webboard/$webb.exe/~WorldVillage/new [1998, December 10].